A Level Media Studies

TV

for

A Level
Media
Studies

Roger Martin

Hodder & Stoughton

A MEMBER OF THE HODDER HEADLINE GROUP

Orders: please contact Bookpoint Ltd, 78 Milton Park, Abingdon, Oxon OX14 4TD.
Telephone: (44) 01235 827720, Fax: (44) 01235 400454. Lines are open from
9.00–6.00, Monday to Saturday, with a 24 hour message answering service.
Email address: orders@bookpoint.co.uk

British Library Cataloguing in Publication Data
A catalogue record for this title is available from The British Library

ISBN 0 340 738 111

First published 2000
Impression number   10 9 8 7 6 5 4 3 2 1
Year   2005 2004 2003 2002 2001 2000

Cover photos reproduced with kind permission of Mersey TV and Carlton.
Typeset by Multiplex Techniques Ltd, Mill Brook Road, St Mary Cray, Kent BR5 3SR.
Printed in Great Britain for Hodder & Stoughton Educational, a division of Hodder
Headline Plc, 338 Euston Road, London NW1 3BH by JW Arrowsmith, Bristol.

CONTENTS

ACKNOWLEDGEMENTS

I would like to thank the following, for their help in producing this book:

My Editor, Melanie Hall, Richard Harvey, Charles Garland, the BFI, the British Library, the Newspaper Library, The Imperial War Museum Reading Room, and my students past and present.

This book is dedicated to my mother, Rose.

The author and publisher would like to thank the following for permission to reproduce copyright text and illustrative material:

Associated Press, p. 142.
BBC, pp. 45, 55, 59, 71, 82, 88, 124.
BFI, pp. 47, 73, 80, 83, 108, 110, 111, 115, 126.
Corbis, pp. 8, 33, 90.
Her Majesty's Stationery Office, pp. 3, 4, 6, 7, 15.
Mersey Television, p. 102.
The Kobal Collection, p. 50.

Every effort has been made to trace copyright holders but this has not always been possible in all cases; any omissions brought to our attention will be corrected in future printings.

INTRODUCTION

This book has been written to provide students with an opportunity to deepen their study of television to a degree not provided by A-level text books that attempt to cover the whole syllabus. This book has a narrower focus: it looks only at television.

Television has stood at many crossroads and now it stands at another. Change is not merely imminent, it has begun and in a way that will transform the communications and cultural landscape more than any other event before it, excepting the moment of television's arrival in the 1930s. If you are reading this book anytime after two years from its initial publication, many of these changes will already have materialised and you will be living through them.

Just look for a moment at a brief sketch of television's history. It begins in 1936, although initially only for three years before being turned off by a world war. After the war it enjoys a revival, still as a monopoly, until the mid-1950s, when the BBC was joined by its commercial cousin, ITV. Now there is cable, satellite and digital television, with a current expansion of the ways in which we use 'the box in the corner': interactive television has arrived. The only option unavailable to broadcasting institutions is *not* to change. It was once said that the only constant in history is change and television is no exception.

This book has been written on the assumption that knowing about the past is helpful in understanding the present. But the history that is here is not, primarily, the history of the development of technology. Where the book deals with the history of television, it is rather the history of the development of ideas and policy. A central idea is 'public service broadcasting'. 'PSB' does not now mean what it did to John Reith in the 1930s. It has gone through a process of what could be called negotiated change. However, notwithstanding the legislative upheaval of the late 1980s and early 1990s, PSB still informs the way we think about television.

The shifts and changes of views about public service broadcasting are dealt with in the first chapter. This is followed by chapters on how television is made, and how it is 'read' where I give a guide to the analysis of a television 'text'. The middle section of the book is devoted to an examination of some of the products of television, specifically various forms of television drama, news, situation comedy and sport. Finally, the book turns full circle and returns to a discussion of broadcasting policy looking at the relationship between the state and television. The book ends with a consideration of how television might develop in the future. The hope is that this book will be of use in coming to grips with a range of issues surrounding television, not only for the purposes of successfully completing a course or examination, but because television forms such an important part of our lives, it needs to be examined and understood.

1
TELEVISION: A BRIEF HISTORY

Public Service Broadcasting (PSB) in the UK

The principles of 'Public Service' have informed the way broadcasting has been run in this country since the birth of radio in the 1920s. These ideas have not remained static and views about what PSB means have been in a constant state of negotiation and revision. Even now, when we are no longer on the edge of a new telecommunications age but are firmly within one, the idea of PSB still informs our thinking about what counts as good television and what television should be like in the future. It will be worth our while to spend some time looking at the development, and changing perception, of PSB.

The story of PSB began with radio and the establishment of the BBC. Within a generation of Marconi's earliest experiments in radio in 1895 (incidentally, the year cinema is generally agreed to have begun) radio became a practical reality.

The origins of the BBC

In a primitive form, radio began at the turn of the century. Its predecessors were telegraphy and the radio telephone. Both of these were point-to-point systems of communication. Telegraphy required a physical link between the two points (hundreds of miles of telegraph cable) and was based around the dots and dashes of the Morse code (the use of Morse officially came to an end by international agreement in February, 1999). Telephony transmitted voices, but only from one point to another. The British government, amongst others, was quick to realise the military value of telephony and virtually took control over it during WW1 (it came under the control of the Admiralty) and the government prohibited its commercial development. This didn't survive the war. Marconi and others involved in both the development of radio and the manufacture of radio receivers imposed increasing pressure on the government to allow the commercial exploitation of radio by private companies. Once the war was over, the argument for retaining a restrictive control was weakened.

In 1920 a temporary licence was granted to the Marconi Company allowing them to broadcast from their transmitter at Writtle, near Cheltenham under an injunction not to interfere with secret military transmissions. In 1922 Marconi began regular broadcasts from its London station. This was followed by stations opened by Western Electric in London and Birmingham (who would later win the race for developing sound on film) and a Metropolitan Vicker's station in Manchester. Licences were temporary because the government (in the form of the Post Office) were uncertain how to shape this embryonic industry. On the one hand the frequency range, fixed for each European country by international agreement, was limited and on the other there was great reluctance to go down the road the Americans had followed, a largely unregulated free-market of the airwaves.

A compromise solution resulted in the Post Office inviting a half-dozen of the leading radio manufacturers, led by the Marconi Company, to form a syndicate which would be licensed to broadcast regular programmes. It would be a monopoly company, largely funded by a licence fee to be paid by anyone purchasing a radio receiver. The British Broadcasting Company came into existence in 1922. The advantage to the radio manufacturers was that the broadcasting of regular programmes would stimulate the sale of receivers which would in turn generate funds.

CASE STUDY

John Reith

It is at this point that John Reith enters the story. He was a Scot, an engineer by profession and much influenced by his Calvinist upbringing. As an army officer in WW1 he had been badly wounded: he finished his war running a munitions factory in Canada. It was Reith who was appointed the first general manager of the British Broadcasting Company at the age of 34.

Reith brought with him a deeply ingrained sense of moral purpose that would define for him the role of broadcasting. For Reith the radio became an instrument of educational and cultural advancement for the whole nation. Through the BBC Reith would be able to give the nation the best of all that was excellent, which for him, was enshrined in the values of classical music. The BBC would be the nation's lecture hall, theatre and concert hall.

This is indicative of the paternalistic nature of the early BBC under Reith: giving people not what they necessarily wanted, but what somebody else thought was good for them. This was not so obviously a problem in the 1920s, when if there was dissent from this position, there were not the channels available through which it could be expressed. At least in appearance, there was an apparent cultural consensus which legitimised Reith's position until the 1940s.

As we conceive it, our responsibility is to carry into the greatest possible number of homes everything that is best in every department of human knowledge, endeavour and achievement, and to avoid the things which are, or may be, hurtful.

(Reith, J. Broadcast over Britain, Hodder & Stoughton, 1924 p.34)

It is occasionally indicated that we are apparently setting out to give the people what we think they need – and not what they want, but few know what they want, and very few what they need. There is often no difference. One wonders to which section of the public such criticism refers. In any case it is better to over-estimate the mentality of the public, than to underestimate it.

(Reith, p.34)

> If, from our perspective, Reith seems an intolerable patrician, this needs to be placed into context. He was a man of his time and class: in that sense he had no choice. He did not so much speak the views of his class; his class spoke through him. He was also in the vulnerable position of having to set up a new service, one that had to win widespread acceptance, not least from his political and pay masters, or it would not survive.

The Sykes Committee

However, there were more pressing, mundane questions. Almost right from the start there were problems over the licence fee. Too many people were either avoiding it outright, or paying a lesser fee on the grounds that they were operating experimental, home constructed receivers. The BBC, as ever, wanted a larger fee. It was this and a persistent measure of uncertainty about broadcasting that led the Postmaster General to appoint a committee to review not merely the question of licences, but 'the whole question of broadcasting.' (*The Broadcasting Committee: Report* (Cmd 1951); HMSO, 1923 cited in McDonnell p.10) On the 24th April 1923 a committee headed by Major General Sir Frederick Sykes was set up to carry out such an enquiry. It was the first of many such committees that would sit every few years, to evaluate the condition of broadcasting and its future development. The Sykes Committee was receptive to the views of Reith and endorsed his view of public service broadcasting:

> **We consider that the control of such a potential power over public opinion and the life of the nation ought to remain with the State, and that the operation of so important a national service ought not to be allowed to become an unrestricted commercial monopoly ... the bulk of the revenue for broadcasting must be collected by the State. More over, the regulation of the power and wavelength of each transmitting station must necessarily be undertaken by the Government, in order to avoid chaos. The ultimate control of broadcasting must, therefore, rest with a Minister responsible to Parliament, presumably the Postmaster General.**
> *(The Broadcasting Committee: Report (Cmd 1951) HMSO, 1923 paras 6, 21,22) cited in McDonnell p.40)*

Advertising was considered, but rejected by the Sykes Committee on the grounds that:

> **....advertisements would lower the standard. The broadcasting of advertisements on a large scale would tend to make the service unpopular, and thus to defeat its own ends.**
> *(The Broadcasting Committee: Report (Cmd 1951) HMSO, 1923 cited in Smith, 1974, p.40)*

The Sykes Committee was also concerned that the cost of air time would advantage only the bigger advertisers. From his perspective, Reith could hardly have framed this better himself – he got basically what he hoped for – a national broadcaster, largely free from both commercial and political control.

According to Cecil Lewis, the first Director of Programmes for the BBC (a post he relinquished in 1926) even though the BBC was still a private company, Reith essentially perceived it in non-commercial, public service terms. In his book *Broadcasting from Within*, Lewis summarised Reith's principles:

1) to cater for the majority of the time to the majority of the public, though without forgetting the needs of 'minorities';
2) to keep programming on the 'upper side' of public taste and to avoid giving 'offence';
3) to provide a forum for public debate which would be impartial and free from government interference;
4) to provide religious broadcasts which were both non-sectarian and non-dogmatic.

(Lewis, pp 48–50)

On the recommendation of the Sykes Committee, a Broadcasting Board was established to oversee the BBC, but this was not a success. Following on from the Sykes Committee, the BBC had been licensed to operate for a further three years. Near the expiration of this time, on the 20th July 1925, the Postmaster General appointed another committee under the Earl of Crawford and Balcarres to 'advise as to the proper scope of the Broadcasting service and as to the management, control and finance thereof after the expiry of the existing licence on 31st December 1926'. The Crawford report was duly published on 2nd March 1926. Again, Reith saw his own thinking about the future of the BBC given official endorsement. He wanted the BBC to be a public trust rather than a commercial company and this is what Crawford recommended.

The British Broadcasting Company became the British Broadcasting Corporation under a Royal Charter that ran for ten years from 1st January 1927. Reith was knighted and became the first Director General.

Through the late 1920s and 1930s, the BBC continued to enhance its reputation and popularity as a broadcaster across the whole nation. In its early days, radio was expensive and regarded as a bit of an eccentricity. One event, however, would change that and at the same time show in sharp relief the nature of the relationship between the BBC and the State.

> **British Broadcasting Commission** – As already indicated, we do not recommend a prolongation of the licence of the British Broadcasting Company, or the establishment of any similar body composed of persons who represent particular interests. We think a public corporation the most appropriate organisation. Such an authority would enjoy a freedom and flexibility which a Minister of State himself would scarcely exercise in arranging for performers and programmes, and in studying the variable demands of public taste and necessity.
>
> *(Report of the Broadcasting Committee, 1925 (Cmd 1929) HMSO, 1926 para 5)*

The General Strike

During a period of economic retrenchment following WW1, the coal mine owners attempted to impose wage cuts on the miners. The trade unions responded by calling a general strike, beginning on 12th May 1926. The country ground to a halt for nine days and the Conservative government under Stanley Baldwin resorted to using troops and volunteers to maintain essential services.

The shut-down included the national press. When the BBC was created, one restriction imposed upon it was the '7 o'clock rule'. The press was concerned that a BBC with the ability to broadcast news would be a threat. The Government acceded to press lobbying by severely curtailing the BBC's role as a news organisation: it was not allowed to have such a role. News could only be broadcast after 7 o'clock in the evening and the BBC was not allowed to have its own journalists and had to use the same news agencies as the press. The strike meant that if the BBC were not able to report the news with the shut down of the press, there would not be any, and so the restriction was therefore lifted. About the only newspapers available was the one produced by the trade unions *The British Worker* and another, *The British Gazette*, by Churchill, who was the Home Secretary.

Churchill was an enthusiastic advocate of taking over the BBC and making it an arm of Government but Baldwin was aware that this would probably be counter-productive. Any public perception that the BBC was merely the voice-piece of Government would completely undermine any public trust in anything it broadcast. In any case, Baldwin was of the view that the BBC would already broadcast whatever the Government wished. He had a point. So far as Reith was concerned, the BBC was for the nation which itself was indivisible from the Government; Reith was an ardent supporter of 'the Establishment'. At the same time he was aware of the dangers of being perceived as too pro-government. He had to walk a very fine line. The delicacy of the situation was intensified by the fact that the BBC's Charter had not yet been approved by the Government: if Reith had alienated the Government, the terms of the Charter could have been made more severe than they were. The BBC was in a 'no win' situation. It did cave in to Government pressure. Most famously it succumbed to the Government over a conciliatory broadcast that the Archbishop of Canterbury was intending to make, but never did. Also, the BBC refused the microphone to any union representative whilst giving it to the Government. There was not much else it could do. Believing the strike to be a constitutional threat it was effectively outlawed: legally the BBC could do nothing that could be interpreted as encouraging the strikers.

However, at the end of it all, a mere nine days later, the BBC came out rather well. It had broadcast five bulletins a day (10a.m. and 1, 4, 7 and 9.30 p.m.). If nothing else, it had been able to give the union's point of view and report the strike in a manner that was deemed both conciliatory and reliable. A perception that the BBC would be a mouth-piece of the Government gave way to a reliance on its dependability. The strike might have threatened both the unions and the Government, but it benefited the BBC. Whatever its shortcomings, the reputation that the BBC would garnish for itself as a reliable reporter of news began with the General Strike. But, nevertheless, it would be several years before the BBC would establish for itself a major news operation: it would take another world war for it to do that.

Over the next decade, the principle of public service broadcasting continued to be developed as did the relationship between the BBC and the State. In 1933 the House of Commons debated the role of the BBC. The particular concern was with political broadcasting. The House passed a resolution stating that it would be 'contrary to the public interest' to 'subject the BBC to any control by Government or by Parliament other than the control already provided for in the Charter and in the licence.' The Postmaster General, Sir Kingsley Wood in 1933, summed up the situation thus:

Parliament decided in 1926 that the broadcasting of this country was not to be run as a state institution. It decided that wireless should not be commercialised. It put broadcasting on a basis radically different from that of broadcasting in the United States and continental countries, and finally, a bold and interesting experiment was made by the establishment of a corporation akin to the nature of a public utility corporation. Considerable freedom and discretion were designedly entrusted to the governors of the corporation......

The whole design, so far as I see it, was not to prohibit Ultimate Parliamentary control, but to limit Parliamentary Interference, and to accord to the corporation reasonable liberty of action as trustees of the service in the public interest...

(Speech in Parliamentary debate on broadcasting, House of Commons, 22 February, 1933; Hansard vol.274, cols 1833, 1843 cited in McDonnell)

However, as we shall see, the BBC was subjected to considerable pressure if not outright interference regarding foreign affairs.

Ullswater Report

As 1936 approached, the BBC's Charter was due to expire. On 17th April 1935, the government announced that it had appointed Lord Ullswater 'to consider the constitution, control, and finance of the broadcasting service...and advise generally on the conditions under which the service.. should be conducted after 31 December, 1936'. The report was duly published on 16th March 1935.The report was favourable to the BBC. The point of contention was political broadcasting. Of the committee members, reservations were principally voiced by the then Labour MP (later prime Minister) Clement Atlee.

First, the views of Ullswater. The committee seems to have been exercised mainly by the issue of impartiality:

It must be recognised as inevitable that more prominence is given to the leaders of the political party in power than to the opposition. There are numbers of occasions on which Ministers of State are called upon to make important pronouncements. These naturally have some political flavour and tend naturally to stress the beneficence of Government activities. There is an equally inevitable tendency in the general programmes of the corporation to devote more time to the expression of new ideas and the advocacy of change, in social and other spheres, than to the defence of orthodoxy and stability, since the reiteration of what exists and is familiar is not so interesting as exposition of what might be.

We have been informed by the BBC that criticism on the ground of political, intellectual, and artistic bias comes from the Right and from the Left.

(Report of the Broadcasting Committee, 1935 (Cmd 5091) HMSO, 1935-6, paras 87-9)

Atlee had other concerns. He was worried by the powers inscribed into the Charter (and are so to this day) that enable the Home Secretary, in an emergency and if it is 'expedient so to act' to send troops to 'take possession of the BBC in the name of and on behalf of His Majesty'.

Atlee took issue with what would constitute an 'emergency'.

> **The control of the BBC by the State in an emergency is obviously necessary, but there is a point where it is difficult to decide whether the emergency is really that of the State or the Government as representing the political party in power. The outstanding instance is that of the coal mining dispute of 1926. In my opinion there is no doubt that the way in which the broadcasting system was used by the Government of the day created in the minds of a very large section of the community grave suspicion which has prejudiced the Corporation ever since.**
>
> *(Report of the Broadcasting Committee, 1935 (Cmd 5091) HMSO, 1935–6, p.48)*

This is an issue we shall engage with more fully in Chapter 7. Atlee is drawing a distinction between the interests of the Government, in so far as those interests are identifiable with the interests of the nation, and those of a particular party – 'government' with a small 'g'. One of the interests of the party in power is to stay in power: this, along with any policy decisions with that primary aim in mind, might not be in the interests of the nation. This was a pertinent issue during the Falklands War in 1982.

The birth of television

Like the early history of cinema, the development of television was international and involved many people. In 1884 Paul Nipkow, a Russian, devised the 'Nipkow disc'. Spirally perforated, it would mechanically scan an object and convert the reflected light into electric impulses through the use of photo sensitive selenium cells. By using another disc, theoretically, these impulses could be converted back into an image of the original object. But he did not get beyond the theory and put the idea into practice.

In 1907, working independently of each other, both A.A. Campbell Swinton (a British scientist) and Boris Rosing (a Russian) showed how the cathode ray tube (invented in 1897 by Karl Braun) could be used as the basis of an electronic television system. Campbell Swinton proposed that the cathode ray tube be used in both the scanner and receiver whereas Rosing envisaged it only being used in the receiver. Campbell Swinton's idea was similar to the system that was eventually used. Although he never exploited his idea and put it in practice, he has a strong claim to being the inventor of television.

In Britain, however, the person most associated with early television is the Scot, John Logie Baird. Unfortunately for Baird, he chose the wrong system. Baird opted for a mechanical system, based on Nipkow's disc, not withstanding the fact that both Rosing and Campbell Swinton had shown that an electronic system based on the cathode ray tube was superior. Baird began experimenting with the Nipkow disc in 1922. He produced his first rudimentary pictures about a year later.

By late 1923 and early 1924 Baird was giving public demonstrations in his Surrey studio to journalists and in 1924 he took out a patent for his system. By 1925 he was transmitting crude pictures (of a ventriloquist's dummy called Stukey) to London. Baird was not alone in this work: D. Von Mihaly (Hungary) and Kenjiro Takayanagi (Japan) were also working on mechanical systems. In Russia Boris Grabovsky (who also claimed to have invented television) was working on an electronic system.

Figure 1.1 *John Logie Baird with an early TV*

Source: Corbis

The Americans, not be be outdone, were also active in 'inventing' television. Whilst others were working on mechanical systems, mostly based on Nipkow's disc, Vladimir Zworykin was developing an electronic system first for Westinghouse and later for RCA. Meanwhile, on 7th April 1927, RCA gave a public demonstration of a mechanical system that had been developed by their Bell laboratories. Five months later, in Los Angeles, the 24 year old Philo T. Farnsworth produced the first workable electronic system. A further advance in electronic television occurred in 1928, when NBC (owned by RCA) successfully tested Zworykin's Ionoscope. This was a cathode ray camera that was more efficient than any other because it could operate in lower light.

Meanwhile, Baird was hard at work. After a series of demonstrations in 1928 of his mechanical system, the Post Office recommended that the BBC should allow Baird to experiment in one of its own stations. To begin with the BBC was hostile to the suggestion but was effectively forced to co-operate when the Postmaster General threatened to award Baird his own broadcast licence. On the 30th September 1929, Baird transmitted his first broadcast from the BBC. To begin with the BBC only allowed Baird to broadcast either sound or image, but not both. His first synchronised broadcast came in March 1930. Baird seemed to go from strength to strength including a visit to America where seemingly only the intervention of the USA radio regulator, the Federal Radio Commission (FRC), prevented him from signing a contract with WMCA, a New York radio station. The FRC rejected WMCA's application to broadcast television on the grounds that they did not want a foreigner gaining a foothold in broadcasting in the USA.

The beginning of the end for Baird came in 1931 when RCA acquired a large share in EMI. Aided by RCA, EMI were able to develop an electronic television system far superior to Baird's mechanical system. Baird's system could initially only produce 30 line pictures whereas EMI were producing 180 line pictures. EMI was strengthened in 1933 when they merged with Marconi, forming Marconi-EMI. By now, with their extensive experience of radio, Marconi had developed high-powered transmitters, while EMI had developed their relatively powerful cathode ray Emitron camera. In 1935, a committee chaired by Lord Selsdon recommended that the BBC should start regular television broadcasts with a minimum standard of 240 lines. Parts of Alexandra Palace were converted into a television studio – in fact *two* studios with one for Baird and another for Marconi-EMI. It had been decided that in order to choose between the two competing systems, they should each broadcast on alternate weeks. This was to continue for three months, the regular service having been scheduled to start in September 1936. The Marconi-EMI system clearly outshone Baird's, and his was dropped by the BBC in February 1937. The electronic, cathode ray system had won the day.

The BBC began its television service on 2nd November 1936. In keeping with the public broadcasting ethos established in radio, the service would be free of advertising and funded by the licence fee. The BBC was not the first regular television service in the world, as is sometimes claimed. Germany had had one since March 1935. In fact the route Germany had tentatively taken was different from either the USA or the UK. It was a state controlled system, based around public viewing areas, such as cinemas. It was a crude system using only 180 lines, considerably inferior to both the British and American systems.

Reith had no interest in television, and like many in the BBC regarded it as inferior to radio. This is perhaps not surprising given the classics/humanities/English literature background of many of his senior staff. Television was the plaything of the engineers. Perhaps for this reason, it was able to get away with somewhat less 'worthy' programming. In the first few days of transmission, there was a display of tap-dancing, instruction in building model boats (given by a bus driver – television was seemingly even more egalitarian!) There was comedy (the popular Ben Lyon and Bebe Daniels) and excerpts from a West End play, *Marigold*.

Not very many people were able to watch any of this. For one thing the transmission range (from Alexandra Palace in London) was only about 40–100 miles and it is estimated that there were only about 400 households with what was then an expensive luxury item. Television began to establish itself but only amongst the more affluent middle class. It was expensive: on average a television set cost £100 (the equivalent of about £3000 today). However, on 12th May, 1937, the profile of television was bolstered by the coverage of the coronation of King George VI.

This was the first big television event and the BBC's most ambitious project thus far: the BBC claimed that it was the 'first attempt to transmit a real "outside broadcast"' (Wheen, p.223). Unlike the coronation of Queen

Elizabeth II, coverage was restricted to and from Westminster Abbey – there was no coverage of the actual ceremony. It has been estimated 50,000 people watched the event from distances of up to 60 miles from London.

The effects of WW2

By 1938 sales had increased to 5000. But its days were temporarily numbered. On 3rd September 1939, television ceased to broadcast. The fear was that the transmitter at Alexandra Palace would act as a beacon for German bombers and so it was decided to terminate transmissions for the duration of hostilities. The BBC television engineers were either drafted into the technical divisions of the armed services whilst others (about 50) worked on the development of radar and navigation.

The final transmission shut down half way through a cartoon: the second half would not be seen for another six years.

Post war television

The BBC had a good war. By 1945 it had vastly expanded its news service which gained a reputation that was second to none any where in the world. It also had a standing in the country that placed it at the centre of the national culture. Even before this, Reith felt that he had achieved his goal: he retired as Director General in 1938, becoming Chairman of Imperial Airways. The general radio service had also expanded. Before the war there were only two radio channels: the national service, transmitted around the country via relay stations and a regional service.

By the end of the war there were three national radio services: the Forces Programme, the Home Service and the Third Programme (these would later be recast as Radio 2, 4 and 3). Public service broadcasting was firmly established and the BBC regarded as one of the major cultural forces in the land. But what to do about television?

The Hankey Committee

The issue began to be addressed well before the end of the war. In 1943 the Hankey Committee was established to enquire into the 're-instatement and development of television'. Incidentally, at about this time, the last remaining German transmitter was destroyed in a bombing raid. As the Americans had also ceased transmitting for a while (apart from one or two stations in New York and only on a limited basis), throughout the world, television went off the air.

1943 was a key year for the British. The Germans had been defeated in North Africa. With the U-boats virtually beaten the Battle of the Atlantic had been won and after a ferocious battle with appalling casualties on both sides, the Russians had prevailed at Stalingrad. The Allies were preparing for victory. It was in 1943 that the Beveridge Report was published – the blue-print for the welfare state. It was in this context that thoughts began to turn to considering what kind of television service there should be after the war.

Hankey received many submissions concerning a variety of issues: the number of lines there should be; whether there should be advertising and/or sponsorship; whether the BBC should retain its monopoly. Amongst the many interested parties who made representations to the committee was J. Arthur Rank, one the leading figures of the British film industry. Fearing competition, many in the film industry were hostile to television. Rank, however, was thinking more in lines of collaboration. He proposed that the film industry should work with the BBC in making programmes and screen them on both television and at cinemas. This was not at all far fetched. The Germans had done it and it was already happening in London; Leicester Square boasted the *Scophony*, a large television screen in the Odeon cinema (the Odeon was the cinema circuit owned by Rank). With greater prescience he foresaw a potential market in films being shown on television. Rank understood that television endowed films with a residual value that could easily be exploited without diminishing their theatrical receipts, as there were 'always people who liked to see a film twice or who had missed it on the first release'. Rank believed that television might make films more popular than ever.

On the other matters considered by Hankey, the conclusions were similar to the pre-war report. Hankey endorsed the principle of monopoly ownership for television as well as radio, there being no 'room for two public systems of television in the United Kingdom.' An interesting conclusion in the light of television's subsequent development.

The ever present question was how should television be paid for? There was an awareness that television was expensive and even in the 1940s many thought that direct advertising and/or sponsorship was the answer. Sponsorship was accepted in principle by the Postmaster General and the Television Advisory Committee, but rejected by the BBC.

On the matter of sponsorship Hankey commented, 'We consider that the inclusion of sponsored programmes and even direct advertising ....would be fully justified.' However, the BBC's position prevailed and they remain sponsor free. In the light of current arguments about the future of the BBC and the nature of public service broadcasting, the Hankey Report is interesting reading, as it is a rehearsal of those same arguments.

Although Hankey was prepared to accept the BBC accepting sponsorship and even advertisements he rejected the idea of a separate, wholly commercial broadcaster. '.....until the television service is well developed, commercial interests would not be willing to incur large expenditure for the purpose, owing, for example to the limited audience served.....In these circumstances, and without prejudicing the matter for the future, we feel it would be premature to come to a conclusion on this question.' So a status quo remained so for a decade although it is likely that but for the war, commercial television would have been introduced earlier.

Despite these decisions, the issue of the BBC monopoly had been raised. Some voices were expressing concern that although centralised control was imperative during wartime, it would become redundant with the successful ending of the war (a foregone conclusion by 1944 and a very real probability as early as 1943). For some, 'the BBC's monopoly of broadcasting, of such national utility in wartime, was an unacceptable restriction of freedom in peacetime.' (McDonnell, p.19)

A new government

After the war in 1945, the Labour party came to power with a landslide result. They were opposed to any commercialisation of the broadcasting and renewed the BBC's Charter in 1946 keeping the monopoly intact and without – what had by now become with any Charter renewal – the usual enquiry.

Labour's argument was that the BBC should have time to adjust to peace. Their one concession, in a White Paper published in 1946, was to extend the Charter to five years and not ten. The White paper reaffirmed the principle that only a monopoly could guarantee that all sections of the population would be offered a 'balanced' range of programmes. One critic of this decision was Sir Frederick Ogilvie, a former Director General (October 1938 – January 1942). As was common in those days for the expression of outrage, he wrote to *The Times*.

Sir
It is good to see that you, Sir, support the plea for an enquiry into broadcasting. And it is much to be hoped that the question of the BBC Charter, when it comes to be debated, will not be regarded, in Parliament or outside, as a mere trial of strength between the Government of the day and the opposition of the day.

What is at stake is not a matter of politics, but of freedom. Is monopoly of broadcasting to be fastened on us for a further term? Is the future of this great public service to be settled without public enquiry, by Royal Commission or otherwise, into the many technical and other changes which have taken place in the last 10 years?

Freedom is choice. And monopoly is inevitably the negation of freedom, no matter how efficiently it is run, or how wise and kindly the boards or committees in charge of it. It denies freedom of choice to listeners. It denies freedom of employment to speakers, musicians, writers, actors and all who seek their chance on the air.

.......The BBC itself, good as it is, would gain vastly by the abolition of the monopoly and the introduction of competition. So would all the millions of listeners, who would still have the BBC to listen to, but would have other programmes to enjoy as well. So would all would-be broadcasters gain. If rejected by the BBC, they would have other corporations to turn to.

(The Times 26th June 1946)

These arguments would be used forty years later when, once again, the question of what kind of broadcasting we should have would be debated.

Whilst there was only one monopoly broadcaster, the principle of public service broadcasting advocated by Reith was secure. With the BBC standing alone, it made sense that they should offer a range of audiences a variety of programmes, all with some sense of 'quality' – and be publicly funded. However, once broadcasting was opened up to a broader market, this position became more difficult to sustain. In the late forties the fight against the BBC monopoly was on, and throughout that period gathered momentum in parliament and from commercial interests. The upper echelons of the BBC marshalled their arguments in defence of Reithian principles. Unfortunately, these arguments often appeared to the public to be 'too close to moral and cultural snobbery and too far removed from public taste.' (McDonnell, p.22).

The Labour government eventually constituted an enquiry into broadcasting under Lord Beveridge. Beveridge was no stranger to major government enquires: in 1943 his name was on the blueprint of the welfare state: the Beveridge Report. The Committee looking into broadcasting sat 62 times and received 233 memoranda over a period of eighteen months. The committee concluded that the BBC monopoly should remain intact. The report placed much emphasis on the 'social purpose' of broadcasting. Competition was rejected; the grounds being that it would be 'imperfect competition', 'the physical conditions' of broadcasting not allowing more than 'three or four broadcasting authorities of equal rank.' Also, the Committee considered that 'to make broadcast programmes directly and automatically dependent on the preferences expressed by listeners would be contrary to the pursuit of the highest social purpose of broadcasting which is in the last resort education.'

The report was presented to Parliament on 18th January 1951. This was followed, seven months later by a White Paper that closely followed Beveridges's recommendation. Only one member of the Committee had raised a dissenting voice. This was Selwyn Lloyd, then a Conservative MP. The minority report he produced argued that a commercial radio and television system should be set up to compete with and complement the BBC. Reith's 'brute force of monopoly' was a danger to personal liberties. He did not, however, advocate a complete free market on the lines of the United States. Lloyd advocated a system mid-way between the American and British models with television overseen by a regulatory authority like the Federal Communications Commission of the United States, but with more power.

The end of monopoly

Before Beveridge's recommendations could be put into effect, there was a change in government and the Conservatives came to power. This probably did no more than accelerate the inevitable. The arguments for at least a measure of free market in broadcasting had been circulating since the inception of radio in the twenties and they had not gone away. The advertising industry in the UK had watched with envy, as across the Atlantic first radio and then television had been milked for all their commercial worth. Gradually, in the UK, the years of post-war austerity were giving way to a measure of prosperity; people had more money to spend and the economy was expanding. The pressure for a commercial television channel increased from advertisers and entrepreneurs alike, all of whom could see the commercial potential of television. The Conservative party, now in power, was sympathetic. A new White Paper was written: this was the first time a government argued for the end of the broadcasting monopoly.

The Conservative White Paper (1952)

The essential points of the White Paper were:

- There was recognition that the monopoly had done much 'to establish the excellent and reputable broadcasting service for which this country is renowned'.
- The BBC should remain intact and 'should be the only broadcasting organisation having any claim on the revenue' from the licence.
- The BBC should not carry advertising.
- Provision for competition within broadcasting should be made.
- License for any broadcaster would be granted (and, if necessary, withdrawn), by the Postmaster General.

What followed was an impassioned debate, on both sides, about the future of broadcasting. The Labour Party argued that commercial television would be 'a national disaster'. The Church also expressed its anxieties, with the Archbishop of York claiming that the second channel should be resisted 'for the sake of our children' (op. cit.). The recently formed National Television Council circulated alarming stories of the philistinism that stalked the airwaves of the USA. On the other side of the debate, the Popular Television Association, supported by television manufacturers, the advertising industry and Conservative MPs campaigned for commercial television; shrouding their commercial interests in a cloak of democracy and a call for the end of paternalistic broadcasting – they advocated 'people's television'. Winston Churchill was the Prime Minister and an advocate of competition.

The coronation of Elizabeth II

During the course of the debate provoked by the White Paper, King George VI died. The coronation of his successor, Elizabeth, on the 2nd June 1953, became the single most important event broadcast thus far in the history of British television. It was also the world's first international broadcast on this scale. It was not only technically significant, but it fuelled the debate about the future of television. For the supporters of the BBC it provided positive evidence of the value of public service broadcasting, bringing to the nation, unfettered by advertising, a historical national event.

This time the actual coronation was recorded. The BBC had five cameras in the Abbey and fifteen along the route of the procession, all linked by five Mobile Control Rooms. All of this was facilitated by twenty-nine miles of cable laid down by the Post Office. The actual crowning was recorded by the BBC's smallest cameraman, Anthony Flanagan, tucked discretely away amongst the orchestra. As Francis Wheen comments, Flanagan's job was not an enviable one. 'As a BBC report noted, his back "was menaced by a ring of steel-sharp cello pegs"; he was also hit on the head every time the orchestra's conductor, William McKie, brought down his baton.' (Wheen, p.226) That day the audience was huge. Although there were only 2 million televisions in the country, it was watched by 20 million. 'The BBC estimated that 7 800 000 people watched it in their own homes, another 10 400 000 watched it in the homes of friends and 1 500 000 watched it in pubs and cinemas.' (Wheen, p.226). Through a highly complicated technical procedure, it was relayed to France, Holland and West Germany.

The coronation had two instant effects. Within months the ownership of television sets almost doubled and a clause was written into the Television Act 1954 stipulating that no programme about the royal family could be interrupted by advertising. It was out of the haze of heated debate that this Act had emerged. It established the Independent Television Authority (ITA) under Sir Kenneth (later Lord) Clark

> The BBC's pictures were sent from London to Dover by three radio links working in tandem; another link carried them to the French coast, at a point near Cap Blanc Nez, from where the signals travelled by further radio links to Mont Cassel in Northern France and onwards to Paris. There the 405 line pictures were converted into 819 lines for French television; but the original 405 line signals were also sent on across Belgium to Breda, in Holland, where they were converted to a 625 line standard, the one used by both Holland and West Germany. The quality of the pictures at the end of all this country hopping was astonishingly sharp. At 11.25 a.m., less than an hour after the crowning, RTF in Paris cabled the BBC: 'VERY URGENT QUALITY IMAGE PASSABLE DEPARTURE FROM BUCKINGHAM PALACE EXCELLENT FROM 10.30 STOP SOUND PERFECT STOP PUBLIC CROWDING ROUND PUBLIC RECEIVING SETS AND CINEMA HALLS FULL STOP REACTIONS ENTHUSIASTIC STOP BRAVO'.
>
> *(Wheen, F. Television,* Century Publishing, *1985, p.228)*

who was then Chairman of the Arts Council. The ITA was tasked to provide a service initially for ten years.

The birth of Independent Television

In the political circumstances it was inevitable that those advocating the end of monopoly would prevail. But there was solace for the monopoly supporters in the extent to which public service principles still informed the new arrangement: a United States style free-for-all was not going to be permitted.

The ITA opted for a federal structure, initially based upon the population areas of London, Birmingham and Manchester and ending up with fifteen regional companies, including two for London - one operating during the weekdays and the other at weekends. The companies forming the new network were all contracted to the ITA to whom they had to pay a fee. The ITA owned the transmitters and laid down the criteria by which the companies were selected in the first place. The contractors were chosen according to both their financial resources and their programming plans, which had to conform to what was virtually a public service remit. A range of programmes had to be offered, including religious, educational, children's and a wide range of entertainment, drama and news. It was decided that news should be handled by a separate company, paid for by the regions. This would assure financial and therefore editorial independence: this became ITN.

Neither the new television companies nor the programmes they made were completely unregulated. 'It would be necessary to introduce safeguards against possible abuses, and a controlling body would be required for this purpose, for regulating the conduct of the new stations, for exercising a general oversight of the programmes and for advising on appropriate matters.'

Any new 'corporation' would own and operate the transmitters, renting from the Post Office any connecting links between stations. These facilities would be hired to the private companies that would make the programmes. The new corporation, the Independent Television Authority (ITA), had a number of powers.

1. To call for programme schedules and scripts in advance.
2. To require the companies to make sound and visual records of programmes for subsequent examination.
3. To forbid the broadcasting of specified classes of matter.
4. To regulate advertisements.

In addition, the new corporation was enjoined to make provision for religious broadcasting; the impartial broadcasting of political matters and it would not be allowed to broadcast its own views: the BBC was already operating along these lines.

The arrival of independent, commercial television precipitated a revision of what the BBC understood as 'public service' broadcasting. This began with a new

> Most of the misgivings which have been expressed about commercial television are based on the assumption that it could be provided only by what is usually described as 'Sponsoring', that is, that advertisers would hire time on the television transmitters and provide and control their own programmes. This however is not so; the Government has decided as a basic principle that there should be no 'sponsoring' and the responsibility for what goes out on the air shall rest with the operator of the station, and not on the advertiser...
>
> *(Broadcasting: Memorandum on Television Policy (Cmd 9005) HMSO 1953 Cited in McDonnell, p.32)*

Director General. Sir Ian Jacob's appointment (1952) was not long before the new White Paper. He brought with him the belief that if the BBC's tradition of public service was to survive, it had to adapt to the new broadcasting circumstances and public mood. Under Jacob, public service became to mean extending programme choices without attempting to direct the taste of the audience. Whilst public service broadcasting still embraced the intention to 'inform, to educate, and to entertain the public' it had to do so whilst developing 'to the maximum the potentialities of the medium as a means of communication.' In addition, 'the corporation must try to satisfy the needs and tastes of the full range of listeners and viewers.' Whilst Jacob's views of public service broadcasting were firmly rooted in Reithian ideas, we can see a shift in his thinking. He not only accepted entertainment (after all, even Reith did) but he encouraged it: 'There should be no lack of light entertainment and triviality alongside the more serious and informative, but it should be of a kind which avoids indecency, and does not exploit vulgarity, violence and tawdriness.' His acceptance of the legitimacy of popular taste was endorsed by the BBC Chairman, Sir Arthur Fforde and marked a continuing process of refinement, if not redefinition, of public service broadcasting that continues to this day.

A third channel: BBC2

The Pilkington Report (1962)

It would seem that each decade wrought great changes on the broadcast landscape: the 1960s were no exception. On the first day of the new decade a new Director General, Hugh Greene assumed office. Greene was in place in time to have to deal with the next great change in television: a third channel. Greene was a man of much experience. During WW2 he ran BBC broadcasts to Germany. After the war he became head of psychological warfare in Malaya: 'he had effectively charmed Communist rebels out of the jungle.' (Black, p. 153). From this experience, Black writes he had formed 'a number of principles which, he said, applied to any overt form of propaganda'. It had to hold, interest and inform its audience. It must have its roots in national character. Most important of all it must be based on the truth.' Black comments, probably correctly, that his experience during the war and in Malaya equipped Greene admirably 'for the job of impressing Pilkington'.

In 1960 another Committee of Enquiry into the future of broadcasting had been set-up this time under Lord Pilkington. The most important outcome of this particular enquiry was going to be particularly significant: a third television channel had been advocated and both the BBC and the independent television companies wanted it. Both the BBC and ITV made submissions to the Committee. The first three years of Greene's tenure at the BBC was preoccupied with Pilkington and he (the BBC) won. The Pilkington Committee was greatly concerned with what it regarded as the 'triviality' of certain ITV programmes 'and what it perceived as a lack of public service mission within the commercial system'. ITV did not help their case with their submission, which seemed to Pilkington to define 'public service' in giving the public what it wants. In many respects, the Pilkington Committee report is a restatement of Reithian values. This is evident in the following extract:

Because, in principle, the possible range of subject matter is inexhaustible, all of it can never be presented, nor can the public know what the range is. So, the broadcaster must explore it, and choose from it first. This might be called 'giving a lead': but it is not the lead of the aristocrat or arrogant. It is the proper exercise of responsibility by public authorities duly constituted as trustees for the public interest.

The antithesis, 'broadcasting should give the public what it wants, and not what someone thinks is good for the public', is, then, a gross over-simplification of a complex and continuing problem; a statement which presents unreal extremes of view as though they were the only choice.

(McDonnell, J., Public Service Broadcasting, *Routledge, 1991, pp. 42–43)*

The report noted that both the BBC and the main ITV companies regarded both extremes as untenable. The report quotes the BBC's view that 'the tendency should be to keep "a little bit ahead of public opinion, leading to some extent but not thinking all the time in doing good" '. This does, of course, mark a shift in 'classic' Reithian thinking, insofar as public taste is being taken into account at all. As it was, the independent television companies came into a good deal of criticism from Pilkington, who were blamed for 'debauching' public taste. On the other hand, the BBC was praised for its commitment to public service broadcasting and professionalism. It's clear, in retrospect, that the BBC under Greene had marshalled by far the most professional and persuasive campaign. They got what they wanted on all the main issues: a rejection of any funding through advertising, the maintenance of the licence fee and a second channel, BBC2. The ITA, on the other hand, was instructed to place a much firmer grip on the independent companies and gain a much firmer control over their output. Pilkington's legislative outcome was the Television Act (1963). This had the function of imposing upon commercial television an enhanced public service remit, which would last until 1990. For the first time, in fact, commercial television (ITV) was described officially as a 'public service'.

2(1) It shall be the duty of the Authority:

(a) to provide the television broadcasting services as a public service for disseminating information, education and entertainment;

(b) to ensure that the programmes broadcast by the Authority in each area maintain a high general standard in all respects, and a proper balance and wide range in their subject-matter, having regard both to the programmes as a whole and also to the days of the week on which, the programmes are broadcast;

(c) to secure a wide showing for programmes of merit.

(Television Act 1963, 11 and 12 eliz. 2c. 50cl.2(1)A–C)

This led, for a while, to an outstandingly successful model that only became untenable with the development of new technologies and the accompanying explosion of new channels. For a while the channels were in competition for audiences, *but not for finance.* This enabled both the BBC and independent television to flourish. Whilst the BBC had the guaranteed finance of the licence fee, independent television had a monopoly on television advertising. The BBC had a long established reputation for excellence, a reputation that ITV wanted to ape. Many felt this led to an unsatisfactory convergence of taste and standards that seemed to exclude many people in what was increasingly seen to be a culturally diverse nation.

Technical advances

Along with the advent of BBC2, two significant and related technical changes occurred around this time. Up until the advent of BBC2 on 20th April 1964, television had been broadcast on VHF using 405 lines. Whilst the quality of this standard had been acceptable to audiences (looked at today it seems very grainy) it was not adequate for colour television, which BBC engineers and others had long been preparing for. The Government and the BBC agreed that BBC2 should be used to test new technology and this included the new transmission standard of 625 lines which was compatible with colour. This did, however, necessitate a new television set. Colour was introduced three years later in 1967. The full transition to 625 lines took about twenty years. The manufacture of 405 sets ceased in 1997 and between 1982 and 1985 VHF transmissions were phased out by both the BBC and ITV. To begin with, BBC2 was only available in the southeast of England. Later in the year, about two thirds of the population were able to receive BBC2, but to do so they had to buy a new television. To begin with, broadcast time afforded the new channel was very modest, just four hours per evening. By 1974 this had increased to 60% of the time BBC1 was on the air. BBC2, however, had not just been conceived as a medium for testing new technology; its brief extended to developing new ideas for programming. In this it achieved some success. One of the ideas it tried out, only to abandon, was themed evenings with programmes worked around a particular film genre or a topical issue. After three months the idea was dropped, not to be resurrected until Channel Four came on air in 1982. It seems that the idea quickly lost favour with the BBC because it created a scheduling problem. It was hard to synchronise the programmes of the two BBC channels. Schedulers wanted 'junctions between the two channels, such that when one programme finished on BBC2, another would start on BBC1, etc., thereby facilitating audiences moving from one channel to the other, reducing the risk of them switching to ITV. The fear was that 'theming' would limit the choice of programmes available to the schedulers, making it harder to find ones of compatible length to 'dovetail' in the schedules. There was also the possibility of an audience not appreciating the theme so it could be lost for the entire evening.

Amongst the programmes with which BBC2 scored a notable success was the mammoth documentary series, *The Great War*. It was the precursor of a form of documentary that became very popular. It ran to twenty six parts, consisting of archive footage and interviews with surviving participants. It must count as an early co-production, having been jointly produced by the BBC, the Canadian Broadcasting Corporation and the Australian Broadcasting Corporation. Written by a team of historians, it drew on the reminiscences of more than 50,000 survivors of the war.

Another success was the talk show, now a staple of television schedules. This was pioneered by BBC2 with *Late Night Line-Up*, a cultural programme offering a critical appraisal of the BBC's output. As such, it was a precursor of something like *Late Night Review* (BBC2) rather than celebrity based chat shows such as *Clive Anderson All Talk* (BBC1), which were both running in 1999.

BBC2 made its mark with drama as well, most memorably with the twenty-six part adaptation of John Galsworthy's *The Forsyte Saga* which was transmitted in 1969. This had two distinctions: it was the last series to be recorded in monochrome and the first lengthy television adaptation of a major book. It is also worth noting that it had extensive overseas sales, including the USA and (unusually for the time) the Soviet Union.

Colour television

The long awaited colour transmissions began on Saturday, 1st July 1967. The BBC was the first European network to do so. The Americans had had colour since 1953. The genres that most effectively exploited colour were natural history programmes and documentaries. Of the latter BBC2 produced some monuments to the form, the two most significant being Lord Clark's thirteen part series on art, *Civilisation* (1969) and the magnificent *The Ascent of Man* (1972–73). The scale of *The Ascent of Man* was truly epic, not so much in its length (thirteen parts) but its range. Presented by Dr Jacob Bronowski, it embraced science, art and philosophy in a way that showed the interrelationship between them. Bronowski had clearly invested a great deal of himself in the series; the manner of his presentation was an awe inspiring demonstration of learning, wisdom and compassion. Andrew Cassell is right when he describes the programme as 'pushing television to its intellectual limits' and marking 'an important moment in the history of the medium.' (Cassell, p117).

The Annan Report (1977)

The Annan enquiry into broadcasting was originally proposed by the Labour Government in 1970. But there was a change of government and the proposals were shelved. In 1974, with another Labour government in power, the Annan Committee began its enquiries. At the same time, the franchises, now in the gift of the new IBA, were extended to 1976 and the BBC Charter until 1979 and then further to 1981.

By this time the Independent Television Authority, who had since 1954 been the overseer of commercial television, had a change of name commensurate with the extension of its role. The Conservatives were keen to exploit the commercial opportunities of radio and in 1972 passed the Sound Broadcasting Act which brought into being a local radio system. This was, in part, a response to highly popular pirate radio stations, such as Radio Caroline, which were broadcasting from boats off-shore. Despite the fact that such activity was outlawed by the 1967 Marine Broadcasting (Offences) Act, they flourished. Now that radio was brought within the remit of the ITA, its name was changed to the Independent Broadcasting Authority.

A month after the passage of the Sound Broadcasting Act, the BBC completely revamped its own radio services. Until now there had been the Light Programme (which offered popular music and light entertainment), the Home Service (which was largely talks, current affairs and drama) and the Third programme, which was renowned for classical music, not least through the BBC's own orchestras. They were renamed Radio 2, 4 and 3 respectively. Aside from these services, the BBC started another, Radio 1, which broadcast nothing but pop music.

The seventies were a highly fractious period at just about every level – socially, economically and politically. Broadcasting was obviously not immune from this and the debates that ensued were partisan and frequently acrimonious. Independent television came in for its own share of criticism, as did the BBC. On the one hand the BBC was regarded as a bastion of the socially and culturally privileged and on the other as a squalid den of dissident left-wing propagandists, especially as viewed by Mary Whitehouse's 'Clean Up TV Campaign' who in the sixties and seventies monitored what were perceived to be moral transgressions committed by television. On top of that television was becoming increasingly expensive and inflation was eating away at the value of the licence fee. It was not a good time, except that is, for programmes: news, current affairs and drama were flourishing.

It was a current affairs programme that caused a breach between the BBC and the Labour Party. Soon after the Labour defeat in 1970 the BBC transmitted a documentary about what life was like for people who had once had power and had now lost it. The programme was called *Yesterday's Men*.

Ex-labour politicians, especially Harold Wilson, ex-prime minister objected to the title. In fact, they objected to the whole tone of the programme and claimed that they had been misled by the programme makers. Wilson had previously been scarred by an interview conducted by David Dimbleby. Wilson had objected to a question about the amount of money he had made from his memoirs. Annan's eventual proposal was that neither the BBC or ITV should get the fourth channel. In the end this met with little opposition from either the BBC or ITV.

Whilst reaffirming the principles of public service broadcasting the Annan Report singled out a central difficulty: how could broadcasters provide 'good' programmes when there was no agreement on what 'good' might be?

John Reith, who created public service broadcasting in this country, was undoubtedly determined to use broadcasting as a means for making a better society. Yet much of what people today consider to be good broadcasting would have been rejected by his definition of that term. Too often those who advocate such a policy seem to suppose that social and moral objectives could be formulated, agreed, and then imposed, on the broadcasters. No doubt they can in totalitarian countries. They cannot here. We do not accept that it is part of the broadcasters function to act as arbiters of morals or manners, or set themselves up as social engineers.

(McDonnell, p.68)

The last sentence in this is significant: it represents the first disavowal of the Reithian principle that broadcasters should be 'arbiters of morals or manners'. There is here an expression of uncertainty that runs throughout the history of attempts to define 'public service broadcasting'. It is probable that the only era of broadcasting to manifest any kind of certainty about this was that of Reith. As we have seen, he was clear enough: he would never have brooked any politician imposing anything upon the BBC. The issue, however, did not arise because of an ideological congruence between him and the government; to a large extent they shared the same values.

The Annan Committee submitted its report in March 1977. It contained 174 separate recommendations. The first was to underwrite, again, the principles of public service broadcasting: 'Broadcasting should continue to be provided as public services, and should continue to be the responsibility of public authorities.' Other proposals were:

- Each Broadcasting Authority should have its own sources of revenue and should not have to compete ....for exactly the same source of finance.
- The BBC should continue to be the main national instrument of broadcasting in the United Kingdom.
- The BBC should continue to be financed from the revenue of the broadcasting receiving licence.
- Proposals for financing the BBC from taxation or any form of advertising should be rejected.

The Committee also proposed that the BBC should lose copyright on its programmes listings. It was recommended that both the BBC and IBA should lose control over local radio services: it was recommended that these be placed under the control of a Local Broadcasting Authority.

As we have already mentioned, the Annan report was not a wholesale endorsement of Reith's notion of public service broadcasting; in fact there was a radical shift. The Reithian notion of public service broadcasting was to offer the best ('best' defined by the cultural values of his class) to as many people as possible. In the Annan report there is a marked shift from this position: there is a move towards redefining public service broadcasting in terms of accommodating minority interests.

Annan published his report in a Britain markedly different to that of Reith's. Technology had changed; the broadcasting environment had changed; society had changed. Britain, since the 1950s, had become increasingly multicultural. Attitudes towards authority had changed; people were less deferential. Popular culture had asserted itself – apart from anything else it had become, since the 1950s, a major economic force. Annan was anxious to reflect the cultural diversity of the country through a new broadcasting institution. He was not particularly anxious to give it to commercial television and the BBC were already operating a second channel. They recommended that a fourth channel should be operated by a new Open Broadcasting Authority. Following the ideas of Anthony Smith, Annan conceived the fourth channel as being rather like a publishing house, commissioning new programmes rather than making them themselves such as the BBC and IBA franchise holders. In the hope of encouraging greater diversity, the OBA would be free of the programming obligations imposed upon the BBC and the IBA.

Channel 4

1979: another election, another government. With a huge Tory victory, Thatcher set out on a crusade on behalf of economic liberalism, the basic tenet being that the state has little business being involved in business. 'There is no society, only individuals.' Broadcasting was not to be left out of the extensive and widespread process of de-nationalisation and de-regulation that the Tories set about pursuing: broadcasting was to be opened up to the free market and made more competitive. The Annan report was largely discarded, except for the new channel. Channel Four (C4) was placed in the hands of the IBA rather than the OBA, but apart from that its character largely reflected the recommendations of the Annan Report. Its remit was to provide innovative and minority interest programming. It was protected from the harsher winds of the free market by being funded by the ITV regions through a 13.6% levy on earnings from advertising. In return, the regions gained revenue by selling advertising space on C4. The idea was that the system would free C4 of having to worry about ratings – it having a brief to provide minority interest programmes. It did take a while for the new channel to establish a strong advertising profile, but it did eventually happen once advertisers realised that, although relatively small, the C4 audience tended to be young Bs and C1s – relatively high earners. Despite the buffer provided by ITV and growing ratings, C4 has never been completely free of ratings concern. Aside from the obvious fact that broadcasting a programme is pointless if nobody is watching it, there was always at least the potential of pressure from both the ITV companies and the government if the channel became unpopular and did not generate a sizeable audience. The ITV companies wanted to make a profit from C4 advertising space and the Treasury would have to fit the bill if the channel made a loss. As a result of the Broadcasting Act of 1990, C4 became a public broadcasting service in January 1993. Still within the remit of the Independent Television Commission, it is fully independent of the other ITC companies and now sells its own advertising space.

Jeremy Isaacs

Jeremy Isaacs was appointed as the first Chief Executive of C4. Isaacs had an impressive record, both as a programme maker and executive. In the sixties he had produced two 'flagship' current affairs programme: Rediffusion's *This Week* and the BBC's *Panorama*. In the seventies he became Controller of Features and then Director of Programmes at Thames, where he was responsible for the epic documentary series, *World at War*. Protesting at what he regarded as unwarranted intervention by the Independent Broadcasting Authority (IBA) he left in 1978. The IBA had banned a Thames documentary, *The Amnesty Report*, which was critical of the Royal Ulster Constabulary in Northern Ireland, alleging brutal treatment of IRA suspects. Isaacs handed the banned programme over to the BBC, thereby making his position at Thames untenable. This mix of high-profile programming experience and clear evidence of independent thinking made him an ideal candidate. His letter of application was a distillation of C4 programming policy and the following list is a summary of the points made in his application:

- To encourage innovation across the whole range of programmes
- To find audiences for the channel and for all its programmes
- To make programmes of special appeal to particular audiences
- To develop the channel's educational potential to the full
- To provide platforms for the widest range of opinion in utterance, discussion, and debate
- To maintain as flexible a schedule as practicable to enable a quick response to changing needs
- To make an opening in the Channel for criticism of its own output
- To accord a high priority to the arts

- If funds allow, to make or help make films of feature length for television here, for cinema abroad.

The structure of Channel Four

Commensurate with these aims were his plans for the structure of C4. As 'Four' was not going to make its own programmes, it was clearly going to have to commission them from the programme makers themselves. The Chief Executive appointed a staff of fourteen commissioning editors, each responsible for a specific area of programming and two film purchasers; ITN was commissioned to provide news.

All of the Commissioning Editors are members of the Programme Committee, which is chaired by the Chief Executive (currently Michael Jackson). This committee decides which of the many ideas submitted should be turned into actual programmes. The next level in the structure is the Acquisition Department. The acquisition team negotiates with the programme supplier over such matters as contractual arrangements and budgets. The Programme Finance Committee, also chaired by the Chief Executive, gives final approval to the commissioning of a programme. Once a programme has got the go-ahead, the Finance Department, allocates finance to the programme makers at various stages of production, and monitors expenditure. The completed programme is then passed on to the Presentation Department which is responsible for scheduling and on-air promotion. Finally, the Transmission Department, headed by the Chief Engineer, organise the transmission of the programme. Other departments include Marketing, Business Development (who manage the commercial exploitation of the programme, including overseas sales and any 'tie-ins' or 'spin-offs' such as books, CDs, video cassettes, etc.) and Administration and Industrial Relations.

FilmFour

One of C4's most significant successes has been its involvement in film. Right from the beginning it became involved in film production, offering a considerable boost to independent film production in the U.K. Many films backed by C4 have achieved considerable success, such as *My Beautiful Laundrette* (1985), *Four Weddings and a Funeral* (1994), *Shallow Grave* (1994) *Trainspotting* (1996) and *Wonderland* (1999). C4 also backs films made outside the UK.

In 1998 C4 launched FilmFour Ltd and FilmFour Channel. FilmFour Ltd makes, distributes and sells films; FilmFour Channel carries independent films from around the world on satellite, cable and digital television. Since the launch of C4 in 1982, it has backed over three hundred films.

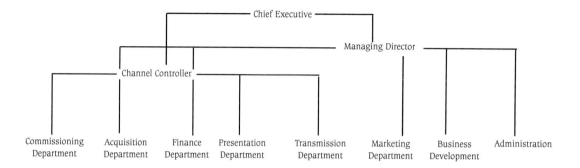

Figure 1.4 *Channel 4 executive structure*

In other areas, too, C4 can be seen to have fulfilled its brief for alternative programming. At its inception in 1982 it launched what has often been the most controversial soap in the UK: *Brookside*. This has tackled many sensitive issues: domestic violence, incest, drugs, religious cults and many others, generally following episodes with information on help lines.

C4 has showcased some American shows that went on to acquire cult following such as *Friends*. Other successful imports include *Frasier, NYPD Blue, Homicide – Life on the Street* and *Ally McBeal*. Other recent significant contributions made by C4 include its Bollywood series which increased awareness in the UK of Indian cinema. To date, there is sparse evidence that the changes to C4 brought about in 1993 (when C4 became responsible for its own funding) have diminished its commitment to its original brief of providing alternative programming. It seems that far from being in competition with the other independent companies for advertising, C4 complements them by providing an audience demographically different to the average ITV audience: it is generally younger and wealthier. C4 has also adopted innovative scheduling practices, using specific themes to package programmes for a whole evening, weekend or even a week, a practice initially piloted by BBC2.

Broadcasting Act 1981

The main features of this Act were to incorporate C4 into the IBA and set up the Broadcasting Complaints Commission. At the same time the BBC's Charter was renewed for another ten years. New ITV franchises were granted until 1989, the previous ones having ran for over thirteen years. There were a few changes to the make-up of the regions: Southern Television was replaced by TV South and Westward was replaced by TV South West. Tyne Tees and Yorkshire became two separate companies. There was one other new development: breakfast television.

Breakfast television

The strategy to open up television to greater competition (in the same way that franchises were open to bids) included the decision to create a separate franchise for early morning television. Breakfast television was launched in the UK by the BBC, ahead of its commercial rival with a programme much influenced by American formats consisting of a blend including news, interviews and aerobics all presented in a homely, populist style. After a competitive bid, the IBA awarded the breakfast franchise to TV-AM, partly on the strength of the personnel involved, but also on their commitment to 'a mission to explain'.

TV-AM had made an impressive submission and had a team of presenters as star-studied as any television programme, including David Frost, Michael Parkinson, Anna Ford and Michael Jay. But they ran quickly into trouble. They were pre-empted by the BBC Breakfast News, which was lighter in tone and TV-AM failed to gain an adequate audience. The original programme was pulled and replaced by *Good Morning Britain*, fronted by Anne Diamond and Richard Keys. Greg Dyke, a successful programme maker with a populist touch, was brought in to revamp the programme. Amongst his innovations was Roland Rat – a puppet that almost achieved cult status: it was hailed by the tabloids as the saviour of TV-AM. But the original 'mission to explain' was rapidly ditched and the new programme was heavily criticised. If *Good Morning Britain* had been in the original proposal, it is unlikely that TV-AM would have won the franchise. Breakfast television in general took a long time to get over the 'tacky' image that was afforded it by TV-AM.

The Hunt Report (1982)

Another change that impacted on television in the eighties was cable. In March 1982, the Conservative government set up a committee under Lord Hunt of Talworth to enquire into the expansion of cable. The committee was given six months. The main outcome was the Cable Authority. As with many of the previous reports into broadcasting, the concerns of Hunt were still with public service broadcasting. Cable was seen as being 'as supplementary, and not as an alternative or rival, to public service broadcasting.' To emphasise this point, the recommendation was made that all cable service should:

> **carry all free BBC and Independent Television services as part of their basic programme package, both so that no one should be deprived of them by a decision to connect a cable system and also preserve the habit of national viewing alongside the new channels which will cater more for special interests and also be more locally oriented.**

In addition to the stricture on terrestrial channels, the Hunt report recommended:

- Cable operators not allowed to obtain exclusive rights to certain major national sporting events
- Pay-as-you-view initially not permitted as a method of payment for individual cable programmes
- Programming not to be regulated in terms of range or balance
- No quota on the amount of foreign material
- A new Cable Authority to grant franchises for specific local areas, programmes only regulated on a 'reactive' basis' i.e. only *after* transmission and an initial franchise period of ten years

- No limit on the number of cable channels
- The press, Independent Television companies and local radio allowed to own cable channels, but not political or religious organisations
- Cable to carry unlimited advertising

The Peacock Report (1986)

This would be the final enquiry into broadcasting before yet another fundamental change of satellite. Prior to the Peacock Committee beginning its enquiry, there was a general awareness that broadcasting was changing in important ways, and where it was not, it should be. In one sense, the arguments had turned full circle. Once again, the issues that had exercised broadcasters and politicians in the 1940s were doing so again: should the BBC take advertising? Should there be a state broadcaster with a public service remit and if so what should that remit be?

The Thatcher government was essentially liberal in its economic thinking in the sense that it did not favour state intervention in economic matters: markets, it believed, should be left to regulate themselves. Few areas of public policy were untouched by this economic philosophy. This included broadcasting. Subject of considerable debate was the licence fee. Advocates of the free market (Peacock was amongst them) argued that it should go on the grounds that it was effectively a regressive tax which had to be paid by owners of televisions whether they watched the BBC or not. Supporters of public service broadcasting insisted that it was essential, that it was right for the BBC to be funded in this way as it was effectively a public asset and without it BBC programming would fall victim entirely to commercialism.

Amongst Peacock's eight proposals were:

- BBC1 should be funded by advertising
- The IBA should be replaced by 'a body more akin to the Federal Communications Commission in the USA' which has few regulatory powers concerning programming being mainly concerned with licensing broadcasters and administering the wavelength spectrum.

The 1990 Broadcasting Act (see later) was based on the Peacock Report and although it did not embrace the idea of the BBC losing the licence fee and carrying advertising, it did include proposals for a 'light touch' regulator.

De-regulation in the 1990s

We saw earlier that prior to the early 1980s, the broadcasting economy was mixed, based on balance between public funding and private enterprise. The arrangement was successful because the two institutions concerned were not in competition for the same sources of revenue. When C4 started in 1982, nothing really changed, because C4 did not compete with ITV; far from reducing its income, C4 was yet another source of revenue for ITV.

The 1980s were a period of great change for broadcasting in the UK. The Conservative government led by Margaret Thatcher were determined to deregulate broadcasting and introduce competition. From the mid-1980s, onwards a very lively debate ensued about the future of television, especially with regard to the funding of the BBC. As one quango, interest group and parliamentary committee after another gave its views, rumours flourished. Thatcher herself would almost certainly have been happy for the BBC to have been privatised and forced to take advertising – ever since the Falklands. Thatcher was hostile to the BBC's coverage of the war, because she did not think it sufficiently partisan, for example, she was annoyed by their tendency to refer to 'British ships' and 'British forces' etc., rather than 'our ships' or 'our forces'. The BBC's position was that its responsibility was to report the conflict as impartially as possible.

She probably saw the BBC as a bastion of privilege and a smug, cultural high-ground as well as being filled with disaffected socialists, congenitally hostile to the Conservatives in general and her in particular. Then there was the *Death on the Rock* scandal. In 1988 Thames made an investigative documentary about an incident that occurred some months earlier on Gibraltar. A squad of plainclothes SAS troops intercepted and shot three members of the IRA. They were almost certainly there preparing for a future bomb attack.

However, what happened during the fatal confrontation between the SAS and IRA suspects has never been satisfactorily explained. The SAS and the Government claimed that the three suspects were armed and making ready to fire their weapons. The SAS, so this version goes, acted in self defence. What the Thames documentary seemed to suggest, however, was something quite different. Drawing on a number of eye-witness and expert accounts, they demonstrated that the official version was simply not true. A more sinister account emerged that suggested the three suspects had virtually been executed. The government put pressure on Thames not to transmit the programme on the grounds that it may prejudice an inquest on the incident. IBA lawyers advised that there were no legal grounds for not transmitting the programme and Thames went ahead with broadcasting the programme on 28th April 1988. Lord Thomson, Chairman of the IBA, said that the film makers were 'simply doing a normal, professional journalistic job and one they were fully entitled, in our view, to do.' (source: British Film Institute).

Thames' intransigence infuriated the Prime Minister, Margaret Thatcher and fuelled her conviction that television had to change. She clearly regarded the longer established commercial broadcasters such as Thames as being no better than the BBC. It was time for a change. Mrs Thatcher's economic liberalism, free-market ideology was to be applied to broadcasting.

Irrespective of who was in power, the world of television was changing so much and so quickly that sooner-or-later the BBC would have had to take stock and consider its options. The BBC, along with every other broadcaster, was going to have to compete and survive amidst an ever increasing number of channels. Not only that, but the nature of those channels was going to change, bringing either threats or opportunities. Satellite and cable had long arrived and digital was next.

To begin with Thatcher wanted to remove in total any public service requirement of commercial television. The plan was to remove the IBA and replace with it with a 'light touch' regulator who would have no power to dictate what programmes were made and broadcast. The television franchises would be distributed purely on the basis of an auction: whoever, on the day, produced the fattest brown envelope. In November 1988 the government published a White Paper called *Broadcasting in the 90s: Competition, Choice and Quality*. Its main proposals formed the basis of the subsequent Broadcasting Act 1990.

The Broadcasting Act 1990

The Broadcasting act heralded a number of changes in the way commercial television was administered. In brief these were:

- The dissolution of the Independent Broadcasting Authority and Cable Authority. The Independent Television Commission (ITC) was set up to replace the old IBA and the Cable Authority – the two were effectively merged. Radio, previously within the remit of the IBA, came under the new Radio Authority.
- Provision made for a fifth channel, and a sixth (if technically feasible)
- The requirement that ITV should commission and schedule programmes through an independent body (this became Network Centre)
- A requirement that independent television and the BBC should apportion '...not less than 25% of the total amount of time allocated to the broadcasting ......of a range and diversity of independent productions.'

(Section 6h p.16 Broadcasting Act 1990)

Distribution of the franchises

The Act was not entirely the retreat from public broadcasting values that was originally feared. Although the franchises were auctioned, provision was made for a 'quality threshold', although, in most cases, this was easily met: as well as having a viable business plan, the programming plans had to meet certain criteria. In some circumstances it was possible for an applicant submitting a lower bid to be offered a franchise.

In the event, although TV South (the pre-1990 Act franchise holder) had submitted the higher bid, the ITC were not satisfied with their business plans and it was Meridian who won the franchise.

In addition to the range of programmes expected, the minimum programming requirements stipulated by the act were:

- regular news and current affairs programmes
- regional programmes
- schools programmes
- religious programmes

The aspect of the Act that came in for most criticism was the method by which the franchises were to be disposed: through an auction. As mentioned, previously contractors were appointed on the basis of their programming plans; now it was to be the size of a cheque, subject to the satisfactory compliance with certain minimum programming criteria. Apart from anything else, the cost was considerable. The sum that each successful contractor bid was not a one-off payment, but an *annual* payment. In addition to which, a fee had to be paid to the ITC. In regions where competition was strong, the amounts offered were high. Not only was this money that would not be available for making programmes, but there was also the danger that some contractors might overreach themselves in their bids, so becoming financially weaker and vulnerable to either going under completely or being taken over. Furthermore, there is evidence that some companies harnessed their resources by cutting programme investment and laying off staff in preparation for a high bid. The London franchises were

(4) ....the Commission may regard the following circumstances as exceptional circumstances which make it appropriate to award the licence to an applicant who has not submitted the highest bid, namely where it appears to the Commission –

    a)   that the quality of the service proposed by such an applicant is exceptionally high; and

    b)   that the quality of that proposed service is substantially higher than the quality of the service proposed

        i)   by the applicant who has submitted the highest bid, or

        ii)   ....by each of the applicants who have submitted equal highest bids.

(Section 17 (3) p.17 of the Broadcasting Act, 1990)

hotly contested: Carlton beat Thames with a bid of £43.17 million – a sum that has to be paid to the ITC each year. On the other hand Central Television faced no competition: their bid was a derisory £2000! The failure of Thames to gain the London weekday franchise must have given the Thatcher Government some satisfaction, in the light of the *Death on the Rock* episode. This may have been somewhat overshadowed by the failure of one of Thatcher's favourites, TV-AM, to win the London breakfast franchise, which went to GMTV. The auction system was widely attacked and thought to be a very unsatisfactory way of handling television: it is unlikely to be used again.

Regulation of programme content

Much of the Act is concerned with the regulation of television, some of which does reflect a concern for a public service ethic.

The ITC does not have the power of 'pre-publication' censorship: it can only act after the event. The ITC was enjoined by the Act to establish a code setting out minimum standards of programming. Details of this are given in the case study in Chapter 8.

The act also makes provision for:

- Independent production

Both independent television and the BBC under the terms of the Act are obliged to apportion '...not less than 25% of the total amount of time allocated to the broadcasting ...... of a range and diversity of independent productions.' (Section 6(h) p.16 Broadcasting Act 1990).

- Changes in funding of C4
  As mentioned earlier in the chapter, prior to the Act C4 was funded by the ITV regions; in return they sold advertising on C4: this guaranteed C4 financial security, permitting it to fulfil its brief of offering original and innovative programming – a brief it still has. Subsequent to the act, C4 has sold its own advertising.
- Provision for C5
- Limits on ownership

Under the Act no franchise holder could retain more than two licences and no newspaper proprietor could own more than 20% of a franchise holding company. This requirement was changed by the Broadcasting Act 1995. The two-licence limit was replaced with an ownership limit of 15% of the total television audience. The new Act permitted, for the first time, newspaper groups to control television companies. Both the Mirror Group and News International were barred because they both owned more than 20% of the total national newspaper circulation. They were, however, able to invest further in cable and digital services, which they did.

Channel Five

The provision made in the 1990 Broadcasting Act for a fifth channel led to another auction. Applications for the new franchise were invited in April 1992, but few were forthcoming. By the time of the deadline, three months later, there had been only one, from Channel Five holdings, which was rejected by the ITC on the grounds of weaknesses in its business plan. In 1995 the franchise was re-advertised and awarded to Channel Five Broadcasting. This was a consortium of Pearson (who own Thames Television and *The Financial Times*), United News Media (who own Anglia Television, 76% of Meridian Television, *The Express, Express on Sunday, Daily Star* and about 120 UK magazines) and CLT who are a Luxembourg based broadcaster. The consortium was led by Greg Dyke (appointed Director General of the BBC in 1999) and Lord Hollick, the owner of United News Media. Channel Five Broadcasting's bid, at £22 million, was not the highest, but the ITC concluded that they offered the widest range of programming. Some major technical problems had to be confronted and this probably put off some potential bidders. For one thing it had a very patchy transmission area, only reaching 70% of the population and in fact by 1999 only 55% were getting high quality reception. There was also a problem with its signal, which interfered with domestic video recorders. Almost £150 million had to be spent on a nationwide video re-tuning operation. Channel Five started broadcasting on 30th March 1997. Like C4, it does not make any of its programmes. Unlike C4, it has not made an impact with any innovative programming. By 1999 its scheduling had become heavily reliant on films, US imports (*Lassie, The Roseanne Show, The Oprah Winfrey Show,* etc.) and repeats (such as *The Ruth Rendell Mystery*). Its own contribution seems to have been largely to daytime television with programmes such as *Open House with Gloria Hunniford*. They have had themed weekends and have commissioned programmes such as the documentary series *Family Confidential*.

In 1998 Channel Five was attracting a weekly audience of only 20 million. Its biggest audience was 4.5 million for the Poland versus England football match on 31st May 1997. One distinction that Channel 5 does have is that it was the last analogue franchise to be awarded.

Satellite television

Satellite television has been the catalyst of change in the market place and how we think about television, including the issue of public service broadcasting. Although it began to emerge in the eighties, it was not until the early nineties that the full impact of satellite began to be felt. The rise of satellite coincided with, and in some ways induced, a number of changes in television both within the UK and internationally. The name of the game, so to speak, has been deregulation. The old legislative regimes have been inadequate to the task of dealing with the accelerating rate of technological change and their implications in terms of changing markets and audience viewing behaviour.

CASE STUDY

BSkyB

In the UK Rupert Murdoch's BSkyB has dominated satellite broadcasting since the early nineties. Murdoch has been able to achieve this by virtue of the sheer size of his organization and the concomitant ability to raise money and take risks. News Corps is a huge organisation which includes substantial assets in several countries. In Australia, a share of Channel 7 and several newspapers; in America, newspapers, magazines, Twentieth Century Fox, Fox Television (which has now become the fourth network), a publisher (HarperCollins) and even a baseball team, the LA Dodgers; in the East, the largest satellite broadcasting operation, Star and in the UK he has News International (The Times, Sunday Times, News of the World and the Sun), the British division of Harper & Collins and, of course, BSkyB.

In 1981 after a trial period of one year Sky Channel (as it was then called) started broadcasting as a cable supplier across Europe. It was owned by Satellite Television plc, set up by an English television producer, Brian Haynes. Haynes (who used to make programmes for Thames) was influenced by Ted Turner and Jim Bakker. Both started using satellite in the 1970s – Turner to broadcast baseball and Bakker – leader of a Christian fundamentalist sect – his own brand of religion. It was Haynes' idea to create a pan-European television satellite service, first with cable, but eventually using direct broadcast satellite. Haynes managed to gain access to the European Space Agency's Orbital Test Satellite (OTS), originally intended exclusively for telecommunications. He then managed to persuade Euresat, an inter-governmental agency which controlled the European use of satellites. Having raised what today would seem the ludicrously small amount of £4 million, he was able to get started, and began by broadcasting to Malta. Costs were low in those days, which was just as well as Haynes ran the whole operation on a 'shoestring'. Satellite time was only £300 an hour and programmes could be purchased for about £100 per hour. The channel was called Satellite and it worked. But by 1983 Haynes had got through £4 million and found that he needed to find another £6 million. This proved difficult but in stepped Murdoch – with £10 million for a controlling interest in Satellite Television plc. By now developments in technology were going apace. The Americans had developed smaller, cheaper, medium-powered satellites whose signal could be picked up by a small dish: this became the basic technology of DBS (Direct Broadcast Satellite). Communications satellites are geostationary, that is to say that at a certain height and speed, they retain a fixed position relative to the Earth on points on a 'ring' that circumscribes the Earth. This notional ring is called the Clarke Ring (named after the science fiction writer). At an international conference in 1977 (WAR77) the various interested countries were awarded 'slots' in the Clarke Ring.

CABLE SATELLITE TELEVISION	Star TV BskyB Foxtel Fox News Channel (V) Asia	Sky Latin America Fox Broadcasting Fox Family Channel Fox Television Stations The Health Network	Fox Sports Net FX Sky PerfecTV! Fox Sports Latin America
FILM	20th Century Fox Fox 200 Fox Studios	Fox Searchlight Fox Animation Studios	Fox Music Fox Home Entertainment
BOOKS	HarperCollins Regan Books	HarperCollins UK Zondervan	HarperCollins Australia
NEWSPAPERS	UK TITLES *The Times* *The Sun* *The Sunday Times* *News of the World*	AUSTRALIAN TITLES *Post-Courier* *Herald Sun* *The Australian* *The Daily Telegraph* *The Sunday Telegraph* News Corp also owns many state-wide papers plus over 90 regional and local papers	NEW ZEALAND TITLES Independent Newspapers (50%) – 90 weekly and suburban newspapers US TITLES *New York Post* FIJI TITLES *The Fiji Times* *Nai Lalaki* (Fijian language) *Shanti Dut* (Hindi Language PAPUA NEW GUINEA TITLE *Post Courier* (60%)
MAGAZINES AND INSERTS	*TV Guide* *SmartSource* *Times Literary Supplement*	*The Weekly Standard* *Times Educational Supplement*	News America Marking Time Higher Educational Supplement
OTHER	LA Dodgers Mushroom Records	Ansett Australia Festival Records	PLD Telekom National Rugby League

Figure 1.2 *The Murdoch media empire (News Corporation in 1999)*

Murdoch had for a long time wanted to break into television, but was prevented from acquiring licences in either Australia or Britain because of cross-media ownership rules. Having acquired Sky in 1983, he later began to supply cable operators in the UK under the terms of the Cable and Broadcasting Act 1984, which did not have the same stringent ownership rules. But he was not the only player in the field. In 1982 the British government had granted the BBC a licence to start a direct broadcasting satellite service (DBS). The BBC intend to use a satellite built by Marconi, GEC and British Aerospace. Not withstanding the IBA joining the scheme and providing cash, the costs were prohibitively high and in 1985 the project was abandoned. In 1986 the IBA began the search for a contractor to have another go, this time to provide a service with, to begin with three, but later five DBS channels. A consortium was put together comprising of Pearson, Reed International (publishers), Granada, Anglia Television and Virgin (who later dropped out). The consortium was called British Satellite Broadcasting (BSB). But, not withstanding their head start, they were delayed by technical problems and did not make it in time. They were beaten in 1989 by Sky.

Figure 1.3 *Rupert Murdoch*   *Source: Corbis*

Sky was based in Luxembourg so was not within the control of the IBA. Murdoch had managed, as he would so often again, to circumvent state regulators. Sky was a subscription service offering four channels: Sky One, Sky News, Sky Movies and Eurosport. It was not until 1990 that BSB went on the air, with their distinctive square aerial ('squarial'). By then, however, Sky had stolen a march and BSB was doomed to failure. But Murdoch, himself, had to take risks. He almost went bankrupt while BSB was being launched and Sky was losing £2,000,000 a week. Luckily Sky was part of a huge multi-media conglomerate with a gambler at its head and *The Sun* turning over a substantial profit: Murdoch would survive. The twin problems were luring enough subscribers and advertisers to what would later become BSkyB. Advertisers would not come until there was an audience, not withstanding a 25% discount on terrestrial advertising rates. He had to move dishes into homes. Here his newspapers were useful. Throughout the early nineties one could not open a copy of a News International paper without finding an offer for a cheap satellite or even a free one given away as a prize: the Sun, News of the World and Today (now defunct) were used to heavily publicise BSkyB. Subscribers were attracted mainly by cheap subscriptions and sport. The latter became the mainstay of his marketing strategy which reached fruition by the end of the nineties. By this time he had gained sole broadcasting rights on a number of sporting events in the UK and had even bought up a number of baseball and football teams in the US. In 1999 he even made an abortive attempt to buy a major English football team, Manchester United.

But what of BSB? They came on the air in April 1990 and went off in November 1990. Murdoch had a clear field, with a sympathetic government led by a prime minister (Margaret Thatcher) who was anxious to maintain the support of *the Sun*, which she got. Because Murdoch managed to evade the regulator (the IBA) he was free to broadcast just what he liked. Wanting to avoid production costs, he offered largely a diet of American fare, especially films, purchasing the rights of a great many. BSB, however, was subject to IBA rules and had to originate a substantial proportion of its own programming. By late

1990 it had spent £1.25 million pounds, but its market penetration was only one in fifteen households. Sky and BSB 'merged' (in all but name it was a take-over) to form British Sky Broadcasting (BSkyB), which began operating as a five channel service in April 1991. Sky went from strength to strength, becoming the world's most successful pay television operator. By 1999, Sky wholly owned eleven channels and jointly owned another ten.

WHOLLY OWNED	JOINTLY OWNED
Sky 1	Nickelodeon
Sky News	QVC
Sky Travel	Paramount Comedy
Sky Soap	Granada Plus
Sky Sports 1	Granada Men and Motors
Sky Sports 2	Granada Good life
Sky Sports 3	History Channel
Computer Channel	National Geographic
Movie Channel	Sky Scottish
Sky Movies	Playboy TV
Sky Movies Gold	

Table 1.1 *Sky channels*

In 1998 it made another advance, this time into digital television. Of the two digital service providers that were operating at the end of the nineties (the other being On-Digital) BSkyB's was the largest, both in terms of the number of channels on offer and the number of subscribers. Another development came in 1999 when BSkyB became the first UK broadcaster to provide interactive televised sport: it is a 32.55% shareholder of British Interactive Broadcasting. BSkyB has also created its own production company for film and drama.

As the case study shows BSkyB has an impressive record of expansion, but there is some evidence to suggest that there is a degree of apathy towards satellite and cable. In 1999 a fifth of all homes had a satellite dish, but this was not reflected in the viewing figures.

BBC	43.9%
ITV	39.1%
Channel 4	10.7%
Cable	8%
Sky	4.3%

Table 1.2 *Viewing figures in Spring 1997*

The other main satellite operator in the UK is Flextech. The major shareholder is Tele-Communications International Inc; others include Cox Communications, Pearson, US West and BBC Worldwide.

Channel or studio	Holding	Programme type
Brava	100%	Films – horror, humour
Trouble	100%	Teenage soap, drama
TCC	100%	Cartoons, games
Challenge TV	100%	Interactive games
UK Living	100%	Women
Maidstone Studios	100%	Production facilities
Action Studios	93%	Adventure park
HSN Direct	62%	Home shopping
Playboy	51%	Soft porn
UK Gold/BBC	50%	Old BBC/Thames footage
Sell a Vision	50%	Home shopping
Discovery Channel	48%	Science, nature and geography
Kindernet	31%	Dutch children
EBN	30%	Business news
GMTV	20%	Channel 3 franchise
STV	20%	Channel 3 franchise
Parliamentary Channel	15%	Westminster coverage
Sega		Interactive video games

Table 1.3 *Flextech's interests*   (The Media Guide, 1999)

Cable

In America, cable television has been a major competitor to terrestrial television since the seventies. In the UK, however, it was much slower to take hold. Starting in 1983 it had, by the beginning of the nineties, achieved less than 20% of the penetration it had achieved in the USA (Doyle, p.36). One significant reason for this is the greater construction costs of the infrastructure: in the UK cable has to be laid underground and the costs of this are very high.

Cable operators in the UK fall into two categories; Franchised Cable Systems and Unfranchised Cable Systems. The franchised operators include the Multiple Systems Operators (MSOs). They have exclusive rights to provide multi-channel services through a large, purpose-built cable system: the franchise period is fifteen years. There are twelve major MSOs including Atlantic Telecom Group (Atlantic, British Telecommunications (BT)), Cable & Telecoms (C&T), Cable and Wireless Communications (CWC) and Comcast Europe (Comcast). Unfranchised Cable Systems have a restricted channel capacity and a shorter franchise period of three years; there were eight such companies in 1999.

All of the MSOs offer substantial channel packages, including Sky and all of the main terrestrial broadcasters, which they have to do because of the Cable and Broadcasting Act 1984. In the eighties it was probably the case that many people were content with the choice offered by the four terrestrial channels. Before satellite became available, cable did not offer such a great increase in programme choice. In addition, the lack of investment in cable meant that most people did not have the option and went to Sky. This situation, as far as cable is concerned, has probably been exacerbated by the arrival, in 1999, of a choice of digital services.

> The difficulty in cable is in laying the wire which will permit interactivity and laying them in a discreet, conservation-minded manner rather than doing what you've done, which is stretching wires all over the United States. That's one of the reasons why cable hasn't worked in the United Kingdom. If we had been allowed to run them on telegraph poles and just run the cables then it would have happened quicker. But the costs of digging trenches and burying them have, so far, prohibited them.
>
> *(David Plowright cited in Doyle, p.37)*

Digital television

As of 1999, the future of the BBC and public service broadcasting seems secure. The form it will evolve into and the manner of its funding will probably be in a constant state of negotiation. The immediate issue is how the BBC is going to finance digital television. One proposal is that a £24 surcharge on the standard licence fee should be paid for a digital licence. This would replicate the procedure adopted by the BBC when colour was introduced. Time will tell whether the strategy adopted by the BBC of competing internationally and retaining its commitment to a broad range of programme making is more likely to ensure its survival rather than the other option, of limiting its remit to a narrower definition of public service broadcasting.

Broadcasting Act 1996

The government published a follow up bill to the 1990 Act in December 1995. Its two main functions were:

- To make new provision for digital broadcasting
- To replace the Broadcasting Complaints Commission and the Broadcasting Standards Council with the Broadcasting Standards Commission.

It also strengthened the ITC's powers to protect regional programme production and amend the restrictions on ownership.

Multiplexes

Because of decompression several digital channels take up the same spectrum space as one analogue channel. Clusters of digital channels are called multiplexes. The 1996 Act made available six multiplexes, each capable of providing between two and six programme channels. The BBC was allocated the one with the widest geographical coverage. ITV, Channel 4 and S4C (Wales) were allocated one between them and Channel 5 was given half of the third. This has made it possible for other services to be provided by the terrestrial broadcasters such as the BBC, putting them on a more competitive basis with satellite.

Multiplex A	S4C in Wales; Gaelic programmes in Scotland
Multiplex B	On Digital Multiplex: Granada Plus, Sky Movies, Carlton Select, BBC Horizon, Sky Sports
Multiplex C	On Digital Multiplex: BBC Style/Showcase, Sky 1, the Movie Channel, Carlton Films, Granada Good Life
Multiplex D	On Digital Multiplex: Carlton Entertainment, Public Eye (including Sky News), Granada TV Shopping, Granada Sports Club, BBC One-TV
BBC Multiplex	BBC 1 and 2, 24 hour news, BBC On Choice, BBC Inform
C3/C4 Multiplex	Digital 3 and 4, Channel 3, Channel 4, Teletext, ITV 2, C4 Film on Four

Table 1.4 *Digital TV*

Since the end of the nineties, both the BBC and ITV have started the first phase of this by broadcasting their analogue services on digital in widescreen; this was a requirement of the 1996 Act. They are now free to develop other services available only on digital channels, such as Film Four, offered by Channel Four, a subscription service available on both Sky Digital and On Digital. Such services are sure to expand.

The USA: from radio to television

As with Britain, the arrangements that the Americans made for television were determined by their experiences with radio. Britain and America took different approaches to constructing their respective national broadcasting systems. In practical terms, radio began in America at the turn of the century. As a result of a highly successful demonstration of his radio to Queen Victoria, Marconi was commissioned to relay the results of the 1899 America's World Cup held off New York. *The New York Herald* paid Marconi $5,000 for what amounted to an immediate transmission of the result at the end of the race. No great distance was involved but it 'caught the imagination of countless middle class American men and women and boys in the opening decades of the twentieth century.' (Baker and Dessart, p.10). This highly publicised event thrust Marconi and radio into the foreground. The rudimentary technology began to become popular, to the extent that amateur operators interfered with naval communications. This led to the Radio Act of 1912. Shortly after this, the loss of the Titanic would highlight wireless communications. It was the first time the new SOS was sent on wireless telegraphy and it also led to perhaps a less well known incident that had major repercussions in the development of radio and ultimately television in the USA. The distress signal was picked up by a young radio operator, David Sarnoff, who relayed the news of the disaster to the press. Sarnoff would later play a key role in the development of both radio and television. Before the First World War, the UK had a virtual monopoly on radio technology, principally through Marconi. After the war the US President, Woodrow Wilson weakened this control by creating a consortium of the American Navy, Westinghouse and General Electric: from this came the Radio Corporation of America, better known today as simply RCA. Within a decade, David Sarnoff became its president.

Radio flourished in the 1920s. Starting from zero, by the end of the 1920s, sales of receivers reached $850 million per year. In one year alone, RCA stock leapt from $85.25 to $549 per share. The decade was boom-time across all industries when merger followed merger. Baker and Dessart cite the best selling non-fiction book as being Bruce Barton's *The Man Nobody Knows*, 'which depicts Jesus as history's greatest executive' who 'would be a national advertiser today,' the implication being that amongst other things, Christ was a brilliant salesman. Radio rode the wave of this economic surf. In January 1926, RCA formed the National Broadcasting Corporation of America (NBC). RCA owned half of the new company, General Electric 30% and Westinghouse the remainder. A leading radio station, WEAF, was purchased from AT & T who had, by then, realised that they could make more money from broadcasting by charging other companies for the use of their long distance lines, and that was precisely what they would do for the new company.

The logic was the same as in the UK with Marconi and the BBC. RCA would make the sets; NBC would make the programmes. Not only that, but the first big network, NBC, was born. This was followed two years later by another network, United Independent Broadcasters (UIB). The company's name was later changed to the Columbia Phonograph Broadcasting company and finally, in 1928 it became the Columbia Broadcasting System (CBS). More detail on the history of these networks is given later.

This was the time when, if it was to happen at all, regulation would have been best put in place. But it was not. That is not to say that many people did not envisage a public service function for radio. In fact when RCA formed NBC it announced:

Any use of radio transmission which causes the public to feel that the quality of the program is not the highest, that the use of radio is not the broadest and best use in the public interest, that it is used for political advantage or selfish power, will be detrimental to the public interest in radio, and therefore to the Radio Corporation of America.

(Baker, W.F. and Dessart, G., Down the Tube,
Basic Books, 1998, p. 12).

For Sarnoff radio was the 'greatest educational tool in history.' However, another function quickly presented itself: advertising. Herbert Hoover, the Secretary of Commerce (and President in 1928) was openly opposed to the use of radio for direct advertising, but reluctant to impose regulation, left the matter in the hands of the industry. However, some form of regulation was inevitable, for the same reason that the British preferred a monopoly system: the limited available spectrum. By 1926 the airwaves had become overcrowded and were verging on anarchy, a state of affairs which did not go unnoticed by the British. Commercial radio had been assigned to two narrow bands on the spectrum in 1924. One was for the broadcasting of the normal station fare, excluding weather and government messages, which had to be broadcast on the second channel. In the case of distress signals being transmitted, broadcasting had to cease and all the frequencies kept open to receive them.

Radio Act of 1927

Out of the Radio Act of 1927 (about the same time the new BBC started broadcasting) came the Federal Radio Commission (the forerunner of the Federal Communications Commission). The prime function of the Commission was to administer the distribution of the available frequencies. Within the legislation there was no explicit reference to either education or advertising, only a vague reference to 'public interest'. But this reference came to nothing, owing to the pervasive faith in self-regulation.

As is well known, the bubble burst in 1929. Wall Street 'crashed'. In 1932 there was a new president with a New Deal. Amidst the storm of legislation carried out by the Roosevelt administration was the Wagner–Hatfield Amendment calling for the annulment and redistribution of all radio licences on the basis of 'public interest'. It failed to be ratified. In 1934 the Federal Communications Act was passed which did little to weaken the hold of commercial interests on radio. The New Deal had little impact on radio. By the end of the thirties, as in Britain, television had arrived. It would be subjected to as little regulation as its forebear.

The arrival of television

Television took hold quicker in the UK than in the USA. One explanation offered by Baker and Dessart is that 'commercial broadcasters were so fabulously wealthy from radio alone that they may have felt little incentive to make the necessary investments.' (Baker and Dessart, p.17). Notwithstanding some experiments carried out by NBC and CBS in 1928, the public did not get their first glimpse of television until 1939 at the New York World Fair. Even the interest this stimulated was not allowed to mature: as in the UK, television went off the air until after the war. The large scale manufacture of television sets did not commence until 1946; by the 1950s television was expanding with a momentum comparable to that of radio in the 1920s. 'In 1950, 10 percent of American households owned a TV; in 1955, 67 percent; in 1960, 87 percent; and in 1965, fully 94 percent were television households.' (Baker and Dessart p.18). There was, however, little interest in anything so uncommercial as public service broadcasting. In 1952 the Federal Communications Commission (FCC) wanted to create seventy VHF channels, with some set aside for education, but nothing came of this as Congress failed to come up with the appropriate funding.

The 1950s were an unstable period for American television. Very rapid expansion was matched with numerous corruption scandals, damaging warfare between the broadcasters and amongst the corrupt quiz shows and some highly innovative drama. All of this was played out against a background of a paranoid fear of communist subversion that seemingly threatened every aspect of American life from the legendary apple pie to democracy itself.

The most high-profile scandal was in 1959. A young, middle class, 'preppy' academic, Charles Van Doren had been built up as a national hero on one quiz show, shooting him and it to the top of the ratings. But the bubble burst when it got out that Van Doreen was being fed the questions and answers in advance. The resulting scandal rocked American television and indirectly gave a boost to the principle of public service broadcasting. It led to the 'fairness doctrine'. The quiz scandal appeared to demonstrate to many the lack of wisdom in allowing television to be virtually regulation free and driven by the engine of profit: it had seemed to have got out of control. Another illustration of this was the way in which CBS had dropped the estimable Ed Murrow's current affairs programme, *See it Now* with a quiz programme (not *the* quiz programme). After the scandal broke, however, it was itself replaced by a documentary series, *CBS Reports*.

The 'fairness doctrine' meant two things:

- The FCC obliged each television station 'to broadcast programmes that dealt with controversial matters of public importance'.
- Any programme presenting largely one side of a controversial issue had to be followed by the presentation of alternative views, if not in a single programme, then over one or more in a reasonable period of time.

The fairness doctrine would survive for twenty five years.

Technical rivalries

At the outset, American broadcasting was subject to a narrow concentration of ownership. It was inevitable that the big radio networks would exploit their strength to develop television. NBC–RCA gained a dominant position early on, in fact RCA have always believed that they invented television. It was RCA who unveiled television at the New York World Fair in 1939. 'It was the central exhibit in RCA's grand, futuristic pavilion shaped like a huge vacuum tube.' (Brinkley, p.51).

One cause for this concentration of ownership was the decision by the FCC in the forties to use only the VHF frequency. This could carry only twelve national channels and three or four television stations in the larger cities. It was the two big networks, NBC and CBS, that attracted lavish amounts of advertising money and by the same token could afford to contract expensive stars – as they had done a decade or so earlier with their radio networks. Local television stations who wanted to enjoy the largesse of the networks and get their programmes, with the stars and the advertising, had to become an affiliate.

The process was inexorable. Originally conceived as a *local* system, American television became a tightly controlled *national* grid emanating from the two largest networks: NBC, CBS along with the smaller ABC. For a while there was another, struggling desperately to survive: Du Mont.

The growth of the networks

Once owned by Paramount until the FCC squashed their attempt to get into television (no Hollywood studio with an antitrust indictment could own a licence) Du Mont went out of business in 1955. There is a nice irony here: it was bought by Rupert Murdoch and formed the basis of his own television company, Fox, which is effectively now the fourth network.

ABC grew out of an off shoot of NBC. In 1943 the Federal Communications Commission ruled that NBC were in violation of antitrust laws and they were forced to divest themselves of one of their two television networks. The two networks were then called Red and the Blue. Sarnoff used the Red Network for generating profits whilst the Blue was devoted to less profitable, but more prestigious cultural programming such as classical music and drama. The less popular Blue network was sold for $8 million to Edward J. Noble (a sweet manufacturer).

The newly autonomous Blue network was renamed the American Broadcasting Company (ABC) and it became the third national network. The cutting to a smaller size of NBC was a fillip to the less successful CBS, which began to progressively grow until in 1948 it became the dominant broadcaster. The person behind this achievement was William S.Paley, a long-time competitor of NBC's David Sarnoff.

Paley had a passion for the arts but was a great popularist and seemed to have an instinctive grasp of what made popular entertainment. Like Sarnoff, Paley was in at the beginning. He bought a controlling interest in United Independent Broadcaster, which operated a struggling network – the Columbia Phonograph Broadcasting System. He was 28 and it had cost him $400,000 (raised primarily through family connections).

In September, 1928 Paley became its president and the network acquired a new name: CBS. Paley then began to take on the much bigger NBC. From a meagre twenty affiliates, Paley began to assemble a nationwide empire that would eventually rival Sarnoff's NBC. His first coup was in 1929 when he sold 50% of CBS to Paramount. Paramount, the largest of the Hollywood studios, was anxious to diversify into radio having converted to sound only a year before. However, the timing was bad.

Being the biggest, the studio had the greatest assets: 1200 theatres and 3 studios. But these assets became liabilities. At about the time Paramount bought a share of CBS, Wall Street crashed and years of depression followed. Paramount rapidly plunged into deficit. Facing bankruptcy, desperate measures had to be taken. One was to sell its share of CBS in 1932. By then the network had acquired ninety-two affiliates. NBC's national coverage was so great they did not have to seek out sponsors and advertisers: they came to them. Unlike NBC, Paley had to aggressively seek sponsors and he did this by launching his own series of programmes.

With these programmes the growth of CBS was steady. For a while its programming emphasis was on news and built up what, in news terms, became a legendary roster of journalistic stars such as the great Edward Murrow who through his live broadcasts, became for many Americans, the voice of London during the Blitz. Others included William L. Shirer, H.V. Kaltenborn, Elmer Davis, Raymond Gram Swing, Eric Sevareid, Robert Trout and Charles Collingwood.

Both in the UK and America, radio news came into its prime. NBC may have outstripped CBS in audience ratings and advertising, but in news CBS became the leader. *CBS World News* Roundup became a flagship programme.

By then the networks were well established: NBC, CBS and ABC. (This situation didn't change until towards the end of the nineties when they were joined by a fourth, Fox Television, a subsidiary of News Corp). One of the most far reaching outcomes of the rise of the networks was the massive increase in advertising.

In 1948 Paley managed to strike a blow against NBC by poaching some of its radio talent and with them went some of their advertising potential. In offering a potentially lucrative scheme whereby artists were allowed to save large amounts of money in taxes, he lured away the likes of Frank Sinatra,

Jack Benny, Red Skelton and others. Paley enabled his new stars to set their shows up as companies and sell them to CBS. As Paley had hoped, the audience followed the stars to CBS and as the ratings increased, so more radio stations became affiliates: many of these radio stars would later form the core of CBS television.

The networks move into television

Television, however, was something else in which NBC stole a march on CBS. Sarnoff was keen to develop television partly because he was fascinated by it, but also to exploit the new technology and create a new domestic market in the sale of television sets. It seems that Paley half-heartedly went into television just to keep pace with his rival. A year after Sarnoff started the first experimental station, CBS started one.

Six months after NBC began broadcasting from the top of the Empire State Building, CBS started up from the top of the Chrysler Building. However, radio was Paley's business and he had no interest in television: where he could, he did his best to delay its development. When NBC sought permission from the FCC to sell advertising on its experimental station, Paley opposed it on the grounds that it threatened radio: he won. Advertisements weren't allowed to be carried until 1941. The next battle was over colour.

CBS Laboratories, under Peter Goldmark, had come up with a way of achieving high quality colour pictures. Seeing this as a way of leap-frogging over Sarnoff in the television market, Paley applied to the FCC to have the Goldmark colour system accepted as the television standard. However, the FCC could not get round the problem of the Goldmark mechanical system being incompatible with the electronic system already in use. If it was accepted as the standard all other television sets would immediately be rendered obsolete.

Sarnoff stepped in and urged the FCC to restrain from making a decision, promising that within six months he would have an electronic colour system that was compatible with the current monochrome sets. It took ten years to resolve. Court case followed court case until finally the FCC approved the CBS system – only to reverse its decision.

Eventually Sarnoff and RCA won: they began broadcasting in colour in 1953. This was the same year that Twentieth Century Fox, in an attempt to claw back audiences, launched CinemaScope with the release of *The Robe*. Most of the other studios followed suit with their own versions of wide-screen.

As in the UK, television did not really take-off until after WW2. In the UK it took the Coronation, the arrival of ITV and cheaper televisions. In 1946 (when television broadcasting resumed in the UK) only 0.02% of American households had television: both countries began the post-war years on more-or-less equal terms. But expansion in the US was rapid. 10,000 sets were sold in 1946: in 1947 the figure was not far short of 200,000. By 1950 9% of American homes had a television. As Les Brown put it, 'Within a mere ten-year span, from 1945 to 1955, television went from a failed idea to one of the necessities of modern life. Five years later it was the biggest and most influential mass medium ever known.' (Smith, 1998 p.151).

What Paley had set in motion was an intensely fought battle between competing colour systems. The drive for colour was determined by a number of factors. For one thing it was now standard for cinema. Audiences expected it and monochrome tended to be used only as a deliberate aesthetic choice for films that aspired towards a certain kind of 'tough' social realism, such as *On the Waterfront* and *The Wild One*.

Paradoxically, the desire for greater realism was one reason why television searched for colour. There was the technological imperative: research scientists wanted to develop it for its own sake. On the other hand, for whatever reasons colour was wanted, it was wanted and new markets would be created and exploited by whoever managed to develop a system.

The National Television System Committee

From the 1940s onwards technical standards for television had been supervised by the National Television System Committee. One of the first actions taken by the NTSC was to lay the down the broadcast standard of US television as being 525 lines and FM sound. In 1941 30 stations ceased to be classified as being experimental and were permitted to carry advertising. Commercial television looked as if it were about to enter a boom period of expansion. But then the war came. Everything went into reverse. The manufacture of television sets ceased and all but six stations went off the air and they were used largely for civil defence purposes. Both Sarnoff and Paley had good wars. Sarnoff was a communications consultant on Eisenhower's staff and Paley was assigned to the Office of War Information with the rank of Colonel. Sarnoff ended up with the rank of general and ever after insisted that he was so addressed.

The institutional form American television took was inevitably shaped by radio. It was the big radio networks that created television and it was funded in the same way: through commercial sponsorship and advertising. Not that there was unanimity about this: there were voices in America (right from the earliest days of radio) who argued for some form of public service broadcasting. The reason why commercial interests were – and are – dominant is not only because of the power of the networks, but because of the place of broadcasting within the American constitution. Any kind of state control has always been seen to be at odds with the First Amendment: the right of free speech. But without state intervention there was never going to be a regulated, public service broadcaster.

Public service broadcasting in the USA

By 1948 the number of licence applications for television had escalated to the point where a freeze had to be imposed on all new stations. Four years later, in 1952, a UHF band was opened and one of the FCC Commissioners, Freda Hennock, forced through an allocation of frequency space for 242 non-profit educational television stations. It was not until 1962, with the passing of the Educational Television Facilities Act, that the federal government provided money for public service broadcasting. It provided for $32 million over five years. It was not a free-for-all give away bonanza, however. There was a fund matching clause. Educational television stations were to be given an average of $6 million a year for updating equipment, but only if, dollar-for-dollar, the same amount was raised locally. This gave rise to one of the defining features of public service television in the USA: local, voluntary funding. It led to 354 local fund-raising groups.

The most significant intervention in the development of public service television came next not from the federal government, but from the Carnegie Corporation of New York. Like the Ford Foundation, this was a philanthropic foundation set up by liberal industrialist, Andrew Carnegie. Now dead (he had retired from business in 1901 to give his full attention to the Carnegie Foundation) he had made provision for the future. In his deed to the corporation, he specified that 'I give my trustees full authority to change policies or causes hitherto unaided when this, in their opinion, has become necessary or desirable.' (Baker and Dessart, p.221)

The Carnegie Corporation saw educational television as falling within the 'broad rubric of education and concern for underprivileged groups.' (op.cit. p.221). It funded the Carnegie Commission on Educational Television which sat for three years. Its conclusions advocated not educational television per se, but 'a third form of television standing somewhere between educational (now called instructional) and commercial television. The title of the report gave the language a new term and foretold a new American institution: *Public Television: A Program of Action.*'

As a direct result of the Carnegie Commission report, in November, 1967, President Lyndon Johnson signed the Public Broadcasting Act of 1967. The commissions recommendations on funding, however were not accepted. One proposal was that there should be a tax on television sets of 2% rising to 5 %. This would have provided revenue of about $100 000 a year. This was, of course, remarkably close to the British system. It was rejected by Congress.

The commission's recommendations for the structure of public television were also rejected. It had proposed that a single agency be established, the Corporation for Public Broadcasting (CPB), which would manage programming and the interconnection of the stations. This was prohibited by the Act on the grounds that 'it might result in centralised promotion and scheduling, which could, in turn, facilitate public television becoming a fourth network.' (op.cit. p.25). The Corporation for Public Broadcasting, instead, had the prime role of distributing federal funds around the public service broadcasting stations. A way had to be found, however, for managing the interconnection between stations, after all, programming as well as funds had to be shared. To this end, in 1969 the Public Broadcasting Service (PBS) came into being. There has often been a tension between the two organizations: CPB had the authority to decide which programmes received federal funding and the PBS had a role in programme planning and even funding. Tensions were inevitable and over the years the balance of power between the two has oscillated.

PBS had its worst years during the Nixon and Regan years, both of whom were actively hostile, believing that it was infested with 'liberals'. Some of the most vituperative attacks came from Vice President Spiro Agnew who was also hostile to commercial television, which he believed to be biased towards liberalism too. He was forced out of office by a corruption scandal.

During the terms of hostile governments the PBS was starved of funds and had to rely heavily on local fund raising, public appeals and advertising. This has led to accusations of these non-profit broadcasters spending as much time raising revenue as commercial stations do on raising advertising. This seemed to be the inevitable fate of a public broadcaster not sufficiently provided for by the State. There have also been accusations that PBS programming all too often is not sufficiently differentiated from commercial television. Some see this as the inevitable consequence of forcing public service broadcasting to compete with commercial television without anything like their resources.

Notwithstanding the problems and shortcomings of the PBS, it has established over thirty years an admirable record as an effective public service broadcaster. It has appealed successfully to minority groups and has been frequently successful in producing popular and innovative programming. Its work in children's programmes has been very influential, with international successes such as *Sesame Street*. Its MacNeil–Lehrer Report has made a significant contribution to television journalism, providing a real alternative to the news coverage of the commercial networks. Perhaps not widely known amongst UK audiences (unless they are careful readers of end-credits) are the number of high quality co-productions that they have made with the BBC and other broadcasters in the UK. The public service broadcasting company most committed to co-productions with the UK has been WGBH Boston in dramas as diverse as *Middlemarch* (BBC, 1994) and the police series, *Touching Evil* (Anglia TV, 1998).

Figure 1.4 *Scene from Middlemarch*
Source: © BBC

CASE STUDY

Hill Street Blues (NBC, 1981–87)

Quality programming is not the sole province of public service broadcasting. Certainly since the eighties a number of American dramas and sitcoms have achieved high audiences both there and in the UK. In his book, *Television's Golden Age*, Robert J. Thompson offers an explanation as to why such quality productions were produced in the eighties and nineties in particular. By the 1980s, the networks were feeling threatened by cable, which had considerably fragmented the audience. This and the possibility that audiences were tiring of formulaic television, created a climate ready for innovative programming. Because cable was encroaching on network audiences, rating thresholds at which a programme was withdrawn, became lower, thus giving new programmes a better chance to establish themselves. Another important factor was the removal of the Television Code in 1982. The Code had placed limits on the number of commercials that could be aired each hour and restricted programme content, in particular language, sex and violence. In line with this, the networks own internal standards departments became less severe (the networks all have their own in-house censorship through which all programmes have to pass before they are allowed to be transmitted). The first of what Thompson calls 'quality programmes' was *Hill Street Blues*. It began when the head of the NBC network, Fred Silverman, decided that they needed a new gritty police drama. He had a few ideas about what the programme might look like: he thought an ensemble of actors might be a good idea and he was much taken by the style of the film, *Fort Apache, The Bronx* (1981). It was suggested that Steven Bochco and Michael Kozoll should do it. Both were with MTM Enterprises, a successful production company started by the comedy actress, Mary Tyler Moore and her husband, producer Grant Tinker. The company had been founded in 1970 around the *Mary Tyler Moore Show*. By 1980 it had gained a reputation for critically and commercially successful programmes. It also had a reputation for giving its creative people a lot of freedom. To begin with, neither Bochco or Kozoll were interested in working on another police show; they both had a lot of experience writing in the genre and knew it well. Eventually they took up Silverman's offer and went to work on what would become *Hill Street Blues*.

It had a very large cast compared to most television series of the day; there were thirteen principal actors. The precinct captain was Frank

.....Hill Street Blues was like nothing else before it on prime time. The audio-visual style was the first thing to strike the new viewer. Each episode opened with a scene of the morning roll call at Hill Street station, the law enforcement centre of a ghetto precinct in a big unnamed city. Unlike the clean, steady, beautifully lit scenes of other network television, however, this one had the look of a low-budget documentary. Shaking cameras seemed to be roaming around the room in search of subjects, sometimes correcting their focus right before our eyes. The sound track was just as chaotic. Overlapping conversations in a style that would be compared to the movies of Robert Altman could be heard under and around the main dialogue of the roll call sergeant's recitation of the crimes *de jour*. Music wasn't incorporated at all in the roll-call scenes and only sparingly throughout the episodes, contributing to the sense that this show didn't sound like all the rest.

(Thompson, R.U., Television's Second Golden Age, *Syracuse University Press, 1997, p.68)*

Furillo (Daniel J. Travanti), a liberal officer, who preferred negotiating to shooting. Serving under him was an odd-ball collection. There was a dishevelled plain-clothes officer taken to growling and who allegedly had once taken a bite out of a prisoner, Mick Belker (Bruce Weitz) and an ex-Vietnam vet, Lt. Howard Hunter (James B. Sikking) who headed-up the station's 'swat' (Special Weapons and Tactics) team and who, unlike Furillo, had a strong predilection to 'cleaning' the streets with maximum fire-power. Also there was the fifty-plus station sergeant, Phil Esterhaus, who had a seventeen year old girl friend who was still at school.

Figure 1.5 *Scene from Hill Street Blues*
Source: BFI

It was not just in the style of its narrative structure and tone that *Hill Street Blues* was exceptional. Typically, several plot lines would run through an episode, cross-cutting from one to another. Resolution was far from guaranteed: in its form it was closer to an elaborate soap opera rather than a standard police drama and narratives would run from one episode to another. After the first series, NBC insisted that in each episode there should be at least one complete story. The immediate legacy of *Hill Street Blues* was a hospital equivalent, *St Elsewhere*, also made by MTM. It was perhaps the most influential television series of the decade, spawning many imitations. Its influence was still evident in the late 1990s on both sides of the Atlantic in series such as *NYPD Blue* (produced by Bochco), *Homicide – Life on the Street* and in the UK, *The Cops*.

US 'quality' imports

Programmes usually included in lists of 'quality' US imports: *M*A*S*H* (CBS, 1972–83) *Hill Street Blues* (NBC, 1981–97), *St Elsewhere* (NBC, 1982–88), *Twin Peaks* (ABC, 1990–91), *Cagney and Lacey* (CBS, 1982–88), *LA Law* (NBC, 1986–94), *Cheers* (NBC, 1982–93), *thirtysomething* (ABC, 1987–91), *Frasier* (NBC, 1993–), *Northern Exposure* (CBS, 1990–95), *The X-Files* (Fox, 1993–), *NYPD Blue* (ABC, 1993–), *ER* (NBC, 1994 –), *Friends* (NBC,1994–), *Homicide - Life on the Street* (NBC, 1995–), and *Ally McBeal* (Fox, 1997–).

Is there a future for public service broadcasting?

There is no guarantee that public service broadcasting will survive – here or in the USA. In both countries there are powerful voices who argue that *all* television should be able to survive – or not – in the open market. The question is whether or not there is a place for the kind of programming that would not survive in an open market. Whether or not the proliferation of channels that we are experiencing will make provision for the challenging and sometimes difficult programmes that we are occasionally shown and whether television will in the future offer a rich and varied choice, has yet to be demonstrated.

ESSAY QUESTIONS

1 What conditions led to the UK having a monopoly broadcaster?

2 What were the factors that led to the end of the BBC monopoly?

3 'In spite of the commercial pressures on broadcasting, the principles of Public Service Broadcasting are still upheld in Britain today.' Discuss.

4 'Public Service Broadcasting bears little resemblance to what was envisaged by Lord Reith.' What evidence is there to support this view?

5 What are some of the difficulties confronted by American public service broadcasting?

FOLLOW UP WORK

1 Investigate in more depth the effects of World War II on the broadcasting industry. Produce detailed notes and sources.

2 Analyse one week of television. Include at least four terrestrial channels and, if you can, one satellite/cable/digital channel. Identify what you consider to be the public service aspects of the programming.

3 Conduct your own survey of television use in your college or school. Your aim is to find out how far the BBC has managed to retain its audience in the face of competition from new media and broadcasters.

4 What American programmes are currently broadcast by the BBC, ITV, C4 and Sky? In what ways might they be said to conform to or challenge the values of Reithian public service broadcasting?

5 What are the arguments for having large broadcasting companies? Give examples from both the UK and America.

SHORT ANSWER QUESTIONS

1 When was the British Broadcasting Company formed and what was it?
2 What was the '7 o'clock rule'? What led to its repeal?
3 What was the significance of the 1953 Coronation for television in the UK?
4 What body regulates American television?
5 Why might television have developed quicker in the UK than in the USA?
6 What are the four critieria described by C.A. Lewis for public service broadcasting?

2

ANALYSING TELEVISION

A number of terms are used to describe the process of television analysis: deconstruction and textual analysis are two of the most common. What they describe is the process of working out how a television programme, or 'text', works; 'works' in the sense of communicating a meaning. This meaning will not be fixed.

The word meaning is best understood as a verb: it is what happens as a result of an interaction between the text and the reader. The text might remain the same, in the sense of the marks on the page or the images on the screen, irrespective of who is reading/viewing it, but the meaning will not be. Readers/audiences are always different, they bring different experiences and values to their reading, and make differing interpretations. This might suggest that when it comes to making sense of a text, whether we are talking about a piece of writing or flickering images on a screen that 'anything goes'. In a sense, it does. Often cited is the concept of the 'preferred reading': preferred by whom? The author, publisher, critic, teacher – reader? 'Preferred readings' are merely the dominant readings arising from what might be called 'interpretative communities',

The purpose of analysis is to achieve a greater understanding of what a text is communicating both in terms of specific themes and its value system – its ideology. The exercise might be also evaluative and it could, of course be both. Popular reviewing in newspapers and magazines tends to be evaluative, although the criteria upon which such assessments are based are rarely made explicit.

The process of analysis begins with deciding what you aim to get out of it. In classroom and examination conditions that is easy; it's done for you. You will be told to analyse a film or programme in order to comment on its relationship to its genre, the values represented by the characters, and so on and so forth. There are specific areas that have to be looked at, to begin with in a largely descriptive manner; in the first instance structure and style. There is a measure of objectivity about both of these; deciding what they actually mean is where critics begin to part company. This is fine – in fact it is to be expected. Texts are polysemic – they have clusters of shifting meanings rather than one fixed meaning. Academic critical writing is not dissimilar from scientific writing – it follows a similar protocol. A problem is stated, the working methodology explained, an interpretation offered and supporting evidence provided.

Style and form

The two basic elements of a text that have to be considered in analysis are style and form. Form is the **structure** of a work, how its constituent elements are arranged. Style is how it is visually rendered and how sound and music are deployed. Both form and style will employ a number of codes and conventions which will be dependent on the genre and even the period in which the programme was made. The visual and narrative conventions of a soap opera, for example, are usually different to those of a sitcom. Soaps will tend to use a greater variety of locations than sitcoms and they have more characters. Soaps have continuous narratives: sitcoms have single-episode narratives (refer to the chapters on soap opera and sitcom).

Style, form and content

Bordwell and Thompson describe style and form as 'the general system of relationships among the parts of a film'. (*Film Art*, 1997 p.479). The problem is separating these out from style and content. In the end, this cannot be done – the distinction between form, style and content is ultimately artificial, although useful for purposes of analysis. After all, we respond to a film, television programme or a book as a *whole*: when experiencing a text, we do not isolate narrative structure or its visual style, although we might afterwards as part of an analysis in order to understand how the constituent elements relate to each other. *The X-Files,* for example, deploys the basic structure of a crime narrative, insofar as an episode, or series of episodes are predicated on the resolution of an enigma that has to be resolved. But *The X-Files* is visually rendered in a style that invokes other genres, most evidently film noir and science fiction. The narrative content is also inflected in a manner that transcends the detective story, again invoking science fiction, but also urban myths of extra-terrestrial visitations and government inspired conspiracies. All of these come together as a whole whilst viewing *The X-Files*: any response will be determined by an interaction of all the elements.

Figure 2.1 *The X-Files*
Source: The Kobal Collection

The fusion of form and content can be illustrated by a consideration of the sign itself. Saussure showed that the sign consists of two elements: the *signifier* and the *signified*. The signified (which, for our purposes, we can take as corresponding to form) is the physical essence of the sign, its physical form, whether that be (as here) a configuration of marks on a page or sounds, as in speech and music. The signified is the mental concept referred to by the sign. 'Dog', both as a series of inscribed marks and also as enunciated sounds through speech, refers to the concept of 'dog'. Equally, another configuration of marks on the page – which I will not embarrass myself by attempting – a drawing – would be yet another signifier alluding to the same concept. Clearly the signifier and the signified cannot exist without the other. I cannot allude to the concept of dog without giving it some kind of representation.

Another important aspect of the sign is its polysemy – the fact that a sign will generate clusters of meaning rather than just one. Roland Barthes argued that the range of meanings a sign carries can be constrained through a process of anchorage, which might be a caption, its juxtaposition with other images/sounds or in some other way manipulating the context in which the sign is used. A red light, for example, might mean a whole range of things, but place it in the context of a system of traffic lights at a road junction and its meaning becomes very precise indeed.

Signs accrue meaning through two orders of **signification**, that is levels of meaning.

The first order of signification is **denotation**. This refers to the literal relationship between the sign and its referent (that to which it refers). The assumption is that this relation is objective and value free: an image of a corgi would have the same value as one of an Alsatian, they are both simply 'dogs'. Likewise, an image of a Rolls Royce is just an image of a car. In practice, of course, it does not work like this, because there is no such thing as a value free order of signification except in mathematics: $1 + 1 = 2$ is a purely denotative statement.

The second order of signification is **connotation**. This refers to the cluster of culturally generated meanings that accrue to a sign. These are both attitudinal and evaluative. Going back to our dog, 'corgi' will have a range of connotations including wealthy middle class domesticity and even the Queen, which will then set into play a range of other meanings. The Alsatian, on the one hand, might well provoke a range of different connotations such as 'fierceness', 'guard' and so on. It could even, as with the corgi, connote 'cuddly pet'; it rather depends on who you are. Film and television, as does all art, fully exploits the connotative potential of signs.

- **Codes** – the way a signifying element is organised. An example is light: the lighting codes of a programme like *The X -Files* are different to those of *Only Fools and Horses*. In *The X-Files*, the dominant code is chiaroscuro; the deployment of light in such a way that there is both an emphasis on shadows and the contrast between light and dark.
- **Conventions** – refer to general 'rules' that determine the features of a certain kind of text. For example, the narrative conventions of soap opera include having a 'cliff hanger' at the end of an episode; it would be *unconventional* for a sitcom to end in tragedy.

Approaches to narrative

There are several specific narrative theories, or models, which are useful as analytical aids. Most of the established theories are derived from literary studies, but they are generally applicable to film and television, because they are both narrative based media.

Seymour Chapman

A useful starting point is the distinction between **story** and **plot** made by Seymour Chapman. Essentially, story is made up of all the events that occur in chronological order. That is the way we usually summarise a book or a film, we distil the major events into a précis. *Mildred Pierce* (1946) for example, is about a women who has a daughter from an unsuccessful marriage, dotes over her and to give her as much as she can, creates a successful restaurant. She marries another man, Monty, who seduces her daughter who then kills him. Mildred attempts to take the blame for the murder, but she is unsuccessful. At the end she is reunited with her first husband. This sums up, reasonably accurately, the story of *Mildred Pierce*, but it is not what you see in the film. Like many 1940s film noir thrillers, much of it is told in flashback with the film beginning at the *end* of the story.

It opens with a woman entering a building, a gun being fired and a man falling to the ground mumbling 'Mildred' – we are supposed to think she did it. What I am describing here is the plot which is the manner in which events are presented in the text. For this Chapman uses the word discourse, 'the modus of presentation'. Story and plot need not necessarily be the same thing, or as Jean-Luc Godard, a French film maker put it, every story has a beginning, a middle and end, but not necessarily in that order. Chapman's distinction between story and plot is similar to the distinction between fabula and syuzhet made by the Russian Formalist Viktor Shklovsky in his book *Theory of Prose (1990)*.

> The concept of plot (syuzhet) is too often confused with a description of the events in the novel, with what I'd tentatively call the storyline (fabula)...the storyline is nothing more than material for plot formation.
>
> *(Shklovsky, p.170)*

Tristan Todorov (1939–)

Events in a story have a causal relationship with one event leading to an other in a pattern of cause and effect. The very notion of 'cause and effect' implies a change in a state of affairs. For Todorov, the primary function of narrative is to solve a problem.

It is this that forms the basis of Todorov's theory of narrative. His model begins with a state of equilibrium, a condition in which everything is in a state of order. This state of equilibrium is disrupted either by a force of some kind or through the actions of an individual. The narrative progresses to a restoration of equilibrium, or order.

Todorov breaks the narrative process down into five stages

- A state of equilibrium at the outset
- A disruption of the equilibrium by some action
- A recognition that there has been a disruption
- An attempt to repair the disruption
- A reinstatement of the initial equilibrium

(Branigan E., Narrative Comprehension on a Film, *Routledge, 1992, p.4)*

Vladimir Propp (1895–1970)

Propp was a Bulgarian literary theorist. In his seminal 1922 work, *The Morphology of the Folk Tale*, he analysed something like 400 Russian folk tales. He found that across all of these tales, not withstanding apparent differences, characters and their actions can be categorised into clearly defined roles and functions which are summarised here:

Roles

- The hero: seeks something, to fulfil a 'lack' of some kind
- The villain: opposes the hero, tries to make the hero fail
- The donor: aids the hero by providing an object with magical properties
- The dispatcher: sends the hero on a quest of some kind
- The false hero: pretends to be the hero
- The helper: assists the hero in some way
- The princess: doubles up as a reward for the hero and the object of the villain's plot
- Her father: will reward the hero (often by giving the hero his daughter)

Narrative functions
Preparation

- A community (a kingdom, family, etc.) in a state of order
- A member of the family leaves home
- A prohibition or rule is imposed on the hero
- The prohibition/rule is ignored or broken
- The villain makes an attempt at reconnaissance; tries to find something out about the hero
- The villain learns something about his victim
- The villain tries to deceive the victim to gain an advantage
- The victim is deceived and unknowingly helps the villain

Complication

- The state of order is disrupted
- The villain harms a member of the family
- A member of the family lacks or desires something
- This lack is made known to the hero who is sent on a quest
- The hero plans action against the villain

Transference

- The hero leaves home
- The hero is tested, attacked, interrogated; the hero receives either a helper or magical agent
- The hero reacts to the donor
- The hero is transferred to the location where he will fulfil his quest/task

Struggle

- There is a struggle between the hero and villain
- The hero is branded
- The villain is defeated
- The initial state of order is restored/the lack fulfilled

Return

- The hero returns
- The hero is pursued
- The hero escapes/is rescued
- The hero arrives home or some other place; he is not recognized
- A false hero makes a false claim
- The hero is given a difficult task
- The task is accomplished

Recognition

- The hero is recognised
- The false hero/villain is exposed
- The false hero/villian is transformed
- The false hero/villain is punished
- The hero is rewarded (marries the princess and is granted wealth/power)

These functions should not be seen just as events, actions or characters in themselves, but as elements in a narrative which can occur at different places. The same action can have a different meaning depending on where it occurs. The building of a castle could mean:

- In one tale, the breaking of a command not to build it
- In another story the castle might be the solution to a task
- In yet another the building of the castle might be in preparation for a wedding

On the other hand, two different events might have the same meaning: a king giving a hero a sword can mean the same as a princess giving another hero a horse.

There have been attempts to apply Propp to film and television. It seems to work well with *Star Wars*, which is a kind of folk tale. Will Wright adapted Propp in an analysis of the western. In his book, *Six Guns and Society*, he describes four underlying western plot structures. Wright's criticism of Propp is that his insistence that all thirty one functions have to appear in order is too restrictive. Propp is difficult to apply to films and television dramas, which are often more complex narratives than the folk tales with which he originally worked. Propp is useful, however, in drawing attention to the importance of structure in a narrative and the similarities between seemingly different stories.

Branigan

Edward Branigan's model is, in some respects, a distillation of Todorov and Propp. Its usefulness lies in its relative simplicity and that it closely follows the way we tend to remember films.

- Introduction of setting and characters
- Explanation of a state of affairs
- Initiating event
- Emotional response or statement of a goal by the protagonist
- Complicating actions
- Outcome
- Reactions to the outcome

C A S E   S T U D Y

Analysis of an episode of *The Cops* (BBC1, 19th October 1998)

The analysis of narrative in television is complicated by the fact that some texts have multiple narratives. *The Cops* is a case in point and this is one of the signifiers of its realism. The complexity and narrative density might be regarded as simulating the rhythms and textures of real life. It is more likely, however, that this 'realist effect' is a function of the *difference* between the narrative strategies and style of *The Cops* and earlier police dramas. In its day *Dixon of Dock Green* was regarded as 'realistic'.

This is the first episode of the first series of *The Cops* (see also Chapter 5).

It is set in a northern town and based around a fictional police station. The main characters in this episode are: Melanie, a probationary officer; Giffin, a sergeant; Roy, an older, very experienced officer regarded as his superiors as effective, but old fashioned; Danny, again experienced, but gentler and Jaz, a young Asian officer, who has embarrassed his father by joining the police. The first episode of *The Cops*, like that of *Z-Cars*, was designed to introduce both these characters and the area.

Figures 2.2 *Scene from The Cops*   *Source:* © *BBC*

The main lines of action set up in the episode are:

- Melanie's investigation of a death
- Roy's pursuit of Vince, whom he blames for the death of a friend and colleague
- Mike and Natalie's dealings with a teenage couple who have stolen flowers from a cemetery

- Jaz, who wants to be moved from the area he patrols because he lives there
- The settling in of a new station sergeant, Giffin, fresh from the Metropolitan Police

For a one hour episode this seems to be rather a lot, but not all the lines of action are accorded the same 'narrative space' (the amount of plot-time taken up). It is usual for multi-narrative television dramas to prioritise one or two lines of action. In this case it is 'Melanie's story', but there are at least two other significant narratives, Roy's and Danny/Natalie's. At certain points they intersect, but it is possible to extrapolate each of them out separately for the purpose of analysis.

Melanie's Story

- Night club (her identity is not revealed to the audience
- Arrival at police station (it is revealed she is a police officer)
- Officers assigned tasks
- Melanie responds to a call from a block of flats – a tenant complains that a fluid is seeping through his ceiling; a disabled man (Raleigh) lives upstairs.
- Melanie refuses to break in – leaves
- Called back, she finds the neighbour has broken in – Raleigh is dead and in an advanced state of decomposition (hence the fluid oozing through the ceiling below)
- Scene of crime (SOC) officer arrives, followed by Roy and Danny (at the beginning of this episode they are patrolling together). The new Sergeant (Giffin) arrives.
- Giffin looks at body. Until now, it looks as if no one has visited the old man for some time. Griffin quickly finds out otherwise: marks on the finger indicate a ring has been removed and his pension book has also been used.
- Murder is suspected; Melanie visits Raleigh's daughter, Theresa. During the pictures of the interview, Theresa walks out of the room – Melanie finds her beneath the stairs injecting herself.
- Theresa is taken to the Stanton station and interrogated. She admits to finding the body and not reporting it so that she can use the pension.
- End of the day and episode. Back in the clothes in which we first saw her Melanie is seen walking home. End credits.

Propp

This is far from representing the whole episode; there are as indicated above, another four. But insofar as it extends throughout the episode and briefly involves several other main characters, it is the dominant one. Some of Propp's character roles readily apply:

- The hero: Melanie
- The villain: Theresa
- The donor: the sergeant – explains the clues
- The dispatcher: the sergeant – assigned her to the task
- The false hero: Theresa – pretends to be innocent

- The helper: the sergeant
- The princess: this is the reward; in Melanie's case it is being accepted as an effective officer – this has been her goal.
- Her father: again, the Sergeant, or perhaps in a more general sense the police station itself.

The application of all of Propp's narrative functions do not work in the order in which he arranged them.

Branigan

Now lets use Branigan's model as an analytical tool:

- Introduction of setting and characters: in a sense the whole episode is about this, but specifically this occurs at the police station and when Melanie first meets Theresa.
- Explanation of state of affairs: this happens twice, first at the police station, where the officers are briefed and at Raleigh's flat, when the sergeant explains what probably happened to the old man.
- Initiating the event: at the flat; the sergeant's explanation initiates a potential murder enquiry.
- Emotional response or statement of a goal by the protagonist: both apply to Melanie; she is moved by Theresa's plight (they are both visually linked by the drug taking) and does not want Theresa to face a murder charge.
- Complicating actions: the fact that Theresa has stolen a ring from her father's finger and has been drawing his pension is incriminating
- Outcome: Theresa does not have to face a murder charge, but Melanie is uncertain as to the outcome and is all too aware of the dire conditions to which Theresa will eventually return.
- Reactions to the outcome: Melanie has proven' herself – up to a point; rather she has demonstrated her potential. In terms of the audience, Melanie is transformed from an apparently reckless, drug-taking girl to an effective and compassionate police officer. This is one of the 'meanings' of the episode. This is only the beginning of an analysis that would have to include an examination of the visual style, the language used, the sound and a more complete analysis of the narrative, showing how the different threads relate to each other.

Style

Style and form are not always distinguishable, for instance editing is both a formal and a stylistic element. There are some basic terms and concept which are useful in any discussion of style.

Mise en scene

This is a French term originally used in theatre that means 'placed in the scene'. The term is used to refer to the way in which a director stages a play. The term has been taken up by film and television and used in a similar way.

It is such an important dimension to film/television production that in France the term *'meteur-en-scene'* is used to describe the director.

In film/television *mise-en-scene* refers to the **manipulation of space within the frame**. This includes all of the visual elements such as:

- Setting
- Props/costumes/make-up
- Body language (gesture/movement)
- Point of view of camera
- Shot size
- Lighting
- Use of colour/monochrome

Some writers have been dismissive about the role of *mise-en-scene* in television because of its inferior quality of image. The difference, however, between the film and television image (although generally still there) is being eroded. In fact recently High Definition television has almost completely eroded any such difference. Conventional television production has improved in every area, from set construction to the quality and light sensitivity of camera lenses, lights and video tape. Digital technology has further enhanced the quality of the television image. Although much image construction in television is largely functional, it is never *wholly* functional. The setting created for every television programme – even a simple interview – in some way or another will have a significance.

There is also a wide-spread view that has been repeated even in very recent writing, that *mise-en-scene* is somehow of no account in television, because the image is less important than dialogue. This is a highly problematic – and inaccurate – assertion. It implies a homogeneity of television output. But it is not homogenous; there are many different television genres with their own formal codes and a range of production values. What aspect of television is being referred to: news, sport, day-time chat shows, drama? What kind of drama? Situation comedy, period drama, 'soaps', etc? A BBC/WGBH co-production such as *Middlemarch* is not going to look the same as a sitcom. Each of these categories of television output have their own aesthetic criteria. But is it true of drama? Not really, especially given that the distinction between 'drama' and film' is now virtually non-existent – the aesthetic criteria used in television drama is often the same as that used for film.

Talking to directors, it is clear that in their own minds they often make no distinction at all between making a 'film' and making a 'television drama'. This has, in part, been encouraged by the institutional convergence of the two media. Films made for television are occasionally given a theatrical release and the large television companies have their own film divisions, for example the BBC and Channel Four (FilmFour).

Setting

It has been claimed that sets on television 'are sparser' than on film and that it is less reliant on *mise-en-scene* than film. For some areas of television programming this might be true, but it certainly is not the case for *all* television. To a large extent it depends on the genre. Some sitcoms are very reliant on verbal humour, such as *Blackadder*; this makes it possible for audio tapes to be successfully released. In anycase, many sitcoms began on radio and on being translated to television retained the emphasis on dialogue. Some sitcoms, however, rely more heavily on *visual* humour, such as *One Foot in the Grave*: such programmes would be less accessible on audio tape alone. This is worth pointing out, because it is easy to make generalisations about television forgetting that television itself is just a medium embracing a number of different cultural forms.

Figure 2.3 *Scene from* One Foot in the Grave
Source: © *BBC*

For all television programmes *mise-en-scene* in general and setting in particular are very important. The setting of *Brookside* is very different to that of either *EastEnders* or *Coronation Street*. Semiotically, these differences are not neutral: they are part of a whole battery of devices through which an audience makes sense of what they are seeing. The sets and settings of *Coronation Street* emphasise a sense of community. The key setting is the pub, a meeting place for all of the characters. Even the name of the pub, The Rovers Return, signifies the notion of a tight-knit, supportive community to which all return should they eventually wander abroad to test out the world beyond 'the street'.

Another key location is Mike Baldwin's factory, which is another communal setting. The homes of the main characters are close together; they are frequently in and out of each others houses. *Brookside* has a very different sense of community; it is more fragmented. In *Coronation Street* almost all the characters are connected to each other in a constantly shifting pattern of relationships. Not so in *Brookside*. There are probably as many characters, but their relationships are configured into more-or-less self contained cells. The characters in *Brookside* are more competitive and aspirational: they are more 'modern'. All of this is suggested in the setting: a modern housing estate with a history that does not pre-date the beginning of the serial (one has the sense that *Coronation Street* has always been there).

Lighting

Lighting has two functions:

- to provide sufficient illumination for an image to be recorded
- to create an appropriate style and mood

Lighting has a number of different components, all of which can be separately manipulated to produce a range of different lighting effects. The basic lighting configuration is called three point lighting. It employs three

...ghts, arranged in such a fashion so as to not only provide overall illumination of a character, but also to 'sculpture' the character and to make him/her stand out from the background.

Three point lighting consists of:

- Key light: this is the light(s) providing overall illumination.
- Fill light: less intense lights used to fill in shadows on characters faces; these lights are used to 'sculpture' faces
- Backlight: this is another form of fill light, it is usually above and behind the character, causing him/her to 'stand out' from the background.

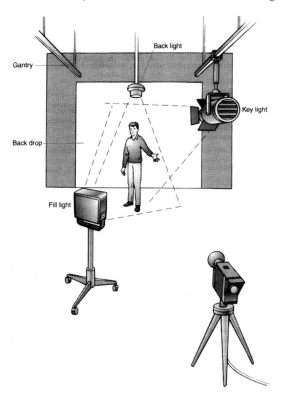

Figure 2.4 *An illustration of the three point lighting system*

These lights can be manipulated to produce different effects. None of these lighting effects 'mean' anything on their own: their filmic significance is determined by their position in the narrative, genre and their relationship to other expressive elements such as camera angle, shot size, etc. and narrative itself.

Lighting is a feature of television production that has improved enormously over the past two decades. Sets can be lit with greater subtlety than in the past. The low-key, lighting of a drama series such as *Touching Evil* would have been very difficult ten or so years ago. Television used to rely heavily on high key lighting, but this is no longer the case. A good example is police drama. No longer do they rely, apart from night scenes, on bright, high key lighting. Lighting for television is approaching lighting for film in the range of tones, both in colour and monochrome, that lighting designers are able to create.

Television genres have their own lighting styles. Game shows always have a very bright level of lighting with concomitant colour values in the decor. Sitcom, too, has traditionally had high levels of lighting, but increasingly there are exceptions. *The Royle Family* and *Rab C. Nesbit* both use light levels lower than is usual for a sitcom. Both of these series, (see the section on sitcom), 'play' with the conventions of sitcom. In terms of both decor, setting and style of lighting *The Royle Family* borrows from the visual conventions of social realism.

The frame

The frame marks the boundary of the image. It is this space that film makers manipulate in order to create meaning. The space within the frame is defined by the size of the shot and its angle of vision (camera angle). A lexicon of shots has evolved which allows us to describe the space within the frame.

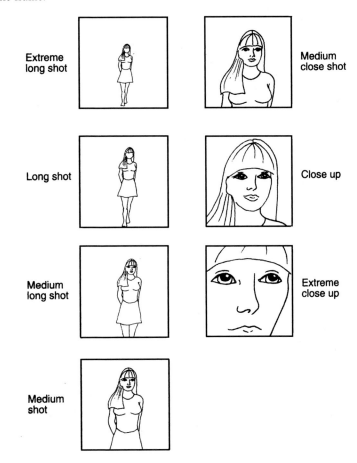

Figure 2.5 *An illustration of various camera positions relating to performers*

Camera angles

Various camera angles are used:

- High angle: this is when the camera is looking *down* on the subject
- Low angle: this is when the camera is looking *up* to the subject
- Point of view shot: when the camera is showing the point of view of a character. This is often an 'over the shoulder shot'; the camera shows us what the character is seeing.
- A subjective point of view shot: when we are 'seeing through the eyes' of the character (a 'subjective camera'). `*The Lady in the Lake* (1946) was made almost entirely with a subjective camera. The entire film is seen through the eyes of the main character, a private detective, Phillip Marlowe: the only time the audience sees Marlowe's face is when he looks in a mirror.

High angle

Low angle

Figure 2.6 *An illustration of the use of camera angles*

Editing

If *mise-en-scene* is the creation of meaning *within* an image, editing is the creation of meaning through the *juxtaposition* of images.

The function of editing is to construct a coherent sense of time and space. Time in film exists at two levels:

- Screen time: the time it takes to watch the film
- Story time: the amount of time that passes in the story (diegetic time).

Time can be *stretched*: an event can be 'stretched' out through a number of devices, for example, by using slow motion or by having several shots from different angles of the same piece of action.

Time can be *compressed* by cutting out that action or actions not essential to the story. The passing of several years can be suggested by cutting from one shot to another in which some element or another signifies the passing of time. It might be a change of the season, moving from summer to winter or characters might have aged, etc. The reduction of time in this way is called a *temporal elision*.

Time can also be *frozen* through a freeze frame (the picture is momentarily stopped and shown as a still).

There are certain conventions that determine ways in which images are combined. The basic rule is that continuity of action is maintained from shot to shot. For example, an action that begins moving right to left, must in every shot continue to do so, unless some device has been used to reorientate the audience. This is the 180 degree rule. The camera must always remain on the same side of an imaginary line bisecting the scene. A simple scenario illustrates the point (see figure 2.7). Imagine that we are in a studio recording an interview. Person A is talking to person B. Camera 1 is on B and camera 2 is on A. If camera 2 was to find itself 'across the line' and recording A from the other side, on screen both characters will be looking in the same direction.

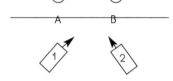

Figure 2.7 *Illustration of camera positions*

the camera must keep on this side of the line: try to visualise the effect of having one or other of the cameras on the *wrong* side.

Another basic rule is the thirty degree rule. Any change of angle on a subject must be greater than thirty degrees otherwise it will not register properly with an audience. Some directors take advantage of the disruptive effect of this: Jean-Luc Godard was one of the first to deliberately do this in his film *Breathless* (1959), but many others have done it since.

Shot matches

Shot matches are important for sustaining the illusion of spatial continuity. When recording a scene that involves cross-cutting between two characters, each character must remain on the same side of the frame.

Each shot must reciprocate the correct line of vision from one character to another. If, for example, in one shot character A is looking down at B, on cutting to show B looking at A, the camera must look up: this is called **shot-reverse shot**.

Cutting on action: moving from one shot to another, an action is picked up by the second shot where the previous shot left off. The illusion is created of the whole action being completed in an unbroken fashion through two or more shots.

These devices, and others, have the effect of disguising the editing, for this reason it is referred to as invisible editing. It is an important feature of realism in film and television. By not noticing the editing, an audience is more readily led into the fictional world (the diegesis) of the film.

ESSAY QUESTIONS

1 With detailed reference to the style and form of any television programme show how it uses its generic features to appeal to its audience.

2 Analyse in detail the opening sequence from any television drama and show how it establishes the narrative and the main character(s).

3 Compare any Australian and British soap. How significant are any differences in style?

4 Take any television drama. What are the narrative problems and how are they resolved?

5 Discuss any one sequence from a television drama of your choice and show its importance to the narrative as a whole.

SHORT ANSWER QUESTIONS

1 What is meant by 'textual analysis'?

2 What are **style** and **form?**

3 What is a sign? What is the difference between 'denotation' and 'connotation'?

4 What is the difference between 'story' and 'plot'?

5 What is *mise en scene?*

FOLLOW UP WORK

1 Take any two consecutive episodes of a soap opera and make a time-line of the main narrative threads.

2 Take any episode of a drama and break it down into segments of action corresponding to Todorov's and/or Branigan's model.

3 Take any episode of television drama and work out how far the characters comply with Propp's model.

4 Compare the narrative structure of an episode of *The Simpson's* with an episode of any soap opera.

5 Take the *end* of any drama. Write a new opening so that the drama is told in *flashback*.

3
TELEVISION IN PRODUCTION

Independent television

In television, 'independent' generally means two different things. In the case of ITV, (independent television) 'independent' refers to the ITC franchise holders. The word was originally used to differentiate the commercial operators from the BBC. Confusingly, however, it also refers to those production companies that do not belong to any of the franchise holders, or for that matter to the BBC. 'Independent', when applied to the media, usually refers to any media organisation that is free of any ties with the major companies. Channel Four has a brief to encourage such companies and give their work a wider audience. 'Independent' also has implications regarding the work itself, suggesting that it is formally, stylistically and in its content, unconventional. How far true independence exists in television is arguable; somewhere down the line even the most independent of independent producers is going to have to deal with a mainstream company. This was ultimately true of Undercurrents, an independent news operation that covered stories concerned with political activism generally ignored by mainstream news. Although their material was distributed on video tape, they were broadcast by Channel Four. Starting in 1994, they closed in 1999 due to financial problems.

Many independent companies have an umbilical relationship with the BBC and the major ITV companies and could not exist without them. Blue Heaven, for example, has collaborated for many years with Meridian, producing the *Ruth Rendell Mysteries* and mini-series such as *The Heroes* (1988).

Overview of ITV

In independent television (i.e. ITV) programmes emanate from two principal sources: the Regions and ITV Network Centre (see below). There are fifteen regional companies all with franchises awarded by the Independent Television Commission. All of these regions (the ITV licensees) will generate many of the programmes they broadcast. ITV Network Centre is an organisation between the ITC and the regional companies which is responsible for commissioning and scheduling nationally broadcast programmes.

Some programmes are purchased from broadcasters overseas, such as America and Australia, but many others come from other television companies within the UK. Since the Broadcasting Act of 1990, 25% of programmes have to come from independent companies: the same stipulation applies to the BBC.

The Licensees

THE 15 ITV LICENSEES				
ANGLIA	CENTRAL	GRANADA	MERIDIAN	ULSTER
BORDER	CHANNEL	HTV	SCOTTISH	WESTCOUNTRY
CARLTON	GRAMPIAN	LWT	TYNE TEES	YORKSHIRE

Fig. 3.1 *Map of 15 licensees*

Most of the ITC franchise holders (the licensees) are owned by four companies. In order of current size they are:

- **Granada** owns Granada TV, LWT, and has shares in BSkyB and BD (British Digital Broadcasting). The Granada group also has substantial interests in hotels.
- **Carlton Communications** owns Carlton TV (the London weekday franchise), Central TV and Westcountry Television and has shares in BDB and GMTV. Carlton also has a 50% share in ONdigital.
- **United News and Media** owns Anglia and Meridian TV and has shares in Yorkshire TV, HTV and C5. They also own Express Newspapers (Express, Sunday Express and Daily Star).
- **Channel Four**

The largest independent is BSkyB. A measure of its size is that Granada's income is only two thirds that of BSkyB.

On Friday, 26th November 1999, United News and Media and Carlton Communications announced their intention to merge, creating a media group worth £7 billion (at 1999 prices). If the merger goes ahead it will control several television franchises, own a 50% share in ONdigital, have substantial business interests in the USA, including Technicolour and own three national newspapers.

The proposed merger has caused concern amongst advertisers, who believe that the consolidation of ITV into two large companies, never mind one, will seriously weaken their bargaining position and lead to a fall in the cost of advertising.

At the time of writing the OFT is examining the rules that limit each large ITV company to 25% of total airtime advertising revenue: UN&M and Carlton will, together, account for 36% of total revenue. If the OFT does not change the rules, the merger will be at risk.

In January 2000, the other major ITV company, Granada, made its own intervention. Granada's interest in the proposed merger is not only that it could leave them weaker than the proposed new company, but they intend to 'hive off' their hospitality interests (hotels, etc.) from their media interests. 'These two companies are our number one targets,' said Allen (Charles Allen, Granada's chief executive) 'There is absolutely no doubt about that: we want to

> The two companies have been under pressure to find a way of becoming bigger to compete more effectively with media giants overseas. They have watched uneasily as Granada, the hotels and media group, has increased its media interests inside the ITV community and elsewhere.
>
> *(The Guardian, Friday, 26th November 1999)*

> Mr Raad (director for media affairs at the Institute of Practitioners in Advertising) said advertisers were very concerned that the merger was taking place while ITV still accounted for 62% of all advertising.
>
> The IPA has already told the office of fair trading that no ITV company should command more than 25% of television advertising revenue until ITV's share of total spending has fallen below 50%.
>
> As it was, ITV's share has been rising, and was too high for advertisers to accept that the three dominant companies should be two – UN&M – Carlton and Granada.
>
> *(The Guardian, Wednesday, December 1st, 1999)*

bulk up our media side ahead of a demerger from our hospitality interests.' (*The Observer*, January 9th 2000). On Friday, January 7th 2000, Granada, in an attempt to undermine the proposed merger, declared its intention to make a counter bid for either UN&M or Carlton. It proposed to the Office of Fair Trading that it should be allowed to do one of three things: bid for Carlton, bid for UN&M or bid for the new merged company.

All of these options, however, would require a change in the same legislation that presently prevents the merger between UN&M and Carlton: the 25% limit on a share of total advertising revenue. The OFT is due to report on the proposed UN&M and Carlton merger in mid-February 2000. Unless the Department of Culture, Media and Sport and the Competition Commission increase the upper limit on advertising sales, the UN&M and Carlton merger will not go ahead. The Government intends to review broadcasting legislation after the next election. The present Secretary of Culture, Media and Sport, Chris Smith, has 'acknowledged that it is important for UK broadcasters and programme makers to be big enough to compete on the world stage. The European commission is also reviewing media ownership rules.' (*The Guardian*, Saturday 27th November 1999)

ITV Network Centre

ITV Network Centre was created in 1993 in order to fulfil a requirement of the Broadcasting Act 1990 that ITV should commission and schedule programmes through a separate, independent body. Network Centre not only commissions and schedules programmes, but its responsibilities also include:

- Broadcasting Advertising Clearance Centre (monitors the standard of adverts.)
- Engineering (sets and monitors the technical standards of programmes)
- ITV2 (the ITV digital channel, available on cable and satellite)
- ITV Sport (co-ordinates the coverage and networking of sporting events)
- Marketing and promotion
- Press and publicity
- Programme and film acquisitions (co-ordinates the acquisition of networked films and programmes)

In 1998 the Network spent £626 million on programmes:

Commissions	£437m	70% of total
Sport	£85m	15% of total
News & Weather	£45m	7% of total
Acquisitions	£45m	7% of total
Other	£14m	2% of total

Figure 3.2 *Chart of ITV Network expenditure* (ITV Annual Report 1998)

Most of this expenditure (70%) was on commissioned programmes and half of this on drama.

Drama	£246m
Entertainment	£82m
Factual	£45m
Children's	£35m
Daytime	£17m
Religion, Education, Arts & Other	£12m
Total for 1998	£437m

Figure 3.3 *Chart of ITV Network expenditure on commissioned programmes*
(ITV Annual Report 1998)

The major ITV licensees such as Granada, Carlton and Meridian are expected to make regular contributions to the Network, but all regions do so from time to time. Regions will either offer programmes to Network Centre or they will be commissioned. Network Centre commissions all categories of programme, including sport and news (the Network Centre acts as a liaison between ITN and the regions). Activities of Network Centre expanded when on 7th December 1998, a new digital service ITV 2 started.

Making programmes for the BBC

The BBC, although a national broadcaster, is also organised into regions, such as BBC Scotland, BBC Wales, etc. They are mainly responsible for generating local programming and news, but they occasionally produce some networked programmes. BBC regions do not have the same degree of autonomy as the ITV licensees. The BBC has, however, placed great stress on its regionalism and throughout the nineties an increasing amount of programming was produced outside London. Under John Birt, the BBC went through what was often a painful process of reorganisation. The key elements of this were Producer Choice and beginning in October 1991, a new bi-media structure whereby radio and television news shared resources, with the aims of enhancing efficiency and cutting costs. Producer Choice brought the market place into the BBC. Programme makers were expected to 'buy in' production facilities at the best available price, which often meant going outside the BBC to independent production facilities companies. Internal accounting practices were also changed: every element of a programme was costed and charged to the production directly.

For example, if a production researcher needed a book from the BBC library, the production would be charged. However, he or she would be more likely to buy it from a shop, because it would be cheaper: the implication of this is that Library Services is being used less.

Another example results from the fact that the cost of studio and office space is charged to the production. The sitcom, *Roger, Roger*, was entirely made at Teddington Studios. It seems that they offered a deal that included not only studio space, but also offices. Critics argue that whilst this might save the production money, it does not necessarily save the BBC money: studios, for instance, are left empty and unused and represent a wasting asset. Whole departments in the BBC have been closed down, including design, costume and make-up: freelancers are now brought-in.

Predictably, Producer Choice has its defenders and critics. One view argues that this and other changes were necessary to improve efficiency and prepare the BBC for new and expanding markets. Still others say that it stifled creative programme making, paid too much attention to news and introduced absurd and costly accounting procedures. They lament what they perceive to be an erosion of the whole character of the BBC as an innovative and creative programme maker.

The new structure

In 1997 the BBC was reorganised into five directorates: BBC Broadcast; BBC News; BBC Production; BBC Resources and BBC Worldwide. The directorates in turn consist of a number of divisions, BBC Broadcast, for example incorporates BBC Broadcast HQ; BBC Television; BBC Production; BBC Regional Broadcasting; BBC Network Radio; BBC Education. Within the directorates, no distinction is made between television and radio, although news managed to resist an attempt to amalgamate television and radio editorially; although they kept separate editors, radio and television have to share correspondents and stories. The accusation has been made many times since that the restructuring of the BBC was part-and-parcel of an accelerating acceptance of commercialism and an erosion of Reithian public service standards.

Most programmes are commissioned by BBC Production, but BBC Broadcast has a statutory obligation to ensure that 25% of network television is made by independent producers. This was introduced by the Conservative government, under Margaret Thatcher, in the Broadcasting Act of 1990. Ostensibly the aim was to stimulate independent production. An alternative view has it that, following on from the Thames *Death on the Rock* episode, the government wanted to weaken the power of the large television institutions, especially in news and current affairs. From this viewpoint, it at worst back-fired and at best simply did not work. The BBC is a very large organisation with many programme making sectors. The 25% ruling only seemed to apply to the organisation as a whole and not individual sectors. This resulted in 60% of light entertainment going out to independent producers, leaving news and current affairs virtually untouched.

There is also a requirement that a reasonable proportion of programmes are made outside London. In 1998 about a third of BBC network radio and television programmes were made outside London and the South East. BBC Production, the core directorate of the BBC, is divided into over twenty departments including: Drama Series; Films and Single Drama; Comedy; Comedy Entertainment; Light Entertainment; Science; Religion; Arts; Music and others. It is at this level that the actual process of making programmes (rather than policy) begins.

Programme making

The precise process followed by any production depends upon its type: sport programmes will clearly be produced differently to drama. In turn, the process of producing a single play will be different to the way a serial is produced. Whatever the programme, however, there are three basic stages of production:

- Pre-production
- Production
- Post-production

Pre-production is concerned with whatever happens to a programme before the cameras start 'turning', such as casting, location finding, set design and construction, costume design, the acquisition of props, the clearance of copyright for any music that is used; basically everything that needs to be done before recording can take place. Production is the process of actual filming/recording and post-production consists of all that happens after the cameras stop such as editing, sound mixing, etc.

The producer

The producer has overall responsibility for a production and is often the only person working on the programme who is involved at every stage, from commissioning, story and script development through to post-production. Overall responsibility for a production means exactly that – being, in the end, responsible for just about every aspect of the show, from the management of the cast and crew to the quality of the final product, the programme itself. Occasionally a producer will also take the role of director. Credit lists will frequently boast at least two producers; an executive producer and a producer. The executive producer has overall responsibility for the series or department but little 'hands on' involvement with a particular episode: that is the responsibility of the producer.

Script editor

This role only applies to a series. Like the producer, s/he is involved at the very beginning. Storylines are worked out with the writers and producer at a 'Story Conference'. Once everyone is happy with the storylines a Commissioning Meeting is held with the team of writers. The storylines are shared out amongst them and off they go to do a first draft of the script. New writers to a series will be given a lot of information about the characters and brief outlines of future stories which they have to 'flesh' out into a complete script. The script editor's job is then to make sure that continuity, both in terms of plot and character, is maintained from one to another.

Production associate/associate producer

The programme budget is the responsibility of the production associate (on some productions s/he is called the Associate Producer). S/he breaks the total amount of money available for the programme into various production areas such as actors' fees, design, etc., and monitors how this money is spent, making sure that the programme does not overspend. Occasionally, this will mean 'trimming' expenditure, such as cutting down on the number of extras to be used or limiting overtime. This can be serious: it might mean the difference between doing a re-take or not or even staying on schedule or going over. Once the deadline in the studio has been reached, penalty payments to the Studio Operatives come into play, and do so every fifteen minutes past the scheduled finishing time.

As well as watching the schedule, the production associate might make themselves unpopular with a director if they have to veto the use of an expensive piece of equipment for a shot, such as a crane.

Director

The director is responsible for *making* the programme. The first thing the director does when s/he comes to a programme is to read the script. At this stage the director is, inevitably, working closely with the script editor and producer. The director has to translate the script into visual terms, first in the form of a camera script, which will show details of camera angles, movement and framing, before translating this to sounds and images on the screen. Being able to mentally visualise a script is an important skill for a good director. As Charles Garland, an experienced BBC producer and director put it, 'You should be able to see a script in your head.'

Figure 3.4 *A TV programme in rehearsal*
Source: © BBC

Having 'blocked' (decided on the position and movements of the actors) the action and worked out how it is to be visualised, the director draws up camera plans, which will be needed by the production team and crew, not least the senior cameraman, lighting supervisor and designer.

Part of the process of devising a camera script is thinking through the action in terms of how it will appear on the screen, that is to say, how is the *mise-en-scene* going to be manipulated? How are characters going to move or be positioned in relation to each other and their surroundings? How are attitudes, thoughts, emotions going to be suggested? How can relationships between characters be hinted at, through gesture and movement? How is light going to be used and how will the frame be composed? All this has to be thought through before the director walks onto the studio floor, but the process of working with actors and the script, as it were *in situ*, will itself generate ideas. Sometimes they will come from other members of the crew or from the cast. There is nothing unusual about this; most directors regard their scripts (camera and dialogue) as useful plans, not as something sacrosanct. Scripts can be changed for a number of reasons which are usually technical, but it might just be a case of finding a better way of doing things. In a soap, especially, actors will often have their own ideas about how their character should 'sound'. However, normally the script is followed as closely as possible.

Production manager

The production manager, with the production assistant, works very closely with the director. During pre-production, amongst his/her most important tasks is drawing up the recording schedule. Scenes are organised into a schedule according to their location and the availability of the cast. For example, scenes that take place in the same location are recorded together, not withstanding their position in the narrative. The process of creating a recording schedule begins with breaking the scripts up into separate scenes. Each scene will have, as Oliver Cookson, a BBC production manager explained, '... the page number of the scene, the scene number, where it is, whether it's day or night.... time of day .... whether it's in the studio or location, how long it is ... the characters involved and a little précis of what the scene is about.' These are first printed out in story order form and then arranged into the order in which they will be actually filmed/recorded. This will form the basis of the recording schedule.

The production manager's role used to incorporate that of both floor manager and location manager (responsible for finding locations), but these roles are now separate. During the recording, the floor manager is in charge of the studio floor, standing in for the director (who will be working from the gallery in the studio or the scanner if on location), relaying instructions to the cast and crew: the floor manager is the voice of the director. Every scene will begin with the production manager calling out the scene and shot number, followed by 'Action!'. All too often this will be followed by 'Reset!' as a retake is prepared.

Production assistant

The production assistant (PA) works very closely with the director and production manager and deals with the administrative workload that every production generates. During the pre-recording phase s/he has to, amongst other things, help to arrange auditions, book artists and type out scripts and storyboards.

During the recording, the PA will sit next to the director either in the gallery or scanner. During a rehearsal or a take, s/he will cue each camera by calling out the camera and shot number. Afterwards, s/he will take notes on each take, the shot is timed and its time-code number written down.

The PA also looks out for any continuity problems, a responsibility shared by make-up, costume and the Assistant Floor Manager (AFM). Parts of a scene might be recorded at different times, sometimes days apart (or even longer). Frequently, a script will call for a scene to be staged in an interior: it might be a simple exchange of dialogue inside a house and will be recorded in the studio. However, if the script calls for that scene to be continued outside, perhaps in a street or garden, there must be consistency in costume, and indeed behaviour and this might have to be recorded on location several days later. Continuity is all about making sure that in each part of the scene, both the interior and exterior and the characters look exactly the same.

After the last shot has been recorded, the PA is still not finished: actors' time sheets have to be filled in; the editing and sound-sypher (the making of the sound track) have to be arranged and music studios booked for the recording of incidental music. If anywhere in the episode diagetic music has been heard playing, from a radio for example, the PA is responsible for getting copyright clearance.

The recording

In addition to set and costume design, the main tasks in the early stages of a production involve casting, finding locations and the drawing up of the rehearsal and recording schedules. At this stage the director is busy working on the scripts; the production manager with the assistant is beginning to arrange auditions and book some of the cast; the location manager is finding locations and the assistant floor managers are organising transport to the studio for the artists and drawing up a rehearsal schedule.

By the time actors are brought in for rehearsals, the production is quite advanced; the script, sets and schedules are complete and all of the accompanying detail, such as booking transport and catering, has been organised. The amount of time spent on a rehearsal depends on the nature of the production: a complex single play will get more than a soap. In most dramas, the first time the actors get together with the director is simply to read through the script. The next rehearsal will focus on 'blocking' actors' moves. After that, if there is an 'after that', rehearsals will be used for fine-tuning performances.

Figure 3.5 *Recording a shot in a television studio © BFI*

During the rehearsal the director will pay more attention to the subtle details of a performance, although care has to be taken not to overdo it; it is the performance during the final recording that counts and it needs a freshness that could easily become stale with an excess of rehearsing.

Finally, there is the equivalent to the 'dress rehearsal' which is called the 'producer's run', sometimes referred to as the 'technical run'. This is usually attended by the producer, as well as the director, the senior cameraman, the lighting supervisor and occasionally the writer. Where a show is being recorded in front of an audience this will normally be done on the same day, probably in the morning.

Recording/filming schedules differ from programme to programme. *The Sweeney*, (see Chapter five), had ten days for a fifty minute episode. *EastEnders* will have a week's episodes (three) taped in a month and *Grange Hill* does four episodes a month. For any television programme, recording will typically begin at 9 o'clock, although there would have been a great deal of activity before that. The studio will have been prepared and make-up artists will have been working for at least an hour. When all is ready, there will be a run through of the day's first scene, followed by slight adjustments to blocking of movements, gestures, the delivery of lines, etc. When the director is satisfied, s/he will go to the gallery with the PA, vision mixer and technical crew who deal with sound, lighting and engineering. The director will be in direct communication with the production manager on the 'floor'. Sitting to the left of the director will be the PA, ready to cue the cameras as the director literally 'calls the shots.' The tension can be palpable, but it is usually very controlled: everyone should know exactly what they are doing. After a take, the director will usually be content to pass on a few words via the production manager but occasionally s/he will go down to the studio floor to speak directly to actors. More usually, the end of a take is followed by the word 'reset' as a retake is prepared. Once the director is happy and the shot has been checked with sound and camera, the next is prepared

What can send a schedule askew is the number of retakes. At the back of every director's mind is the desire for perfection, however, they know that if the day's schedule is not completed it will be carried over to another day. Although every recording schedule includes at least a day or two for 'picking up' lost scenes, no director likes to be behind schedule. Producers do not like it either.

In the studio the director will be able to cover the action with several cameras; a sitcom will have about five, but the number will vary depending on the scale of the action and sets. A director needs to 'shoot' with the editing in mind, making sure that visual continuity is maintained. However, there is usually a 'fall back' known as the 'iso' line (isolated line). This is a camera(s) on a separate line that records independently of the studio cameras. Charles Garland used the 'iso' while making an episode of *The Big Break*, with Jim Davidson. Davidson is an unpredictable, energetic performer. Garland wanted a camera on Davidson the whole time, just in case he did something that would otherwise have been off camera and lost. The 'iso' did the job perfectly.

Post-production

As far as the director is concerned, post-production is mainly to do with editing and sound. Immediately after a day's recording the director will be given a VHS copy of all the takes. This enables the director to do a lot of preparatory work on the editing. Whilst recording, the director will build up some idea of what are the best takes and the PA will have made a record of these. But editing is not just about joining up the best shots. Just as when the director is working in the studio with the actors and new ideas are generated, the same can happen during editing. As well as new ideas, problems will also arise. In the studio, most dramas will use several cameras as this saves time. Each camera can be set up to give a different shot and an unbroken sequence can be constructed by cutting from one to another (this is sometimes referred to as a 'pass'). At the editing stage, it may become apparent that a pass is not entirely satisfactory; one of the shots might not be quite right. The remedy might be to replace it with a shot from another take.

Editing a television programme is normally done in two stages: off-line editing and on-line editing. Off-line is rather like doing a first draft. The director will sit with the editor and together they will build up the programme although some directors prefer to do this on their own. Once this has been done, the tapes and notes are handed over to the on-line editor (it may or may not be the same person) and the final version is made. Once the editing is complete, the sound track needs to be constructed. This process is called 'sound sypher'. 'Sypher' is shorthand for synchronised post-dubbing. It can be, for the uninitiated, an awe-inspiring process, as the sound supervisor can produce whatever sound s/he wants. In fact most of the sounds heard on a television sound track are added at this stage. Sounds have to be given the right timbre and resonance: they also have to come from the right direction, which may well change from shot to shot. This can occasionally be a problem in sitcom. Actors sometimes 'tread on a laugh' which is when an actor begins a line too early, before the laughter of an audience has sufficiently subsided and some of the words are lost. In such instances, the laughter has to be digitally 'trimmed' so all of the line can be heard.

The final part of the sound track is the music. How this is done will, again, vary from programme to programme. It will usually be composed and recorded after the programme has been edited. This is necessary, as the synchronisation with music and image has to be precise. Finally, when everything else is done, the opening and credits are added, and the programme is ready for transmission.

A production timetable

Although all drama productions go through a similar process, the timing will differ. Series tend to have a more rapid turn over than single plays.

CASE STUDY

Production schedules

What follows is the production schedule of a sitcom series of six episodes.

Weeks 1 and 2
Each episode lasts 29 minutes (24 minutes and 30 seconds on ITV). On average, each episode will have twenty minutes in the studio and ten on location (shooting exteriors). All of the exteriors for each episode are shot together in the first two weeks. Six episodes represents a total of 60 minutes which is about ten days filming. Later, the exteriors are edited in with the studio footage, as video inserts.

Week 3
Monday: Read through of the script; blocking of movements. The writer(s) is usually present with the director and producer. Make-up and costume are also present and measure/fit the cast.

Tuesday:	Rehearsal: the sets are marked out on the floor with tape.
Wednesday:	Technical run: senior cameraman; lighting designer; sound supervisor; make-up; costume and writer in attendance. The vision mixer will sometimes be present.
	The 'tech run' is immediately followed by a 'tech meeting' between the director and the senior production crew in which the technical/equipment requirements are discussed, such as the number of cameras, lights, whether any special equipment such as a crane is needed, etc.
Thursday:	Producer's run: the episode is performed uninterrupted: the director/producer gives final 'notes' to the cast.
	The studio is prepared for recording
Friday:	Preparations in the studio are concluded. 5 pm: final 'dress run' for the benefit of the cameras. 7 pm: the studio audience is admitted 7.30 – 10 pm: the episode is recorded.

Weeks 4–8 (episodes 2–6) as above

ESSAY QUESTIONS

1 Describe two important jobs in each of the pre-production, production and post-production departments of a television drama.

2 What does a production manager need to take into account when drawing up a recording/filming schedule?

3 Which people are involved in the studio during the recording of a television drama?

4 Outline the process of production from the initial idea to its transmission.

5 What was 'producer choice' and why was it introduced?

SHORT ANSWER QUESTIONS

1 What are the two franchise holders serving London?
2 What is the ITC?
3 What is Network Centre?
4 What percentage of their total output are the BBC and ITV companies allowed to produce themselves?
5 What are the three stages any production must go through?

FOLLOW UP WORK

1 Script writers will sometimes complain that by the time their work reaches the screen, it has completely changed. What factors in the process of production might bring about such changes to a script?

2 It has been said that the producer's job is to create the best conditions in which the director can make the film/programme. How far do you think this is true?

3 This exercise can be done in the form of a script or storyboard. If you can, video it.

Take a simple domestic incident and storyboard/script it. You might, for example, simply have a person open a door and walk into a room. Does s/he know what is on the other side? How does s/he feel about it – is it joy? Fear? Or uncertainty? This should be reflected in your final product.

4 Take the opening or any other scene from a book or short story you know. Script/story board a television version.

5 Research the making of any television drama. Identify three decisions that effect the final outcome of the programme.

4
SITUATION COMEDY AND SPORT

Situation comedy

The roots of situation comedy, or sitcom, are many and include radio, the theatre and cinema. Indeed, some early sitcom performers had gained considerable reputations in all three before moving over to television in the fifties. Institutionally, the impetus for the BBC to develop the form of sitcom came in the forties. Even before WW2, the BBC had incorporated many well known music hall and variety acts into its light entertainment programmes.

This area of BBC programming expanded rapidly during the war years, supplemented by forces broadcasting. Comedy variety shows became very popular, often featuring elaborate sketches with what became quickly established characters with catch phrases, as in the very popular *ITMA* (It's That Man Again).

ITMA was the forerunner of shows such as *The Goon Show* and *Round the Horne* which in turn influenced early sitcoms such as *Hancock's Half Hour*. Both *The Goon Show* and *Round the Horne* were essentially sketch shows, but they had regularly occurring characters. It was no great leap from *Round the Horn's* Sandy and Julian's shop (or any other of their locations) to Railway Cuttings, East Cheam with Tony Hancock and Sid James.

A decade earlier in American radio, the sketch show had fully developed into half-hour comedy drama. Some of these transferred over to television, the most celebrated, perhaps, being *I Love Lucy* with Lucille Ball and Desi Arnaz which ran from 1951 to 1957. From 1947 to 1951, Ball played in a CBS show called *My Favourite Husband*. It was so successful, that CBS got Ball to develop a television show based around the wacky housewife she had played on radio.

Lucille Ball had been a Hollywood star with an image quite different from her television persona. Paramount had nurtured her into something of a sophisticate. At CBS she had to undertake a transformation into the 'dizzy', scatterbrained Lucy. But it worked, and she became more popular on television than she was in films. The eponymous heroine became a source of considerable wealth and prestige for Ball, as she along with her husband Arnaz, owned the rights to the show which was worth a fortune when syndication rights and re-runs were taken into account.

Lucy reappeared from 1957 to 1960 in the *Lucy–Desi Comedy Hour*. Ball maintained her success when she struck out on her own, taking the show's regular cast with her, to create the *Lucy Show* (1962–68) and *Here's Lucy* (1968–1974). Lucy is one of the most long-lived sitcom characters in television history. Ball made a career out of her namesake, winning four Emmy awards and nine nominations, as well as getting very rich.

The attractions of sitcom are that they are cheap, sharing with other television series/serials the economy of fixed sets, casts, writers, etc. Working with tried and tested crews also reduces costs with savings in time. Minimising costs is important because of all television output, sitcom is probably the hardest to sell overseas: humour does not travel well. There will be the occasional 'hits', such as *Absolutely Fabulous* and *Are You Being Served* in America, but these are exceptions.

What, then, is sitcom? There are three things that link all of the very different shows listed above: two are obvious, the other less so. (1) They are comic; (2) they are based on a simple situation, usually to do with either (or both) home and work; (3) they are based on conflict.

The last is crucial, but then that is not surprising, as all drama is based on conflict. The first of these elements, the comedic, is derived from the other two. The writer of a sitcom has to create a situation which will make us laugh – it is as simple and as difficult as that. As Barry Curtis wrote,

> **'Comedy is measured against a form of pragmatism to which other types of programme are not subjected – it has to make the audience laugh through a certain rate of joke delivery or forms of comic authority or control. The consortium of skills are relatively rare and a small elite of comedy writers and performers much sought after.'**
>
> *(Cited in Cook, J. (ed.), BFI Dossier 17:*
> *Television Sitcom, 1992, BFI, p.4)*

Curtis' point about 'a small elite of comedy writers and performers (being) much sought after' is evidenced from any list of the most popular sitcoms. This is because sitcom is always a risk. The *raison d'être* of comedy is to make the audience laugh – if that does not happen then all is lost. It is not surprising that producers, having latched on to a writer, or a pair of writers, will not want to let him/her/them go, or want to risk an unknown quantity.

It has also been the case that writers, directors and actors have preferred to work together. However, there have clearly been recent attempts by the BBC and independent television to find new talent – an obvious necessity, as none of us are around indefinitely. Not only is new talent being promoted, but new ideas and new forms, hence the innovative series that emerged in 1999, *The Royle Family* and *People Like Us*, both of which, although different, played with the traditional sitcom form.

What is 'funny'?

There are many models of the comedic – many explanations as to why and what makes us laugh. There is, of course, no simple formula: the sheer number of quite awful sitcoms and 'dead' comedians is testament to that! In his *Jokes and their Relation to the Unconscious*, Sigmund Freud sets out what he considered to be the conditions of humour. These include:

1. Mood: 'In a toxic mood of cheerfulness almost everything seems comic, probably by comparison with the expenditure in a normal state. Indeed, jokes, the comic and all similar methods are no more than ways of regaining this cheerful mood.....'

2. The expectation of the comic: 'A similarly favourable effect is produced by an expectation of the comic, by being attuned to comic pleasure.' Freud explains well why I, for example, always laughed whenever Frankie Howard appeared on the stage – even before he said a word, or the shambolic Sergeant Wilson indolently ambled towards Captain Mainwaring. 'In the last resort it is in the recollection of having laughed and in the expectation of laughing that he (sic) laughs when he sees the comic actor come on to the stage, before the latter can have made any attempt at making him laugh.'

Figure 4.1 *Scene from* Dad's Army
Source: BFI

3. 'If we add to this that the generating of comic pleasure can be encouraged by any other pleasurable accompanying circumstances as though by some sort of contagious effect ...' This explains the inclusion of laughter from the studio audience that so many comedy programmes have: it encourages us to laugh at home: we have all experienced it: other people laughing makes us laugh.

Looking at a different viewpoint, in *The Meanings of Comedy*, Wylie Sypher describes the lows and highs of comedy.

At the bottom of the comic scale – where the human becomes nearly indistinguishable from the animal and where the vibration of laughter is longest and loudest – is the 'dirty' joke or the 'dirty' gesture. At this depth comedy unerringly finds the lowest common denominator of human response, the reducing-agent that sends us all reeling back to the realm of old Pan......There we drop the mask

which we have composed into the features of our decent, cautious selves.....any group of men or women, no matter how 'refined', will, sooner or later, laugh at a 'dirty joke'... .... As we move 'up' the scale of comic action, the mechanisms become more complex but no more 'comic' .

(Sypher, W., *The Meaning of Comedy*)

One mechanism of laughter is the unexpected. Hitchcock's principle of suspense is applicable to comedy. He argued that if a couple is sitting at a table and a bomb placed beneath initially unseen by the audience, they are shocked when it suddenly explodes. But this is not suspense; it is a surprise that is over in seconds. Suspense is created by showing the audience the bomb ticking beneath the table throughout the scene. It is the same with comedy. A man walking along and slipping on a banana skin will surprise and perhaps raise a laugh but if the audience sees the banana skin before the hapless victim, there is a kind of comic suspense in the anticipation of the inevitable outcome. Also the situation can be played with. The first man might walk safely past, up-setting the expectations of the audience, only to trip up the next person. Expectations are frequently disrupted by inverting the 'natural order'.

Most commonly the 'order' that is disrupted is that of power relations. Power in this sense may be inflected in terms of age, gender or class. In the extremely successful *Dads' Army*, for example, the bank manager and platoon commander, Captain Mainwaring, was only too aware of his lowly social position, acerbated by the fact that Wilson the bank clerk and platoon sergeant, was public school educated and socially a 'cut above' himself. Based around a squad of seven largely elderly misfits – along with a couple of younger ones – *Dads' Army*, written by Jimmy Perry and David Croft, was first broadcast in 1968 and ran for nine years. It has been repeated on several occasions both on the BBC and UK Gold. It was adapted for the radio, a feature film 'spin off' was made in 1971 and a stage show based on the programme toured the UK between 1975 and 1976.

The inversion of power relations is a common comedic device. *Absolutely Fabulous* inverted the usual mother/daughter relationship, with the former behaving like a particularly explosive adolescent whilst the latter was the epitome of stable maturity. The series was centred around the dissolute life of Edina Monsoon (Jennifer Saunders) and her best friend, Patsy Stone (Joanna Lumley). Their intertwined lives were laced with an excess of alcohol, drugs and sex. Edina's daughter Saffy, on the other hand, was a model of sobriety, good sense and maturity who was for ever having to chastise her mother for her irresponsible behaviour. The visual style echoed the excesses of the characters. Illuminated with a dominant key light, it was a veritable palette of vivid colours, mostly clashing. It was treading potentially dangerous ground as it depended upon a sophisticated, sitcom-experienced audience not coming up with an aberrant reading of the sort that would conclude that the series was *endorsing* the life-style advocated by the two 'heroines'. It did run into trouble in America. Roseanne bought the rights to develop an American version and it was about to go into production when it was called off because of objections by the censors. In an on-line interview (www.abfab.demon.nl/abfaq) Roseanne stated that she had dropped her plans for the show, as the original had already been broadcast in the USA and there were already a number of 'copycat' series.

Figure 4.2 *Power relations in* Absolutely Fabulous
Source: © *BBC*

Behind the comic veneer, quite serious issues are sometimes tackled by sitcoms. Whilst the debate about the proprieties of the ordination of women was raging within – and without – the Church of England, the BBC was running a sitcom about this very matter: *The Vicar of Dibley*. The American sitcom, *The Third Rock from the Sun* did this with gender, which was part of the broader aim of satirising a variety of social foibles and idiosyncrasies. It was based around the idea of a group of aliens from a more advanced planet who, in the process of doing a reconnaissance of the Earth, attempt to blend in by assuming the physical attributes of humans. As time goes by, they also begin to assume earthly emotional characteristics. The essence of the humour came from the attempt to regard much of what we regard as 'normal' literally through the eyes of an alien. Much of this came from the characters. The oldest of the original alien force takes the form of a pubescent boy. The lieutenant in charge of security becomes a women, and so forth. All have to learn the social complexity of their roles as they go along in the process, they unwittingly illuminate some of the absurdities of ordinary life.

Genre and sitcom

Both in the USA and the UK sitcom is a long established and popular form that incorporates many different comedic traditions as well as transcending most of the traditional television genres. There have been police sitcoms (*PC Penrose*, *The Thin Blue Line* and *The Detectives*); medical sitcoms (*Doctor in the House*); war sitcoms (*Dads' Army* and *'Ello, 'Ello'*), at least one combining medical with war (*MASH*); another that ingeniously incorporated war-time melodrama with time-travel science fiction (*Goodnight Sweetheart*); a 'sit com' *Grange Hill* (*Please Sir*); television news (*Drop the Dead Donkey*) and perhaps most oddly in recent times, a sort of Ken Loach/Mike Leigh social realist sitcom – with a touch of Harold Pinter – (*The Royle Family*). In similar 'social realist' territory, perhaps one can add *Rab C. Nesbitt*. There are others that defy easy categorisation such as *The Last of the Summer Wine*. What is clear is that sitcom, more than any other genre, has plundered television itself for its raw material.

Figure 4.3 *Drop the Dead Donkey*
Source: BFI

Most of the generic features that constitute sitcom have arisen largely through the practical contingencies of production, including cost and scheduling. The main elements of costs include:

- cast
- sets
- scripts
- recording and post-production costs.

Most of these costs are smaller with a series than for single plays or other one-off productions. Certainly the cost of sets is lower as they are often used across several episodes. But so too are the costs of actors: by and large, an actor's fees will be less per episode of a series than for a single play. Once crew and cast settle into their roles, rehearsal and production time is again, less than a single play. In the case of independent productions, studio and post-production facilities become cheaper with longer bookings.

Sitcom and generic conventions: form and style

How are these considerations translated into the form and style of sitcom? Let us take narrative first. Most sitcoms (there are exceptions) take the series form rather than that of the serial. The key difference between the two is that with the serial, the narrative is continuous from one episode to the next; one story is told in, for example, six episodes. A series, whilst having continuity in setting and characters, will have a discrete narrative per episode. The appeal for schedulers and the American networks is that any one episode can be watched without reference to a previous one. Single episodes do not have a memory. Characters never make reference to events in previous episodes, so it does not matter in what order episodes are transmitted. They tend to occur in few locations and even these tend to be interiors. This keeps down the cost of set construction and location shooting. Plots also tend to be based around very few characters: again, smaller casts, lower costs.

There are some exceptions to the statement that most sitcoms take the series form, and the argument could be made that they are not sitcoms but comedy-drama serials. One example of this was the long running *Only Fools and Horses*. Written by John Sullivan for the BBC it ran for seven series between September 1981 and February 1991. There were also several 'Christmas specials', the last on Christmas Day, 1996. Although each episode, based around the antics of the entrepreneurial Trotter family, was self contained in the sense that there was always a resolution, there was an element of narrative continuity insofar as events in previous episodes would be referred to. Another example from the late 1990s, and more clearly a serial, was *Red Dwarf*, a comic science fiction based around the misadventures of a small group of dysfunctional space travellers. All of the attributes of the sitcom are there, except that one plot is carried over several episodes, each one concluding on a 'cliff hanger'. Another example from the seventies is *The Fall and Rise of Reginald Perrin* which was similarly constructed as a serial.

Despite the exceptions, a sitcom episode is mostly a self contained 'classical' narrative involving the disruption of a state of order and then the moving towards its restoration. In other words, unlike a comedy sketch show, they have a clear beginning, middle and end – and usually in that order. There is also a sense in which they are cyclic, as concluded by arriving at the point where they started, ready for another episode.

Sitcoms have no narrative history, except as it exists in the mind of the audience. Sitcoms are forever in the present, 'nothing that has happened in the narrative must destroy or even complicate the way the situation is grounded.' (McQueen, p56). Characters in sitcoms themselves always live in the here and now: lessons are never learned from previous episodes. In that sense, characters do not develop. In *The Last of the Summer Wine*, Compo will forever indulge in a futile but nevertheless joyful lusting after Nora Batty. Characters are like the figures on Keat's Grecian Urn; they have ceased to age and are frozen in time. The exception is when a series ends. In the last episode of *Only Fools and Horses*, the elusive fortune was finally achieved; in *Goodnight Sweetheart*, Gary, who had spent so long flitting backwards and forwards between the 1940s and 1990s finally had his dilemma solved for him by becoming trapped in 1945 and so forced to stay with Phoebe. But these are merely modifications of the formula. In sitcom the basic situation remains unchanged.

Associated with the circularity of sitcom is what Philip Drummed has called 'synchronising motifs'. These are the frequently repeated, and therefore highly predictable devices which are employed by most sitcoms. In *The Last of the Summer Wine*, we can reliably expect in any episode that Compo will be hurled into a ditch or river or land in something with lots of water, mud, or generally unpleasant substance. In *Only Fools and Horses*, Rodney will be called a 'plonker', in *One Foot in the Grave* Victor Meldrew will have cause to declaim, 'I don't believe it!'. Corporal Jones, in *Dads' Army*, can be reliably expected to panic and cry out 'Don't panic!'. It is the predictability of these motifs that forms the basis of their humour. It is as if they simultaneously remind us of previous occasions when we have laughed and cue us to laugh again.

The narrative in any sitcom episode will be based around a problem. A classic strategy is for one or more of the characters to be placed, at the beginning, in a relatively minor difficulty or inconvenience. In an attempt to resolve the problem it is exacerbated and the simple problem becomes a complex problem and around its resolution the comedy is woven. Work and home are the recurring settings of sitcoms. Those set within places of work include *Dads' Army, Are You Being Served, Hi de Hi, Drop the Dead Donkey* and there are many more. Work based sitcoms have always run in tandem with those set in the home. In the fifties *The Mary Tyler Moor Show* had the eponymous heroine (a single woman) working for a newspaper, where much of it was based. Many sitcoms since have occupied the spheres of both work and the domestic arena such as *Only Fools and Horses*, *Fawlty Towers* and *Father Ted*.

Since sitcoms have only one or two main locations and few key characters it is not surprising that plots tend to be based around equally few scenarios, basically work or home, and some with elements of both. This is true of the earliest sitcoms. As we have seen, one fifties sitcom went one stage further and actually featured a genuine husband and wife team, Lucille Ball and Desi Arnaz in the long running *I Love Lucy* (1951 – 1957).

If they are not based around work, historically both American and British sitcoms have been based around the family. This is evident from some popular sitcoms of the past: *Father, Dear Father, Not in Front of the Children, Mother makes Three* and *Butterflies* to name but a few. The tradition carried through to the 1990s with *2.4 Children* and *Not in Front of the Children*. Early examples featured married couples *without* children (*I Love Lucy* and *The Dick Van Dyke Show*, for example), a tradition that has more contemporary descendants, such as *One Foot in the Grave*.

Sitcom, representation and ideology

Till Death Do Us Part

Sitcoms invariably rely on stereotypes which are a feature of most forms of comedy. What is at stake, however, is not stereotyping per se, but the attitudes it seeks to encourage in the audience.

The sixties gave rise to an acute example of this in the controversial sitcom *Till Death Do Us Part*, written by Johnny Speight. First screened in 1966, it featured a working class bigot, Alf Garnett, who spent most of each episode giving vent to his many hatreds and arguing with his daughter and socialist, Liverpudlian son-in-law. (It was never clear what infuriated Garnett more, him coming from Liverpool or being a socialist – the appellation 'scouse git' seemed to cover it all).

On the side-lines, making the occasional incursion into the conflict was Garnett's wife, the embodiment of tolerance and patience. Garnett seemed to value only West Ham football team, the Conservative Party, Winston Churchill and the Queen to all of which he granted a simplistic and occasionally touching devotion. For all else he had a vitriolic line in abuse, which was particularly barbed if the target was race.

Garnet was nothing if not a totally reprehensible, narrow-minded bigot. But he was created in this fashion not to encourage or celebrate such attitudes, but to hold them up to critical scrutiny. Not that this always worked, however, as the production office received the occasional odd-ball letter which clearly took Garnett's racism at face value. For a minority, it confirmed their distorted world view.

The audience of *Till Death Do Us Part* reached 18 million. Its popularity was not welcomed in all quarters most notably by Mary Whitehouse who presided over a 'Clean Up TV' campaign. Although she later mollified her views – she thought it 'very clever and funny ..... But once again the thing went too far' (Wheen, p.205).

She complained about, amongst other things, the language, producing, as evidence, the number of times 'bloody' was uttered. In his book, *Television*, Francis Wheen cites Speight as claiming that the cause of the eventual demise of *Till Death Do Us Part* was the appointment of Lord Hill, who was not known for his liberal views, as the Governor of the BBC.

At the end of the second series in February 1968, Speight announced the end of the programme: 'The trouble has been since Lord Hill's arrival at the BBC and I could be the victim of new policies. I would write another series for the BBC but only if this censorship was stopped.' (Wheen, p.205). It was briefly revived four years later.

Similarly, *Men Behaving Badly* could be criticised for its apparent celebration of the antics of Gary and his flatmate Tony.

On the other hand, their 'laddish' behaviour can be seen to be held up to ridicule as an aspect of their perpetual adolescence, from which (it being a sitcom) there is no hope of redemption.

The wide ranging response to television programmes such as *Till Death Do Us Part* and *Men Behaving Badly* is in part explained by the notion of preferred and negotiated readings. The author of a text might well have intended a certain meaning, but that is no guarantee that an audience is going to interpret it in this way.

David Morley, following on from earlier work done by Stuart Hall and others, argues that an audiences' decoding of a text – or other message – will be mediated by a series of factors:

• Age, sex and class
• Cultural identity
• Experience
• Context in which the decoding takes place

In short, the way anything is read will in part be determined by a complex interaction of at least these factors. Even taking into account age, gender, social class and other circumstances, the way a text is 'read' will, in part, be determined by the context in which that reading occurs.

For example, a member of a trade union is likely to interpret a television news item about a strike differently to an employer, just as a determined racist is likely celebrate the jaundiced views of Garnett, not withstanding any implied irony.

A programme that seemed to reproduce, wholesale, the crudest of national stereotypes was *Rab C. Nesbitt*. Nesbitt seemed to boast every reprehensible feature of the pantomime Scotsman: an unemployed, malingering drunkard who had managed to foster in his two sons the same qualities in equal measure, whilst his luckless, benighted wife endured (or not) every calamity he – and they – visited upon her. While she endured, he drank – usually in the company of a set of individuals who were not far behind in his lassitude. But does that make Nesbitt a regressive assault on the good name of Scotland?

As with Alf Garnett, only if taken at face value. The humour of Nesbitt works at different levels. There is the paradox of such an irredeemably lost cause having such perspicacity and wisdom. He sometimes seems like a sage who stands outside the ebb and flow of conventional society, making moralising and witty observations on life as it passes him by. His speech has the quality of raw poetry.

Being a character in a sitcom he is somehow timeless: we do not know where he came from or how he achieved his condition – like all sitcom characters he just *is*. There is also a touching quality of vulnerability about him, Mary and his associates. These are not misfits by choice – it is they who have been chosen. Their humour is their redemption; their weapon.

David McQueen cites John Foster of Paisley University who lived in Govan for eighteen years:

In a sense, Rab represents the way Govanites would see Govan if they tried to make fun of themselves. It's self-effacing humour – but it's also a kind of oppositionalism, which says, 'This is us portraying us in terms of accepted values, in the worst possible light.' It's a self-caricature launched against polite culture.

(cited in McQueen, p.60)

If you wanted to portray an accurate picture of Govan, you wouldn't have two partners living in that house. In terms of the social or family bond, the Nesbitts are like the Waltons, they're romanticised. There are whole blocks of kids in Moorepark, and not one has a father living in the house. So in that respect I think we're upholding the old values.

McQueen, D., Television: a Media Student's Guide, Arnold, 1998)

Nesbitt is, like all sitcoms, an idealisation of the situation it depicts. The writer of the series, Ian Pattison, argues that, socially, *Nesbitt* is totally unrealistic:

An even more generically deviant series is *The Royle Family*. It has to date run to two series. The first was screened, in September, 1998, on BBC2 (this a measure of its unconventional status). It picked up a considerable following, sufficient for the BBC to make a second series and run it on BBC 1 in October 1999.

As a sitcom it is unusual. It is a 'minimalist' sitcom, reducing the genre to its basic elements and inverting some of the dominant conventions. Each episode is about 30 minutes, has a core of five main characters and one key setting.

We have seen that most sitcoms are either set at home or work, with one or two locations. *The Royle Family* takes this to the extreme. It mostly takes place on three pieces of furniture, a sofa and two arm chairs. Occasionally, the action has spilt over into the kitchen. The second episode of series two took place entirely around a dining table in the kitchen.

The Royle Family is a sitcom about people watching television. In that sense it is self-referential, putting in the foreground the act of watching television. Its title sequence depicts a television's eye view of it being watched by a group of people, who, therefore, look directly at the actual viewer. The sequence ends with Jimmy Royle leaning towards the screen (his screen and, seemingly, the viewer's screen) and turning it off.

```
┌─────────────────────────────────────────────┐
│              C A S E   S T U D Y              │
└─────────────────────────────────────────────┘
```

The Royle Family

*T*he Royle Family plays out in real time, that is to say 'story time' and 'screen time' are the same. The style of acting is naturalistic, lacking any affected idiosyncrasies or mannerisms of the kind often associated with sitcom. This style of acting is normally found in drama. Exchanges between characters have the quality of real, off-the-cuff conversation, very often about what is showing at the time on the television. The television always seems to be on, showing actual programmes. The final episode of series two, for example, begins with Jim and Barbara watching *Eastenders*. Their television screen within the viewers television screen creates the effect of a screen within a screen. The humour arises out of what seems to be natural conversation; there are no obvious jokes. The narrative is equally self-effacing. Plots in *The Royle Family* seem almost non-existent but there is a structure. In the last episode of series two there is a clear 'narrative curve.' At the beginning only Jim and Barbara are present. It is Anthony's 18th birthday and Jim is not in the least looking forward to the celebrations carefully prepared by Barbara. Gradually people arrive. First it is Twiggy who gets conscripted to assist a very reluctant Jim to blow up balloons and the inevitable fooling around ensues, with various shaped balloons simulating anatomical parts. But Jim is still not in a party mood.

Figure 4.4 *Characters watching TV in* The Royle Family   *Source: © BBC*

Eventually, all arrive: Denise, their daughter, with her husband Dave; Nana Royle and the neighbours, Mary and Joe Carrol with their daughter, Cheryl ('We're Mary and Joseph like in the Bible, but we've got Cheryl not Jesus). Anthony arrives with his girl friend and Darren. Eventually the banter, teasing and questioning lead to a kind of revelation, the catalyst of which is the most unlikely one of all. Throughout the series Joe has hardly uttered a word beyond 'Yes' or 'No'. Slightly tipsy when he arrived, he removed himself to the back of the room after a speaking of a friend who has only one leg (the point of this discourse seems to be resilience and acceptance of ones lot). Unnoticed by the still slightly fractious group silent, Joe breaks into song. He sings, beautifully, 'I will take you home, Kathleen'. This becomes the 'cement' that 'heals' the group, brings them together and makes them whole. At first seduced by the beauty of the song, Nana succumbs to nostalgia and is reduced to sobbing heavily into the arms of Denise; Anthony and his girlfriend hold hands as if the song has taken away their unease at showing affection; Jim slowly begins to play, in accompaniment, with his banjo. The scene is now complete, only to be undercut. Earlier, Dave had traipsed in with some dog excrement sticking to the bottom of his shoe, which Barbara had cleaned for him. Darren, who has been mesmerised by the television throughout, hardly paying attention to what is happening around him, suddenly bursts out with, 'You can still smell ... in here!' Throughout, most of the characters barely move. Instead the camera constantly shifts and nudges around them, hand-held, as in a true documentary. *The Royle Family* is a rare example of a self-referential sitcom, taking as its subject sitcom itself and the act of watching television.

Sport on television

Since WW2, the greatest single influence on sport around the world has been television. Mainly because of television, some sports have become massive wealth-generating enterprises. Their cash potential has meant the virtual eclipse of amateur sport. Sponsorship, substantial prize money and lucrative television contracts have turned sport into a full-time profession, a fact from which even the Olympics is not completely shielded. The dividing line between a heavily subsidised amateur and a paid professional is murkily blurred: at what point do generous expenses turn into a fee?

The shift from the largely amateur to professional status of sport represents a considerable cultural change. But television has frequently altered the games themselves, both in terms of their rules and appearance. The 'pure' white of the amateur is rapidly giving way to the lurid, spectacular colours of the professional in both tennis and cricket. This sartorial change was introduced by the Australian Kerry Packer in the 1970s. When he signed up cricket players for his World Series games, created for his own Australian channel, he had them wear yellow shirts and blue pads because they looked better on television. But this was far from being the first occasion when television had changed the appearance of sport. In the USA, as early as 1939, NBC, found that the contestants' coloured shorts were indistinguishable on black and white television. They were able to persuade boxing commissioners to permit contestants to eschew their coloured shorts in favour of an arrangement where one would wear a black stripe on white and the other a white stripe on black.

Sports now have to take into account the requirements of television schedulers. One undoubted plus is that 'huge numbers of the previously disenfranchised or simply disinclined to attend a live event, have been able to share in the successes and failures of national teams and national athletics.' (Barnett, p.5) Whatever view one takes on how the Olympics have evolved, television has turned it into a global spectator event of massive proportions.

Figure 4.5 *A historical picture from Wimbledon*

Source: Corbis

As with all the programme categories dealt with in this book, sport is a scheduling staple. It is cheap (although television deals with major sporting clubs have increased over the past few years, largely because of inflationary deals made by Sky) and it has a sizeable demand. It is also as old as broadcast television itself, one of the earliest programming regulars being sport. The first sporting event to be televised was the Wimbledon championship match between G.L. Rogers and B. Austin on 21st June 1937. This was followed on the 9th October 1937 by motor racing – the Imperial Trophy Road Race was televised from Crystal Palace. Almost immediately concerns were raised that would become running sores that would seep through the history of sport on television. Money, of course, was one, but not the most urgent. To begin with various sports bodies were more concerned about the impact television might have on the games themselves, principally attendance.

Television's impact an attendance

The worry was that television would keep people at home, especially when major national events were being televised. In the 1930s, this was hardly a real threat as there were very few households with television (about 2000) and the range from Alexandra Palace was still limited. Concerns were translated into action when, worried about the effect of televising both an England–Scotland match and the FA Cup Final on attendances at smaller matches which were scheduled to play at the same time, the BBC were initially refused permission to televise either of them. Eventually, after much lobbying by Gerald Cook, the Director of Television, permission was granted. On the 9th April 1938 the first ever football match to be televised was played between Scotland and England.

Three weeks later, on the 30th April, the first televised FA Cup Final was played between Huddersfield Town and Preston North End. Much was made of the latter event, not least because it was a Royal occasion. A television was placed in the Royal Retiring Room, but Cook must have been hoping that it was not being watched as 'the preliminaries were disastrous'. Television carried the radio commentary, but for the first half-hour this had failed. Notwithstanding such 'teething' problems, the broadcast was well received and it had a good press the following morning.

Prior to this on the 2nd April 1938 yet another major event was televised – the Oxford versus Cambridge boat race, accompanied by John Snagg's radio commentary. The following year, the Boat Race and the FA Cup Final had their own commentary, but even as television sport was beginning to come into its own, Alexandra Palace closed down for seven years. Within a few months of the 1939 Boat Race and the FA Cup Final, Britain was at war and television was closed down.

Television restarted at 3 pm, 6th June 1946. Aside from a formal opening by the Postmaster General, The Earl of Listowel, it featured 'Mickey's Gala Premiere' (the last item partially transmitted before television closed down on Friday, 3rd September 1939), a variety concert and finally 'The Dark Lady of the Sonnets' by George Bernard Shaw. It was all over by 4.30pm. But by the next day normal service had resumed, with a mix of programmes running from 8.30 a.m. until 10.15pm, when the final news bulletin (sound only) came on. Sport re-appeared for the first time at the beginning of week two.

On Monday afternoon at 3.40 p.m. there was the first post-war sports broadcast, wrestling, or as the Radio Times presciently put it (given what wrestling would become), 'A dramatisation of heavyweight wrestling: Harry Anaconda v Bert Asseratic'. The following year, sporting highlights included the first England–India test match and Wimbledon. By this time the number of households with television had grown to about 25 000.

But pre-war concerns on the part of sporting associations had not gone away. One major worry was that cinema would 're-diffuse' the television picture (show it themselves) and charge for admission. The prospect of this happening was doubly irritating for the sport associations as not only would cinema be financially exploiting their own events, but the associations themselves were not making much anyway, as charges to the BBC were small. This was in part because the number of sets was still relatively small, but also in deference to the public broadcasting status of the BBC. There was a general awareness that the BBC could not afford to make large payments. But, not withstanding this, trouble was brewing for the broadcasters.

It came initially from the Greyhound Racing Association. They led the formation of the Association for the Protection of Copyright in Sports (APCS) who demanded assurances from the BBC that no pirated television pictures would be shown in cinemas. At one stage all of the sporting events that were eventually broadcast in the first few weeks of the return of BBC television were at risk.

In addition to Wimbledon and the Test there was speedway at West Ham and Wimbledon stadiums, the Amateur Athletics Association Championships, racing from Ascot and Varsity Rugby Union from Twickenham. In the end all were broadcast.

Post-war sport on television

The first post-war football match to be televised was the amateur Athenium League contest between Barnett and Wealdstone, although it was interrupted because of poor light. By the end of 1946 Maurice Goreham, Head of Television Service, was able to report, 'We are now getting full co-operation from the majority of sports promoters.'

Goreham had met with only two refusals. The Wembley Pool ice show had declined on the grounds that the television lights might melt the ice. There was also a problem with the middleweight boxing championship to be held on 28th October between Roderick and Hawkins. The BBC could not offer any firm guarantee that cinemas would not show the pictures so the British Board of Boxing Control cancelled the broadcast.

Then, in steps Jack Solomon who was for a long time the best known boxing promoter in Britain. He offered the BBC a fight featuring a 'star' boxer, Baksi, to be held on 5th November, but he backed away when the BBC insisted that he disclose the way he apportioned the rights fee. There was a concern that too much would go to the promoter. Solomon was nothing if not persistent, however, and attempted to introduce commercialism into television 'through the back door'. He offered the BBC another contest, again featuring Baksi against Woodstock. He wanted an announcement shown on television, 'by courtesy of Jack Solomon and Vernon Pools.' He was turned down.

Concern about the effect of television on attendance at sporting events remained. On the one hand some saw television as giving substantial free publicity whilst others thought that fee paying spectators were being kept away. Wimbledon and the rugby and cricket bodies saw that considerable benefits could be accrued from events being televised. Some games at Twickenham were oversubscribed, such as those played between England and France and between England and Scotland.

In addition to increasing attendance Colonel Prentice, who administered Twickenham, told Ian Orr-Ewing, the BBC's Manager of Outside Broadcasts, 'television is a 'Godsend' to him since it keeps all the old gentlemen at home and they write long letters afterwards commenting on the play and don't bother him on the day.'

The publicity given by televising events saw steeple chasing at Sandown park reporting an increase in attendance figures. That year also saw attendance records broken at both the Centre and No.1 courts at Wimbledon. However, the events that seemed to be doing well out of television were leading 'blue ribbon', often international, events. Concern still lingered about the effect television was having on less prestigious sports. Amongst the sceptics was the chairman of the British Boxing Board of Control who reported at the end of 1947 his view that television 'cannot be but detrimental to professional boxing.' (Barnett p.11).

In the case of football there was a lingering suspicion that the televising of key 1st Division and international matches was causing a drop in attendance at other matches occurring simultaneously.

The 1948 Olympics

1948, however, introduced a new dimension to the sporting spectacle: the Olympics. This first to be televised by the BBC was held in London. The technical and logistic challenges were substantial and the fact that the BBC overcame them demonstrated fully how far they had come in covering sport in a single decade.

To begin with there were the obsolescent cameras: the BBC were still using 1930s Emitron cameras. These only had a single lens and a viewfinder that showed an inverted image. The BBC managed to obtain new Image Orthicon cameras from America. These had three interchangeable lenses that not only showed the image the right way up, but also brighter and clearer. The BBC used two mobile units (forerunners of the modern Outside Broadcast scanner); one was in Wembley Stadium and the other in the adjacent Empire Pool. Other events were covered by BBC newsreel units and screened in the evening.

The BBC's coverage was well received and seemed to many to be the final justification for televising sport. Here was a major international event that had previously been accessible only to a privileged few and now, potentially millions, could tune in and watch.

Televised sport in the 1950s

By the end of 1949 the number of television sets in the country had increased to about 50 000. On top of this, some evidence from the USA suggested that television did have a detrimental effect on receipts at live events. A complete ban on the televising of sporting events was proposed by the APCS from 1st January 1950. The declared motive was not financial. An APCS document from 1950 states that 'it is not the object to get more money for the promoters by selling the rights but to protect the whole sporting spectator system,' (Barnett, S., *Games and Sets: The Changing Face of Sport on Television*, BFI, 1990). Because of conflicting interests in sports the ban was only partially implemented and as such came to little.

But the issue of diminished attendance at other, lower profile games, did not go away and became focused on the 1950 Cup Final between Arsenal and Liverpool (Arsenal won, 2–0). On that day there was a considerable short-fall on attendance at matches played elsewhere. Some people were clearly determined to watch the game, come what may.

> In Birmingham there were crowds around the demonstration sets in city stores. One Midland viewer is reported to have been watching at home when he was interrupted by two callers who asked if they could come in and join him. They explained that they belonged to a larger group which had split up and gone in search of television aerials in the neighbourhood.
>
> *(Barnett p.12)*

The Postmaster General set up the Sports Television Advisory Committee (STAC). The various sports associations agreed to allow the BBC to show up to one hundred sports events for an experimental period during which time the new committee would assess the direct and indirect effects of television on attendance.

A report on the Cup Final was inconclusive, in part because of the bad weather, which the BBC argued was the real reason why people stayed away from other matches. The report concluded, somewhat ambiguously: 'There were large audiences for many different kinds of event, even though some of them attracted comparatively small attendances and it is reasonable to conclude that television is helping to develop interest in sporting activities.'

Aside from the FA Cup Final event, evidence given to the STAC was mixed. The Thoroughbred Racing Association of America claimed that television had led to racecourse attendances rising by 15% during 1950. On the other hand, the STAC report quoted research from the National Opinion Research Centre at the University of Chicago which suggested that minority sports did suffer a short-fall in attendances. The National Association of Broadcasters claimed that television actually encouraged people to go to live sporting events; the author of this report, however, was Jerry Jordan, whose father was a vice-president of Ayer and Son, an advertising agency that handled several sports accounts.

There was no consensus of opinion and the STAC report was summarised by G.R. Barnes, Director of Television at the BBC:

1. **Some time must elapse before it is possible to estimate the effect of television on gates.**

2. **It is the televising of important events like the Cup Final and professional boxing which have a marked effect on attendance.**
3. **This effect is greatest on the smallest clubs.**

Little came of all of this, except perhaps to harden the conviction held by the football authorities that television was undoubtedly having a detrimental effect on their gate takings. As a consequence the 1952 FA Cup Final was not televised, the only time this had happened since the war. The reason was that the FA wanted a delay of one week in the broadcasting of the game, a restriction that the BBC was not prepared to tolerate. Only after much lobbying did the FA relent and allow the 1953 Cup Final to be broadcast live: it was by all accounts an outstanding final played between Blackpool (4) and Bolton Wanderers (3).

By 1953 attitudes towards television were beginning to relax and the arrival of commercial television was imminent. The BBC was understandably nervous that they would not be able to compete with the comparatively vast treasure chests of commercial television. Fearing the possibility of being excluded by prohibitive costs encouraged by the potential bidding power of the new independent television companies, the BBC had drawn up a list of 'events from which the BBC would not wish to be excluded.' This list included the FA Cup Final along with international matches, such as Test cricket and 'blue ribbon events' like key racing meetings (Derby, Grand National, St. Leger and Royal Ascot), Wimbledon plus the Wightman and Davis Cups, Rugby Union internationals and the Boat Race.

In the event, the position of the BBC was far more secure than they imagined. In their negotiations with sports promoters, the BBC emphasised that their primary concern was not with maintaining excessive rights, but simply having access to major sporting events. In their turn the promoters showed considerable loyalty to the BBC who were able to secure broadcasting deals for a number of sporting events. This in part was probably due to the reputation the BBC now enjoyed as a premier world-wide broadcaster. Many sports' authorities must have enjoyed the kudos of being carried by such a prestigious organisation and the BBC was now synonymous with great national events.

Certain BBC voices carried with them the very texture of particular sports and, in the minds of many people, were inseparable from them. Dan Maskell and Freddie Grisewood were Wimbledon; Kenneth Wolstenholme, football (for ever associated with England's World Cup victory in 1966); Harold Abrahams, athletics (he was himself an Olympic champion, whose achievements were celebrated in the film *Chariots of Fire*) – and there were many others.

Despite the success of BBC sport, football still held out. Although the Football Association had relented, the Football League had not. The new ITV made a play for the League and, for a while, seemed to have won, but such a conclusion was premature. Midlands Television offered the Football League Management Committee £40 000 for live coverage of matches postponed until 6.15 p.m. Because the BBC were still negotiating, three weeks later this offer was upped by another £10 000. But it all came to nothing and the League decided to reject all offers and postponed indefinitely any question of having their matches televised. It would not be until the 'eighties that a League game would appear on television.

Sport on television in the 1960s

Sport on television did not come of age until the sixties. The BBC had by then found that their fears concerning ITV had been unfounded. The BBC either kept the 'blue ribbon' events they had always covered or shared them with ITV. About the only sport that ITV were able to make almost exclusively their own was professional wrestling.

To begin with ITV had to resolve a number of 'teething problems' and their difficulties made the BBC appear even more adept at the handling of televised sport. The fact that they were by design a regional organisation, without the centralised national networking system that they have today, did little to help. However, they were a competitor about whom the BBC could not afford to be complacent. The impetus to programming innovation of the sort that transformed television news, eventually, but not quite so quickly or dramatically, impacted on sport. However, it was not until 1964 that 'the BBC initiated what was to become the hallmark of British football coverage and the centrepiece of Saturday night programming – recorded highlights on *Match of the Day*.' (Barnett p.17)

Match of the Day was a distinctly televisual solution to the problem of covering sport. At its best, it did and indeed does, provide a balance between often sophisticated analysis, explanation and entertainment. In other words it is 'packaged' to appeal to the aficionado and the less knowledgeable. Insofar as it did not show games live, it was not a threat to club gate revenues.

CASE STUDY

Sport and Money

Television has transformed sport into an industry. It has parallels with the film and other entertainment industries. Like a film, a game is a one off that is produced according to a set of agreed conventions that are understood by the clubs ('producers'), players ('stars') and supporters ('audiences'). Like a film or other text, a football match is played according to rules, but in a manner that will hopefully display both individual and team invention. In other words, a game is about a tension between the familiar (the rules of play) and the unfamiliar (the way the game is actually played).

A professional game is played for a number of reasons. One presumes that the players actually *like* to play and hope to win for the satisfaction of so doing and displaying their personal and team prowess. But games are also played to make money, either directly thorough gate fees or the sale of television rights. And then there is sponsorship.

Many clubs would find it very difficult to flourish without the revenue that comes from sponsorship, which depends almost entirely on television. Manufacturer's will pay to have their brand names and logos displayed around a major ground or, for even higher fees, on the players themselves. Clearly, the more prominent the team and the greater the likelihood that they will appear on television, the higher the fee.

Sometimes a commercial organisation will sponsor an event rather than a team. This kind of sponsorship is older than is generally realised. In the winter of 1861–62 Spiers and Pond, a catering company, sponsored England's first cricket tour of Australia and allegedly made £11 000 out of it (equivalent to about £500 000 at today's rates), and that was without the advantage of television. Substantial though this sum is, it is nothing compared to the fortunes that are generated through television from the salaries earned by players in sponsorship fees.

In 1972 Alex Higgins earned, in one competition, £480. In 1981, on winning the same championship, Steve Davis picked up £20 000. By then, of course, the championship had adopted the name of one of the sponsor's (a tobacco company) leading brands, Embassy World Snooker Championships. Embassy began to sponsor the championship soon after BBC2 started broadcasting it as a two week event and it remains much sought after. Having become the world snooker champion, Davis' own sponsorship value was much enhanced. The following year, in 1982, he was offered £220 000 by a brewery, for 40 personal appearances. And the figures have kept on going up for sponsorship of many events.

The most secure form of sponsorship, of course, is for an event to be owned by a wealthy benefactor. Motives for so doing are many and varied. For large multinational media conglomerates such as News Corporation the reasons are clear enough: gaining control of sporting events became a way of increasing audiences and thus advertising and subscription revenues. But what is the effect of this on sport?

The more commercially oriented sport becomes, the more it tends towards spectacle, much of which is peripheral to the game itself. But perhaps this does not matter very much, except to the purist. After all, sports have for a long time adapted themselves to the needs of television, and one of these is the requirement for spectacle.

From goal mouth to screen

In the beginning the limitations of technology were severe. Public events could only be covered if landlines were both available and accessible. In the thirties the Emitron cameras were heavy, cumbersome and only had a single, fixed focal length lens. This made dealing with relatively large spaces, such as football matches, difficult. Varying distances had to be covered by different lenses and changing them took some minutes leading to vital action being missed. It was not until the BBC covered the Olympics that up-to-date cameras were eventually acquired.

We have seen that television has been responsible for altering the look of a game, timing and even rules. But in what other ways does television transform sport? Clearly, watching a game of football, a cricket match or tennis tournament from the comfort of an armchair in a sitting room is not going to be the same as actually being there. The experience is going to be radically different. But how? And are the differences important in terms of appreciating a game as a *game*?

Is it the case that being present as a spectator is more authentic an experience than watching at home on television? At the stadium one will experience the excitement of being amidst the crowd, perhaps joining in the chanting and singing. One will be carried along by the shifting ebb and flow of a game, brought down at the low points and raised up in a swelling surge of excitement at the scoring of a goal or perhaps even just a near miss. It is an experience that cannot be quite replicated. And of course the spectator at the game is free to look where he or she chooses, whereas the vantage point on television is pre-selected.

'Different from' but not necessarily inferior to watching the same game on television, television possesses its own distinct advantages. One is greater clarity. Furthermore, the viewer can create his or her own coverage of a game with interactive television. This was introduced by Sky in 1999. Conventionally, the camera follows the ball, with occasional wide shots of either a more substantial portion of the pitch or court or even the whole of it, in order to show the dispositions of the respective teams (and, of course, to instil some visual variety).

In fact the television is not so much subjected to the whims of the director as to the conventions that largely determine how a game is recorded. The director does not have a great deal of choice: essentially, the camera will follow the ball. Up until a few years ago that meant covering the pitch with about half a dozen cameras arranged at both goal ends and the flanks. Now, with lighter and more sensitive cameras, producing sharper images and capable of going into tight close-up with zoom lenses, very dramatic shots are now the common currency of televised sport.

The process of translating a game into television can be divided into three components: the visual, aural and contextual. All of these are dependent on the available technology, the various techniques employed and the plethora of decisions made by the individuals responsible for making the programme – crucially the director and/or producer in the scanner (a mobile control room) who call the shots. Perhaps the single most important element of the visual is the facility of instant replay, frequently in slow motion and from several vantage points. This has the dual advantage of embellishing the dramatic impact of the moment and, sometimes, giving an opportunity for analysis. This facility has also long been available on big screens in American football and baseball stadiums and it cannot be long before it is a common feature in British grounds. The function here, however, is probably different: the big screen becomes (for at least one set of supporters) the focus of collective celebration. Sporting purists, however, may feel that there is a thin line between using technology to enhance the appreciation and understanding of a game and turning it into a fizzy spectacle of which the game is only one component. The impetus towards spectacle may in time be seen as the most enduring contribution television has made to sport. This is because sport not only forms a significant part of television schedules, but because, certainly in the case of BSkyB, sport has been used to bring in large audiences which in turn are delivered to advertisers.

Sport is a substantial revenue generator not only for club owners, but for television itself. Sport, as we have seen, has been one of the ways that News Corporation, principally in the UK but also in the USA, has increased its audience share, thus enhancing its appeal to advertisers. The more television exposure a team has, the higher its advertising premium. There is an intimate link between a team or player's status and the ability to attract advertising revenue. This in turn inflates transfer and appearance fees. In recent years the most newsworthy attempt by a television company to gain control of a major football team was in 1999 when BSkyB attempted to buy Manchester United, one of the leading UK football teams and the richest in the world. Murdoch's bid of about £600 million was accepted by the Manchester United Board, much to the chagrin of most supporters and in the face of determined protest. It was deemed to be unacceptable, however, to the Monopolies and Mergers Commission who refused to sanction the sale, on the grounds that the deal was not in the best interests of football as a whole.

ESSAY QUESTIONS

1 How far is sitcom reliant on stereotypes?

2 What sitcoms are there showing at the moment that seem to break with conventions and how?

3 What effects has television had on sport?

4 What effects has sport had on television?

5 The BBC is a public service broadcaster. What is the justification for it showing sport and sitcoms?

FOLLOW UP WORK

1 Think of one sport that is not currently being televised.
How would you do it?

2 Choose three sitcoms currently running on television.
What features do they share?
In what ways are they different?

3 How far are sport and television dependent on each other?

4 What are the attractions for audiences of sport on television?

5 Find out what current or recent television sitcoms started out on radio.
What changes has television imposed upon them?

SHORT ANSWER QUESTIONS

1 What is a sitcom?
2 What did, and do, the American networks find attractive about sitcoms?
3 Bullet point some of the problems the BBC had in the earliest days of televised sport.
4 What sports have been particularly amenable to being televised?
5 Why has television changed the appearance of some sports?

5
SOAP OPERA AND POLICE DRAMA

Soap opera

'Soap opera' is one of the most popular fictional forms on television. A soap is essentially a multi-narrative continuous serial, structured around several characters with some key locations. Soap opera as a form has its roots in the 19th century when it was common practice to serialise novels in magazines as Charles Dickens had done with *The Pickwick Papers* and, later, the *Strand Magazine*, in which Sherlock Holmes first saw the light of day.

Not so many years after Sherlock Holmes appeared the cinema took to the idea of the serial. In August 1912, the front cover of the *Ladies' World Magazine* boasted 'a stunning portrait of a beautiful young woman' (Steadman p.3) created by Charles Dana Gibson, a well known artist of the day. Across the bottom of the cover was written 'ONE HUNDRED DOLLARS FOR YOU IF YOU CAN TELL "WHAT HAPPENED TO MARY"'. Readers were invited to predict how the story would develop with the correct solution winning $100.

In this relatively inconspicuous fashion the first 'chapter play' heroine was created. What happened next is part of film history. In that same summer of 1912, the magazine editor, Charles Dwyer, had met Horace G. Plimpton, the manager of the Thomas Edison Kinetoscope Company, a powerful film production company.

Edison, remembered now for a host of inventions from the electric light bulb to the electric chair, had played a key role in the development of cinema and was the driving force behind the Motion Picture Patents Company. This was known as 'the Trust', which was a cartel of nine of the biggest companies attempting to gain control of the whole industry.

In fact that year they consolidated their position by creating the General Film Company, a distribution company created to handle Trust films. Plimpton suggested that the Edison company make a film version of each month's story and release it in theatres around the country. The idea rapidly caught on and the serial became a staple of cinema through to the 1950s.

Serials on the radio

The genesis of the radio serial drama happened in 1925 when two vaudeville players, Jim and Marion Jordan were appearing in Chicago. Busy as they were, their agent suggested they appear in a radio programme, apart from anything else, it would be good publicity. The result was *The Smith Family*, presented one night a week, with a repeat on Sunday, on Samuel Insull's WENR. 'In this open-end drama of family life, Marion Jordan became the first of the serial mothers, her sources of both delight and anxiety being two marriageable daughters.....' (Steadman p.226)

Serials on the television

Serials made the move to television in 1946 when a single episode of *Big Sister* was televised as an experiment. This was followed in 1947 by the first, but short-lived, daytime serial, *A Woman to Remember*. It was produced by one of the smallest of the networks, Du Mont Television Network (later to be reborn as Fox Television).

In 1950 CBS broadcast *The First Hundred Years*, the first daytime television serial to be sponsored, in this instance by Proctor and Gamble. It was one of the half dozen companies which had dominated the sponsorship of radio daytime serials. One daytime serial from this period, remarkably, is still running. *Guiding Lights* (also a Proctor and Gamble show) ran for its 47th season on CBS in 1999, having been premiered on 30th June, 1952. But it did not start there. *Guiding Lights*, like several other 1950s television shows began on radio, the first episode was broadcast in January 1937.

In American television a distinction is made between 'soaps', such as *Guiding Lights*, which are broadcast between 11 a.m. and 2 p.m. and bigger budget serials called 'primetime serials' such as *Dallas* and *Dynasty* (also, at one time, popular in the UK) which are transmitted in the evening between 6.30 p.m. and 10.30 p.m. Together they form a major component of American television.

Soaps are world-wide phenomena, principally because they are relatively cheap to make and popular. There hardly can be a country with an established television service that does not have a home-grown soap. As in America, in the UK soap began on radio with the long running *Mrs Dale's Diary* (1948–1969). This was very much a product of its time, a post-war drama offering a very traditional representation of the family, with Mrs Dale supporting her husband through thick-and-thin.

By 1969, when it was taken off the air, the sixties were about to give way to the seventies and Mrs Dale began to seem increasingly anachronistic. Overlapping with *Mrs Dale's Diary* was *The Archers*, which, of course, is still running. *The Archers* began as more of an information-cum-educational drama about farming and rural life, but the soap aspects took hold. It has been able to survive because of its ability to keep pace with, and reflect, social change – often to the dismay of some its more conservative listeners.

It was not until 1954, with an eye on the imminent arrival of independent television, that the BBC launched its first television soap, *The Grove Family*. It was transmitted live from the BBC studios at Lime Grove (hence the title) and ran for three years. It featured the 'long suffering father Grove and grumpy but loveable Grandma Grove'. (Wheen, p.143).

ITV's first long drama serial was *Emergency Ward Ten*, a hospital drama that began in 1957. It was screened twice weekly and ran for ten years. It was the forerunner of such medical dramas as *St Elsewhere*, *E.R.*, and

Casualty. Like its three descendants, *Emergency Ward Ten* had all of the formal characteristics of the soap – a large cast of characters and multiple, continuous narratives.

What is historically interesting about *Emergency Ward Ten* is the way men and women were represented in the narrative. The doctors were all men, surrounded by subservient and frequently swooning nurses; a long way from *E.R.* and *Casualty.*

In 1960 Granada launched *Coronation Street* on ITV, the UK's longest running television soap. Another record *Coronation Street* can lay claim to is the longest serving actor: William Roache appeared in the first episode as a young student and continues to appear.

Three soaps started in the sixties: *Compact* (BBC, 1962–1965); *Crossroads* (ITV, 1964–1988); *The Newcomers* (BBC, 1965–1969). *Compact* and *Crossroads* were certainly an advance on the way women had previously been represented in the early radio soaps and *Emergency Ward Ten. Compact* was about the production of a women's magazine; whilst questioning some of the dominant attitudes towards women, it nevertheless reproduced many of the traditional female stereotypes. *Crossroads,* occasionally mocked because of the quality of some of the acting and the frequent apparent lack of stability of the sets, did at least have a strong female character who in the end came to embody the show; Meg Richardson, who owned the motel.

The Newcomers (1965–69) was interesting insofar as it embodied an element of the social realism that became so important in British cinema, theatre and television drama in the sixties. Following the experiences of one family, the programme took as its theme the uprooting of people from long established areas of inner London to new housing estates. The image of people from close-knit communities, moved to a brand new estate characterised by tower blocks, where there was no sense of community was perhaps too bleak. It was not a popular drama and only survived four years.

The only major soap to start in the seventies was *Emmerdale Farm* (1972). Shown on ITV it was originally based around a farm. In 1989 the title was changed to *Emmerdale*, reflecting a shift in focus from the farm to the nearby fictional village of Beckindale. It courted a certain amount of controversy because of the lengths it seemed to be prepared to go to gain ratings, including a dramatic plane crash.

A new era of soaps

The 1980s was another period of birth of new soaps. *Take the High Road* had a rural setting, this time in Scotland. Two of the most significant soaps running on television in the nineties commenced within three years of each other; *Brookside* (1982) and *EastEnders* (1985). *Brookside* is firmly rooted in the tradition of British social realism. From the start it had a policy of being issue-led. Phil Redmond, its creator, has been quite explicit about this, 'I always wanted to do contemporary drama that, while it would entertain, would raise people's awareness of contemporary issues.'

Figure 5.1 *Issues raised in* Brookside © Mersey TV

The issues Brookside has dealt with have not only been topical, but risky, sometimes pushing to the limit the tolerance level of the 9 p.m. threshold (it is transmitted at 8 p.m. and 8.30 p.m. with an omnibus edition starting at 5.05 p.m. on Saturdays). Murder, drugs, patricide, rape, surrogate birth, suicide and homosexuality have all been featured. More than once the show has provided the tabloid press with good copy. Not least was the lesbian kiss. In January, 1985 an episode was screened depicting an established character, a young medical student, Beth Jordache (Anna Friel) kissing a friend who had been uncertain about her sexuality, Viv (Kerrie Thomas). The story had been developing over the previous twelve months. Beth had earlier been involved in two other lesbian relationships as part of a long storyline in which she was seen trying to come to terms with her own identity and sexuality. The ITC received fourteen complaints about the kiss, but did not uphold any of them. The furore was sufficient, however, to cause Channel Four to cut the kissing scene from the Saturday's omnibus edition, screened less than twenty fours hours later. This illustrates the delicate balancing act that has to be performed by institutions producing anything remotely challenging.

The reason given by Channel Four for cutting the scene highlights the difficult relationship between the popular press and the soaps. At one level, they need each other and the soaps like the publicity. Competition amongst newspapers, especially the tabloids, has increased their reliance on entertainment as a source of stories likely to encourage sales. On the other hand, the soaps can feel badly represented. According to a Channel Four spokeswoman, 'the decision was made because inaccurate representations of the scene have appeared in newspapers prior to transmission without our knowledge, which we felt distracted from the original intent and thereby distorted the integrity of the storyline.'

But this was not the only controversy in which the Jordache family was embroiled. As a young child, Beth had been raped by her father, who had also consistently beaten her mother. This was clearly a difficult story-line for any soap to deal with, and it did not end until Beth, coming to the aid of her mother, killed her father. This brought more complaints to the ITC, on this occasion about the explicitness of the murder, involving a kitchen knife. In October 1993, the ITC issued a formal warning to Channel Four when the scene was repeated in the Saturday early afternoon omnibus edition, on the grounds that a large number of children would be watching. This represents a scheduling problem for Channel Four; what might be acceptable fairly late in the evening and close to the 9 p.m. threshold, might not be at 5 p.m. on a Saturday. Beth eventually committed suicide whilst in prison (it was the actress's wish to be 'written out').

Soap and narrative

Soaps have evolved into a distinctive television form. In terms of longevity alone, one will probably have to return to something like the Indian epic *Mahabharaba* (an epic poem of 220 000 lines, probably written at about 500 BC) to find a narrative on the scale of any soap. *Coronation Street*, the longest running British Soap, was first transmitted in 1960. The implications of this in terms of memory are considerable while generations of families have been and gone. Soaps differ in their settings, narrative content and thematic preoccupations, but they all share one common factor and that is a highly distinctive narrative structure, quite distinct amongst all cultural forms. Soaps are without beginning and without end. All soaps attempt to affect the illusion of having always been there.

When a new soap begins it has to bring with it, in the first episode, a pre-history in a way that is unique amongst narrative forms and the audience has to be made privy to this 'memory'. In the first episode of *Coronation Street*, the solution to this narrative problem was strikingly simple. It opens in the street's shop and we learn that the shop is changing hands, and the new owner is being told not only what she needs to know about the running of the shop, but perhaps just as importantly, what she needs to know about her new customers. In they come, one by one and through the gossip we learn all about them. In this first episode, as a character was talked about there was a cut-away and we saw them 'in action'. The first episode of *Brookside* had the Crosby's arrive at Brookside Close from a more 'up-market' part of Liverpool. Down on their luck, they have had to move. As they get to know their new neighbours, so do we. Gossip is an important device in all soaps for keeping audiences up-to-date with events, as few people are either able or willing to watch every episode.

Soaps have multiple narratives, built around the diverse range of characters and their often complex inter-relationships. But audiences would rapidly lose interest if soaps told endless, continuous stories – this would imply the absence of structure, or at least unacceptably loose structures that give little satisfaction in terms of narrative pleasure, and it is narrative pleasure that is soap's key 'hook'. Even in soaps, stories must have a beginning, a middle and an end. The difference between soaps and more traditional narrative texts is that they have a multiplicity of narratives, often arranged in complex patterns. Typically, in a sequence of soap episodes, there will be several interwoven plot-lines, criss-crossing with each other. Whilst closure is achieved with one plot-line, another will still be continuing or others beginning. Conventionally, each episode will conclude on a 'cliff-hanger' or, less frequently (and generally in the last of a week's episodes), there will be a moment of closure, when a long-running plot line is resolved, such as the death or departure of a character.

Notwithstanding the duration of some plot-lines, soaps require narrative strategies that engage both new and infrequent viewers. That would not happen if plot-lines simply took their course without interruption over a long period of time: it would be very difficult for a new viewer to 'catch up'. The solution is to have an overlaying of plot-lines of varying length and at any time, at different stages of development. Christine Gerraghty uses the terms flexibility and variation to describe the way serials reach climaxes of tension or simply stop at a moment of unfinished action, to be held over until another episode. Similarly, there is an ebb and flow of characters. Along with key characters having their cycle of narrative problems, others enter, bringing with them fresh narrative problems, and at their resolution, leave. When, in 1999, Steve Owen arrived in Walford Square (*EastEnders*, main location), it was clear from his general demeanour – and the fact he was there at all – that his arrival would initiate a story-line. This proved to be the case, with a story line that would eventually result in manslaughter with another character wrongly jailed for the offence. This created another narrative problem around Steve Owen: having been acquitted was he to be punished in some other way? Both the writing and the performer, Martin Kemp, managed to create a character able to provoke, almost in equal measure, hostility and sympathy. A character was constructed that, in the language of the tabloids, 'we love to hate'. An advantage that a regular 'soap' has over single dramas is that it can, over time, create layers of complexity around a character, moulding levels of traits that may be contradictory so creating more 'rounded' complex characters. This is an attribute of realism. Such characters can achieve, in the minds of audiences, a high level of plausibility; what Hodges and Tripp call 'modality'.

In line with the need for fluid plot development, the turnover of characters in soaps is high, whilst maintaining a core of regulars who themselves are not invulnerable. Core characters are also cut from time to time, often at the wishes of the actor. This happened, for example, in October 1999, when a very popular character in *EastEnders* left, who had for some time been one of the stars of the show. Ross Kemp, who played Grant Mitchell had announced his intention to leave some months previously; he wanted to develop his career in other directions. This gave the writing team sufficient time to develop a story line that resulted in the character vanishing after a dramatic plot-line resulted in a car crashing into the Thames. This story line, of ill fated dealings with loan-sharks, sibling betrayal and frustrated romance, brought together a number of plot-lines involving several characters. Grant Mitchell had confessed to his brother, Phil, that he had slept with Phil's estranged wife, Kathy, with whom Phil was hoping to be reconciled. Their younger sister, Sam, was having an uncertain relationship with an ex-police man, Beppi di Marco. He had become an ex-policeman as a consequence of interfering with some crucial evidence that would have cleared Grant Mitchell of murdering his wife, Tiffany (played by Martine McCutcheon, who left some months before to cultivate a career as a singer). The manner of his departure, however, left open the possibility of a return. It is this type of on-going narrative complexity, with a pattern of resolutions and beginnings, that is one of the key 'hooks' for an audience.

Advantages of soaps

Finance

Soaps have the same economic advantages as any other regular drama series. Sets, costumes, studio space and other production costs are cheaper

per episode than for a single drama. Actors, too, contracted to appear either over a period of time or a given number of episodes will cost less per episode than for a single drama. Soaps rarely have to pay higher fees for 'stars' – they tend to create their own, and most actors in such stellar positions are aware that their status rarely travels with them: few actors have achieved success after their soap careers. Producers are also able to use a little financial 'muscle', inhibiting extravagant claims for increases in fees, because it is generally known that no individual in a soap is indispensable. A cast might be able to apply pressure *en masse* for changes in conditions of work on the series, but rarely does this work individually. In the balance of power between producers and cast, the former have the advantage.

The same sets, of course, are used week in and week out. *EastEnders*, having three episodes a week and occasionally five, is virtually in full-time production. The programme has a fixed – and closed – studio at BBC Elstree Television Centre in Borehamwood, Buckinghamshire. In the studio some sets, such as the pub – the 'Vic' – are permanent. The most famous element of the set is Albert Square. Albert Square is, in a sense, a real place. It is built of bricks and mortar, but the houses are hollow shells and all of the interiors are shot inside the studio. The bridge, occasionally glimpsed in the background, is only half a bridge and the two ends do not go anywhere. Building Albert Square was expensive, but when that cost, including its upkeep, is distributed over the huge number of episodes that have and will be made, it is very cheap per episode.

There was widespread misunderstanding over the cost of the set for the short-lived soap, *Eldorado*. There was criticism of the construction costs, of £10 000 000 for the set in Spain where real houses were built. It was conveniently ignored by the critics that the set was built for the production of a large number of episodes and constituted a valuable asset that could, and was, sold when no longer required.

When, in the eighties, *Grange Hill* moved to a fixed set, considerable savings were made in production costs. Prior to this, virtually all exterior scenes shot in the fictional school had to be recorded on location. Two parts of a school exterior built at Elstree studios eradicated the need for much location work. The set itself, at about £50,000, was relatively cheap and built on a car park adjacent to a building containing the production offices of *Grange Hill*, *EastEnders* and *South East News*. This building also had a studio on the ground floor. *Brookside*, as is generally known, went so far as to buy part of a housing estate. Again, given the number of episodes that have been made since 1982, the cost is small and Mersey Television also has a very sound asset.

Programme makers

Soaps also have considerable advantages for those who make and appear in them. This is by no means true of everyone involved, but many of the production crew and cast will have contracts that run to several episodes. Not only does that represent a measure of financial security, but everyone involved in the production has time to develop their roles. This is equally true of production staff as it is of actors. Everyone, from production assistants, designers and studio operatives to writers, directors and producers knows the programme intimately. This means that it can be produced quickly without compromising quality. Rehearsals, technical run-throughs, etc., take less time than for a single play.

Advertisers

Advertisers like soaps because they attract audiences. By the same token, television can charge premium rates, but with such a huge audience, as in the case of *Coronation Street* (an average of 15 million) it still works out relatively cheap per viewer for the advertiser. Over the past few years sponsorship has also increased. Cadbury has for some time been sponsoring *Coronation Street* using the slogan 'the Nation's Favourite' along with images of a chocolate version of 'the street'.

Audiences

Viewing figures speak for themselves: soaps are very popular. *EastEnders* and *Coronation Street* regularly attract audiences of 18 million. Why is this? There is the pleasure of the narrative. One of the 'addictive' aspects of any soap, that will often transcend any consideration of 'quality', is the desire to know what happens next. With soap or any other continuous series, final 'closure' is always deferred so they are never-ending. Through the multi-narrative, interweaving structure of soaps, audiences are positioned in a distinctive way. In the traditional novel or film, there is one dominant, linear narrative with the stress placed on the actions of individual protagonists. These strong individuals are the main bearers of the action, responsible for the resolution of a (single) narrative problem, finally leading to narrative closure where all the 'loose ends' are tied up. The emphasis on the individual is further emphasised by the way in which the reader/viewer is placed in a position of omniscience – all knowing and all seeing so the reader/viewer is empowered to look into the hearts and minds of all the characters and granted a knowledge denied all but the author.

Soaps are a variation of the form of a traditional novel or film. The viewer is still placed in a privileged position of knowledge (most of the time) in the sense that they know more than any one character does. The sense of a free-flowing narrative in soaps has been likened to the pattern of everyday life, especially women's lives which are often a balancing act between the demands of home and work.

Police drama

Unlike soaps, police drama generally takes the form of a series, however, it does take other forms. There are mini-series such as *Prime Suspect*, with Helen Mirren or the occasional two hour single dramas such as the long running *Inspector Morse* with John Thaw. There have also been mini-series within a series: with *The Bill* there have been occasional specials narrated over anything from two to four episodes. There have even been police sitcoms such as *The Thin Blue Line* (BBC, 1999) and a spoof observational documentary, *People Like Us* (Carlton, 1999).

Crime fiction as we understand it, began in the 19th century with Edgar Allan Poe. As a fictional genre it rapidly developed and became very popular throughout America and Europe. In the UK, Wilkie Collins created the first British detective in his novel *The Woman in White* (1860). Towards the end of the century, Sir Arthur Conan Doyle created Sherlock Holmes in his first published story, *A Study in Scarlet* (1887). It is perhaps with Holmes, the most famous of all detectives, that the modern crime fiction begins. Holmes had all the attributes of most modern fictional detectives, whether s/he be a private eye or police officer. He was a loner, had his own way of doing things, he was upper class and, above all else, relied on deduction – a process of reasoning – in order to solve the crime. Holmes set in motion a tradition of British crime fiction that survives to this day in television series such as *Inspector Morse*. There are many variations on the same theme, where the basic attributes have been played with, by varying the gender and social class of the detective and endowing them with a variety of eccentricities. Morse, for example, was a loner with a cluster of idiosyncrasies such as a taste for real ale, an old maroon jaguar and a love of opera.

Whatever their differences, all of them solved the crime in the same way: by deduction. Often, experience and deductive powers are set against official police procedure. The solitary detective tends to be 'his own man' with a low tolerance level for officialdom. Ideologically, individualism is favoured over collective action and reason over intuition.

There are several sub-genres of crime fiction which can be broadly divided between police procedural fiction and detective fiction and both have their variations. The antecedents of television crime fiction were long established in film and literature. In terms of films, the most influential were the 1940s and 1950s FBI procedural films that often had a pronounced documentary element to their style, such as *The FBI Story* (1959) and *The House on 92nd Street* (1945). Both of these films, and others like it, were characterised by the occasional use of voice-over narration, an emphasis on police procedure and documentary style footage. The stories would often be based on actual cases. All of these features spilled over into television crime fiction such as the long running series *Dragnet* and *The Untouchables*, both of which appeared on British television in the 1960s. *Dragnet* was a 1950s American police series based on the LAPD (Los Angeles Police Department). It prided itself in its realism claiming that it was based on actual cases and employed serving officers as advisors. It was, for its time, fast paced with a semi-documentary style. *The Untouchables* (1959–1963) also had realist claims. It was set in the 1920s and based on the autobiography of Elliot Ness who led an IRS (Inland Revenue Service) Special Intelligence Unit. They were tasked with assembling evidence of prohibition violations (alcohol was outlawed at the time) by Al Capone. Again, it had a pace and energy that had, until *Z Cars*, eluded the British police drama.

Television police dramas in Britain

In Britain, police dramas began to appear in the 1950s. After the short lived *Colonel March of Scotland Yard* (with Boris Karloff) it was not until *Dixon of Dock Green* appeared that television had its first long running drama which lasted for over twenty years. It was inspired by the 1949 Ealing Studios film, *The Blue Lamp* (directed by Basil Deardon), in which Sergeant Dixon is killed, quite early on in the film, by a young hoodlum played by Dirk Bogarde. *The Blue Lamp* is an interesting example of post-war realism. It sets out to tackle a genuine contemporary social problem, delinquency, in a fairly realistic style (use of actual locations, etc.) yet, at the same time, presents a somewhat idealised version of urban communities. However, it was regarded as being very realistic in its time. Of the film, Lord (Ted) Willis who wrote the film, said of it:

The Blue Lamp was the first film to show the police with some degree of realism .... it's difficult for people nowadays to understand exactly what was new because they have been so accustomed to police series, but it was literally the first film that took people behind the scenes in a police station......It was the first film that showed the kind of humdrum day-to-day life of a policeman behind the counter of a police station or on the beat and his relationships with his clients, as he called them in those days.

(Keating, H.R.F., Crime Writers, *BBC, 1978)*

This, perhaps, serves as a reminder that realism is relative; it is a shifting body of codes and conventions.

Figure 5.2 *Post-war realism in* Dixon of Dock Green © BFI

In the film Dixon is presented as an exceptionally able and experienced police offer who is the lynch-pin of the local community. At the beginning of the film he is seen 'grooming' a young, and inexperienced copper, teaching him not only police-work, but perhaps more importantly, the ways of Paddington Green and its people. The central motif running throughout the film is the importance of *community*. At the end, even the local villains join in the hunt for Dixon's killer, partly out of respect for him, but also because the young delinquent has upset the finely balanced relationship that existed between the criminal fraternity and the police. The criminal is, of course, captured after a dramatic chase. The 'rookie' picks up Dixon's legacy and the final shot of the film is of him walking a London street; Dixon lives on.

And indeed he did. He was resurrected in 1955 by the BBC in the form of *Dixon of Dock Green*. Still played by the original actor, Jack Warner (he played the role well into the 1970s when he himself was over eighty!), Dixon became the epitome of the mythical British bobby. He had a clear and uncompromising sense of what was right and wrong. He, himself, was absolutely incorruptible. He was experienced both as a police officer and as a man: he knew what was right and he knew *people* – his strongest asset. Carried over into *Dixon* was *The Blue Lamp's* idealised image of both community and the police. Dixon was the police writ large. The irony was that at exactly the same time *Dixon* was being broadcast, the Metropolitan Police's CID was going through perhaps the greatest crisis in its history: corruption was rampant. The disparity between what, increasingly, people began to know as true and the image of the police that *Dixon* was offering had little in common. This was one of the reasons that led to the final demise of *Dixon*. In only one episode was there a suggestion that the police might be the same as the rest of us, subject to weaknesses and failings. In one episode Dixon is confronted by a corrupt officer. His sense of moral outrage is palpable as he orders the offending officer to remove his uniform as he is no longer worthy to wear it. Watching this scene, one has the overriding sense, not of a mere uniform being torn away, or even an ethical and moral order, but the removal of the right to belong to a select and worthy community.

Everything about *Dixon* the series and Dixon the character speaks of a firm ideological order. Every stereotypical tenet of white, Anglo-Saxon, middle-class society is maintained. *Dixon*/Dixon stood for social stability and a clear sense of right and wrong. It has to be said that as the series neared the end in the 1970s (for a while it overlapped with both *Z Cars* and *The Sweeney*) its rigid certainties began to wobble a little and moral ambiguity began to insinuate itself into the scripts.

Police drama from the 1950s

From the late 1950s on, the BBC and ITV produced one crime drama after another. In 1957 Granada produced *Shadow Squad* (1957) but the first successful and long running ITV police drama was *No Hiding Place* produced by Associated Rediffusion (1959 – 1966). It featured Johnny Briggs who now plays Mike Baldwin in *Coronation Street*. The police series went through some interesting twists and turns before it settled into anything like a formula (it's arguable that such a formula, in terms of actual programmes, does not actually exist). At about the time *Z Cars* started (in 1962) and Associated Television produced *Sergeant Cork* (1963–1966) with John Barrie and William Gaunt. This had a Victorian setting and Cork was a member of the brand new CID. Apart from the setting, formally it was indistinguishable from any other detective fiction. Cork was the usual idiosyncratic detective, solving crime with inspired acts of deduction. Social class was a prominent motif in the series, as many episodes would permit the blunt Cork to clash with his social 'superiors'. Another variation was *Red Cap* (1964 – 1966), which as the title implies, had a military setting and included Leonard Rossiter (later the star of *Rising Damp*), Ian McShane (*Lovejoy*) and John Thaw (*The Sweeney* and *Morse*).

The two key police drama series of the seventies were *Z Cars* and *The Sweeney*. We have to look across the Atlantic for at least part of the explanation as to why these two shows came about, but another important part of the explanation lies in what was happening to BBC drama at the time and to an increasing perception that *Dixon* was simply out of touch with what was happening in 1960s Britain. The first episode of *Z Cars* was something of an epiphany in the development of the genre. Things would never be the same again and the death knell sounded over *Dixon* and its image of cosy Britain. *Four of a Kind*, the first episode, begins with what is a disturbing image when compared to *Dixon*. Two detectives, Detective Chief Inspector Barlow and Sergeant Watt are standing over the grave of a murdered colleague. Not many police men were 'killed in action' in *Dixon*, except, ironically, Dixon himself in *The Blue Lamp*. The scene in *Z Cars* ends with the declared hope that the killer will 'take the drop' (Britain still had the death penalty in 1962). In the second scene the two detectives are in a car discussing the problems of policing the neighbourhood, a new town (it was actually called Newtown in the series and was allegedly modelled on Kirkby, an over-spill district of Liverpool). This second scene elaborates and extends the image of social unrest suggested earlier: what we have here is a war against crime. Gone is the comfortable relationship between the police and the civil community. In *Z Cars* the police were not an integral part of the community as was Dixon – they stood outside, trying to contain it. The rest of the episode is about the recruitment of a motorised, rapid-response team – the Crime Squad (the Z Cars) which was an elite group of officers tasked to respond to any outbreak of trouble, whatever that might be.

Figure 5.3 *Z Cars* © *BFI*

It is unlikely the officers recruited would have met with Dixon's approval. Each, in their different way, was a non-conformist who would 'bend' the rules if it was necessary. One aspect of the first episode that caused consternation in the press the following day was that one of the officers, P.C. Steele, admitted to hitting his wife (she boasted a conspicuous black eye). In a BBC documentary, *The Death of Dixon,* one senior police officer, who was an inspector at the time, described how on arriving home after a shift, he was approached by his outraged wife, upset that she had just seen a television programme in which a police officer had struck his wife. She was adamant that such things could not possibly happen with real policemen. The Inspector replied that he had only that morning dealt with a similar situation. Art was catching up with life and for many in the audience it was not a comfortable experience.

Dixon was ordered, well mannered and conciliatory: *Z cars* was aggressive, abrasive and even, at times, antiauthoritarian. Many senior police officers were affronted and the Chief Constable of Lancashire withdrew his support for the programme. Ironically in the light of that response, *Z Cars* was ultimately sympathetic to the police. It was the first drama series to deal with the effects of crime on the police themselves. In *Z Cars* the police seemed more like normal people – warts and all. Audiences, for the first time, began to have a glimpse of what policing in a modern city was like. Although today it seems dated, in the 1960s the sense of realism created in *Z Cars* was almost palpable. Right from the start it was a mix of location and studio shooting. In its early days it had an extra 'edge' because it was recorded live with inserts of scenes shot on location. Up until the 1960s, when video tape began to be used, *all* drama was recorded live and there was at least one live drama series, *The Eleventh Hour*, until 1975. It must have been a nerve-racking business for everyone concerned. One imagines that appearing on stage in front of an audience is bad enough, but performing on television, in front of several million people, must have ratched the experience up to another level of terror.

Z Cars gave rise to two sequels, *Softly, Softly* and *Softly, Softly – Task Force* featuring a promoted Barlow and Watt. It also became part of a growing concern about the rise of violence on television, although this was focused largely on American imports such as *The Untouchables*. This would be a concern that would sustain itself to the present day. *Z Cars* was certainly less compromising than its predecessors in its representation of police, crime and society as a whole. In part, this was reflected in its scheduling: *Dixon* was transmitted at 6.30 p.m. on Saturday (a prime 'family viewing' slot whereas *Z Cars* went out at 8.30 p.m. on Wednesday, much nearer the 9 p.m. threshold. 'Reassurance' was built into the very structure of Dixon. It would begin with Dixon himself, emerging from darkness, cheerfully whistling. He would then speak directly to the camera, saying, each time, the same opening words, 'Evening all!' He would then proceed to set out the problem for us. At the end, standing smartly in front of the police station, hands held behind his back, he would sum up the lessons to be learned from what has just transpired. The last thing the audience would see and hear of any one episode was this comforting, avuncular figure assuring them that all was right with the world. *Z Cars* provided no such assurance. Perhaps oddly, both series were as popular as each other, with audiences of between 12 and 14 million.

The police series that stood astride the 1970s was *The Sweeney* (1974 – 1978). It was made by Euston Films, a subsidiary of Thames Television, then the weekday franchise holder for London. The American influence was far more obvious on *The Sweeney* than it had been on *Z Cars*. At times it must have seemed that British television was awash with popular American imports such as *Starsky and Hutch* and *Kojak*. In the seventies and eighties there were a number of attempts to create a British police drama that would match the American product in its pace and action. The most successful of these was undoubtedly *The Sweeney*.

Figure 5.4 *Icon of the 1970s:* The Sweeney © BFI

Following a pilot (*Regan*) in 1974 *The Sweeney* ran for three series, all of which were repeated through into the 1980s, spawned two feature film 'spin-offs' and a crop of imitations. Its subject was the Flying Squad, an elite branch of the Metropolitan Police specialising in armed robbery. Amongst the writing credits two names are prominent: Troy and Ian Kennedy Martin. Troy Kennedy Martin devised *Z Cars* and his brother, Ian, devised *The Sweeney*. The directing credits are, in retrospect, also of interest. Ted Childs directed two episodes as well as producing the series. He would later produce *Morse*, also with John Thaw.

CASE STUDY

Production in a police drama

*T*he *Sweeney* was made on video tape. Each episode ran for approximately 50 minutes. There was a ten day shooting schedule (five minutes of screen time per day). Such a schedule only permitted one location per day. Other production constraints included the stipulation that all filming had to take place within one hour of Euston Studios in Hammersmith and no more than two minutes per episode of exterior night time filming was permitted. The budget was about £50 000 per episode.

Being made for ITV, each episode had to include two 'cliff-hangers' for the commercial breaks. Narrative constraints included considerable restrictions on what could be filmed. No access to public transport was permitted other than to British Rail and then only during off-peak periods. Facilities at airports were rarely made available. Philip Drummond points out that it was 'barred from prisons and other Home Office properties relating to the police service or the law courts, forbidden to stage crime in public thoroughfares, and only cautiously conceded the tangential privilege of filming people and cars entering and leaving New Scotland Yard.' (Screen Education. p.17). In short, co-operation from the authorities was almost non-existent. Advice on police procedure, etc., seems to have been given on a purely informal basis.

If the relationship between the civil community and the police was seen to come under some strain in *Z Cars*, it virtually ceased to exist in *The Sweeney*. The fictional world created within *The Sweeney* presents both the police and the criminal as existing outside civil society and at war with each other. This aspect of *The Sweeney* has been examined by Geof Hurd:

The notion of war is a major strand within *The Sweeney*. It is reflected both in explicit references and implicitly in the structure of each episode; the planning and counter-planning in each camp, the military-style conduct of police and criminals, manoeuvring for tactical and strategic advantage, and the final set-piece battle, often preceded by minor skirmishing, which frequently ends each episode.

(Screen Education, No. 20, Autumn 1976, p.49)

Regan's recognition of this state of affairs, that they are 'at war' with crime, leads to his willing acceptance that unorthodox methods have to be adopted in order to prevail. Essentially, this entails a further recognition that the formal strictures regulating police conduct – the 'rules' – have to be interpreted in a way that does not compromise the ability of the police to effectively carry out their job, which is to catch criminals. As Regan saw it, criminals don't stick to the rules – if the police did, they would be fighting 'the war' with one hand tied behind their back.

A central motif running through the whole series was the permanent state of tension between Regan and his superiors (the 'fifth floor'). Haskins, Regan's immediate superior, acted as an intermediary between him and the 'fifth floor'. In terms of the narrative, his role was to restrain Regan and keep him within tolerable limits. Regan and Carter's occasional transgressions were generally tolerated because they were highly skilled 'thief catchers'. When their conduct was not tolerated, it was Haskins' role to dispense appropriate disciplinary action, usually in the form of a chastisement, delivered in tones that suggested that it was a waste of time. All of this is suggested by the title sequence. In a series of stills resembling a time-lapse sequence, Regan and Carter are involved in a car chase. Stills of an ensuing fight are followed by the arrival of Haskins, shown gesticulating in admonishment towards the two delinquent officers. Authority was not the only object of Regan's suspicion, if not scorn: he and Carter were unmistakably working class and suspicious of those who weren't. One can add to that a degree of techno-phobia and an acute distaste for paper work. Regan was 'a man of action' who achieved results by dint of aggressive determination, the sound application of deduction and knowledge gained from years of experience 'on the ground'.

All these elements came into play in an episode called *Country Boy*, from the second series, transmitted on 17th November 1975. Inexplicably, bank alarms have been going off without any evidence of interference. Regan and Carter are on the case, but the 'fifth floor' deem that they need technical assistance. A detective called Keen comes up from Bristol who is an expert in telecommunications and opera. He has the misfortune to arrive in evening dress (he was at the opera when the call came through). Regan and Carter are immediately hostile. They view Keen as being young, educated and qualified but useless in the field. During the course of the episode Keen proves his worth. Through his knowledge of telephones he leads Regan to the villains. But what really wins Regan over to him is his behaviour under fire. In a shoot-out in a power station, Keen is wounded, but nevertheless, through quick-thinking, courage and accurate shooting, saves the situation. In other words, Keen proved himself in Regan's terms.

The Sweeney's representation of the police had left *Z Cars*, never mind *Dixon*, far behind. Its heroes were two hard drinking, womanising officers who rarely thought twice about breaking the rules and intimidating suspects, or even witnesses. In *Country Boy* Regan threatened to withhold a life-sustaining drug from a rescued GPO technician, unless he co-operated and remained trussed up in a tunnel in order to maintain the villains' illusion that their plan had not been discovered. Where Dixon, and even some of the Crime Squad in *Z Cars*, had wives, Regan was a divorcee who, given the chance, cavorted with a different women each week. In *Country Boy* his misguided advances to a young doctor, whom he believes to be merely Keen's friend, run aground when, at the end of the episode, it transpires that she is his wife.

Real senior police officers hated Regan as much as their fictional counterparts. But according to a BBC documentary, *The Death of Dixon*, most serving officers loved it. One ex-Flying Squad inspector described how every Wednesday at 9 p.m. every seat in the television room at Hendon (the police training college) was full. During its production run, serving officers acting as unofficial advisers fed to the writers and directors actual incidents that were sometime only superficially disguised. A line from one episode, 'I'm not going to hit you, my sergeant is going to hit you,' was, allegedly, based on an actual incident. *The Sweeney* was the begetter of a number of imitations including *Dempsey and Makepeace* (LWT, 1985–1986).

If the police had been concerned about the way they were represented in *The Sweeney*, *Law and Order* (BBC, 1978) must have induced apoplexy. It was a 'mini-series' of four episodes written by G.F. Newman and produced by Tony Garnett (who would later produce another, if less, controversial series, *Between the Lines*). *Law and Order* assumed the view that corruption in the police (the CID) was not simply a case of the odd 'rotten apple', as in *Dixon*, but 'the apples in the CID barrel were continually going rotten and that if they weren't in this permanent state of fermentation, they would not be able to do their job, which is to protect us from criminal despotism' (H.R.F. Keating, p.129). *Law and Order* took hold of *The Sweeney* thesis that to defeat crime, the rules had to be bent and carried it further. Regan and Carter may well have 'bent' the rules, but they were not corrupt: criminals were not 'fitted up' and money never changed hands. Newman has said that he wanted to show the police in a different way.

Newman's argument is that most pre-1980s police drama subscribed to the 'rotten apple' thesis and in so doing maintained the myth (he calls it the 'Lie') of the incorruptibility of the police. His view that the problem went deeper than the odd delinquent officer is explicitly presented in *Law and Order*. In terms of narrative, *Law and Order* was unusual. There were four separate episodes; only in a loose sense was it a serial. Each episode gave a different perspective on the one crime. This is suggested by the titles: *The Villain's Tale*, *The Detective's Tale*, *The Brief's Tale* and *The Prisoner's Tale*. *The Detective's Tale* was particularly controversial, centred as it was on the corrupt activities of a CID detective, Pile.

> 'as they've never been shown before on the television screen, or any other screen come to that, and part of the intention was to actually make a film about the police that stated the case as it is in present day.... I think the main problem...is that the people who make the series, the people who write them, the people who direct them just don't know the realities of police, villains and judiciary. They just don't know policemen and criminals. They haven't experienced policing a metropolis, they haven't experienced crime, so they have nothing to relate to. All they can relate to in fact are things they've seen on television. If you accept that television is art .... then art should imitate life. But all television is doing is imitating other art, I mean they're just imitating Kojak and things like that, American police fiction.
>
> *(Screen Education, No.20, Autumn 1976, p.17).*

Law and Order marked the end of the age of innocence with the police drama. It was, however, atypical of the genre. The late 1970s and the 1980s produced a number of shows that were variously and to differing degrees influenced either by *The Sweeney* or American products such as *Starsky and Hutch*, *Kojak* and *Miami Vice*. All of these tended to be about idiosyncratic officers working in pairs with difficult relationships with their superiors. The BBC's efforts to imitate *The Sweeney* led to *Target* (1977) with Patrick Mower. In 1981 another variation of the same theme came with the BBC's *The Chinese Detective* (1981) about a Hong Kong detective working in the CID. Granada produced a series about a black detective, *Walcott* (1981). Thames played with the idea of the eccentric detective in *Strangers* (1981) featuring a Wordsworth loving detective with a fondness for a pair of gloves he never seemed to remove who was also learning to play the saxophone whilst undertaking an Open university degree: a very busy police officer.

Figure 5.5 *Juliet Bravo*
Source: BFI

In 1980 both the BBC and LWT came up with series featuring women in the lead roles. *The Gentle Touch* (LWT, 1980 – 1983) was another CID series with Gill Gascoine as Detective Inspector Maggie Forbes. Meanwhile, the BBC produced *Juliet Bravo*, which was the exact contemporary of *The Gentle Touch* and ran from 1980 to 1983 also. In many respects *Juliet Bravo* was the more interesting of the two series. In the first episode a new Inspector takes over command of a Yorkshire police station. The new officer, however, is a woman, Inspector Jean Darbley (Stephanie Turner) and this presented a problem, if not for everybody else, then certainly for the station sergeant, Beck, a dour, very experienced and traditional officer with very set views about the 'proper' place of women. The underlying narrative theme throughout the whole series was the struggle of Inspector Jean Darbley to establish her authority, especially over Sergeant Beck which, by the end of the series, she does. *Juliet Bravo* was very much in the tradition of *Z Cars*: the cases dealt with by Jean Darbley tended to be dramatically low-key and often of a domestic nature.

Police drama in the 1990s

The number of police dramas did not diminish in the 1990s. Many of them reflected the post PACE police force. Rising concern about corruption and an increasing distance between the police and the public gave rise to greater regulation and public accountability. The *Dixon* image of the police had been eroded. It was not just the number of high profile corruption cases that had been surfacing since the 1960s, but an undermining of public confidence. This was brought about by a seemingly relentless rise in crime rates and also a series of public order crises which had brought to the nation's television screens images of the police force embattled on the streets of Liverpool and Bristol, with the very people it was supposed to be serving. Most damaging of all, perhaps, were the images of pitched battles between the police and striking miners in 1984. In addition throughout the 1980s and 1990s there seemed to be an endless series of miscarriages of justice, not the least of these were the Birmingham Six and the Guildford Four, where a number of people were wrongly convicted for offences committed by the IRA. A number of reforms came into being during the 1980s, including the passing of the Police and Criminal Evidence Act in 1984 which laid down a number of rules concerned with the treatment of suspects and the handling of evidence.

These concerns filtered through into new police dramas. The most durable has been *The Bill*. First transmitted in 1984, it began as a weekly 50 minute drama. In 1988 it changed to a bi-weekly series of half hour episodes and it remained so for several years. In 1999 it reverted to the 50 minute format. It has also experimented with longer stories, some running over three or four episodes. *The Bill* belongs to the *Z Cars* tradition. It is based around an inner-London police station, Sun Hill. There are no obvious individual stars. Although any one episode, or series of episodes may have a dominant story line, there are usually one or two subsidiary narratives. This, in a less complex way, echoes the multi-narrative form of the 'eighties American series, *Hill Street Blues*.

The 'nineties have seen a boom in the number and variety of police series. As with any proliferating genre, they have all endeavoured to find a 'spin' on the format. *Cracker,* which went through several series in the 1990s, was a variation on the detective format with a psychologist at its centre. He, too had his defining eccentricities: he lived a problematic life style that was dominated by work, drink and gambling. In *Silent Witness* (BBC, 1999) Amanda Burton played a pathologist who invariable became involved in solving a crime. The 'nineties even produced a short lived up-dating of *The Sweeney* called *Thief Takers*. During this period ITV tended to produce 'safer', more traditional police series such as *Heartbeat*, *Inspector Morse*, *The Ruth Rendell Mysteries*, *A Touch of Frost* and *Taggart*. *Heartbeat*, in particular, seemed to be a 'throwback' to Dixon. Set in a northern rural community it oozed nostalgia with its 1960s setting. An interesting series in the early 'nineties was *The Chief*, starring Martin Shaw. It specifically focused on such issues as race and police corruption. *A Touch of Frost*, like Morse, was about a middle-aged detective who eschewed bureaucracy in favour of 'old fashioned policing'. But there were times, as in *Taggart* (set in Glasgow) when the 'heart of darkness' would show through in some of the storylines. Both had a fairly dark visual style, signifying a bleak moral universe which was mitigated by the determination, commitment and frequently the passion of Taggart and Frost. However grim the darker recesses of humanity with which Frost and Taggart had to deal, as with more traditional crime fiction, the police could be relied upon to bring about a satisfactory solution. This was also true of the darkest series that (up to 1999) ITV has screened. This was a mini-series, *Touching Evil* (Anglia TV, 1998), starring Robson Green as Dave Creegan, a detective serving in a special operations unit. Creegan confronts both an international ring of paedophiles and a man who, deranged by grief, holds Robson responsible for the death of his daughter in a botched police operation. But although the personal cost to Creegan is high, the narrative concludes with the paedophiles being 'put away.' The style of *Touching Evil* was reminiscent of *The X Files*. It was characterised by low-key, high contrast lighting, it had occasional captions indicating time and location and although not dealing with the paranormal and extra-terrestrial, it dealt with the extraordinary and highly disturbed states of mind. Many interiors almost looked as if they were shot through frosted glass. The similarity with *The X Files* may not have been accidental as it was a co-production between Anglia TV and WBGH Boston, an American public service station.

In the same period, BBC police dramas were also potentially more unsettling. In the early 1990s there was *Between the Line*, based on the Complaints Investigation Branch (CIB), tasked, as their real-life counterparts, with investigating wrongdoing within the service itself. Whereas all past police series (even, on one occasion, *Dixon*) had occasionally tackled the problem, here was a series almost solely about police corruption. It went further than showing the odd 'bent copper' and suggested that the police force, like any other state agency, could be subject to political manipulation, from within and without. Occasionally the shadowy interface between the police and security agencies was featured. It also seemed to offer a critical insight into what in the 1980s and early 1990s was referred to as the 'canteen culture' of the police force, a metaphor that spoke not only of alleged sexism, but also of a self-protective, closing-of-ranks whenever any of their number was seen to be threatened.

The series was based around a CIB team lead by Superintendent Tony Clark (Neil Pearson). In one episode, *Manslaughter* (transmitted in October 1993) Clark and his team, Inspectors Harry Naylor (Tom Georgeson) and Maureen Connell (Siobhan Redmond) investigate the death of a boy killed by a speeding car. All of the evidence points towards it being a police constable. Their efforts are frustrated all the way by a quiet resistance on the part of both the officers being investigated and their colleagues. The final scene is quite unlike that of most police and detective dramas, in which the audience is doubly reassured by the invincibility of the police and a tidy resolution of the narrative problem. In *Manslaughter* there is no such reassurance. Clark and Connell interrogate the suspect, whom they know is guilty. He is a police officer, P.C. Curles (Shaun Dingwell). As the scene progresses it looks as if it is heading for a typical dénouement, with either the offender being caught out and his guilt revealed or a simple confession. Neither happens. Clark tells Curles that they have the evidence, his finger prints are on the car. But, Curles replies, the prints got there because under instructions from Inspector Connell, he looked the car over when it was first brought in: Clark's case has collapsed. He says to Curles, 'You think you've covered all the angles' to which Curles replies, 'You're the detectives, prove it.' The image freezes on a still of a medium close-up of Clark turning his head to look, in dismay, at Connell. Fade to black and the credits roll. Not all episodes ended in this way, but the element of unpredictability was one of the series attractions. Whether or not Clark and his team prevailed and they 'got their man', there was a sense in the series that they were confronting powerful forces against which simple powers of deduction were inadequate. The series was produced by Tony Garnett who, in the 1960s, produced the controversial drama, *Cathy Come Home*.

Garnett, with the same independent production company, World Productions, went on to make an even more abrasive police drama. *The Cops* (BBC 1998–99) was set in and around a northern urban police station. It was structured like *Z Cars* and *The Bill*, but most of the similarities end there. Like its predecessors, it was based around a police station and a large number of characters. It had a multi-strand narrative structure, oscillating between the personal and professional lives of the officers. It was shot in a distinctive documentary style, emulating the look of cinema verité, with a hand held camera constantly zooming and shifting focus as it seemingly attempted to 'capture' real events as they unfolded. The content was uncompromising, showing in stark detail the problems of policing a run-down inner city area. The police were shown to be as erratic in their personal behaviour as anyone, but also doing an almost impossible job.

The first episode opens with a cluster of girls crowded in a night club lavatory. Shot in a 'raw' documentary style, the shifting camera settles briefly on one girl as she 'snorts' cocaine. Outside on the dance floor she is alerted to the fact that it is 5 a.m. Alarmed, she races out to a taxi with the camera precariously chasing after her. Scrambling from the taxi, with the camera in jerky pursuit, she is seen hurtling towards what appears to be a block of flats. As she darts through a couple of rooms and corridors, it suddenly becomes evident that not only is she in a police station, but she is, herself, a probationary police officer, P.C. Melanie Draper. This unconventional opening set the tone for the whole series.

Structurally the first episode is reminiscent of *Four of a Kind*, the opening episode of *Z Cars*. It served the same function of introducing a number of key characters through a series of parallel narrative threads. One difference between this episode and *Four of a Kind* is the more complex relationship between each of the narratives; there is not only constant cross-cutting between them, but they also interlock. (see Chapter 2). Police drama will probably always be a scheduling staple, partly because we all enjoy encountering the forbidden and dangerous. There is the pleasure and reassurance of a problem neatly resolved and a different kind of pleasure when it is not. Producers like police drama for the reason they like all genre: it provides a ready made production template. Writers and actors like them because of the darker recesses of experience that they can imaginatively explore.

ESSAY QUESTIONS

1 What devices do soap operas/police dramas employ to achieve 'realism'?

2 How would you account for the fascination that soap operas hold for such a large and diverse audience? (OCR, 1996)

3 Compare the representation of any social group of your choice in two or more different soap operas. (OCR, 1998)

4 Why does police drama continue to have such a prominent place in television schedules?

5 Discuss the notion that the most interesting police dramas blur the distinction between right and wrong.

SHORT ANSWER QUESTIONS

1 Why are soaps called soaps?
2 Bullet point the basic features of a soap.
3 Make notes on what the differences are between *Dixon of Dock Green* and *The Cops*?
4 Bullet point the main generic features of police drama.
5 Make notes on the main features that differentiate British and Australian soaps.

FOLLOW UP WORK

1 Several soap operas are now heavily 'trailed' on television. What aspects of these soaps are foregrounded by the trailers.

2 With a storyboard or script, devise your own trailer for a soap opera.

3 Write a brief treatment for a new police drama about either the fraud squad or dog handlers. Devise three or four main characters.

4 What features would you highlight in order to make your programme attractive to a potential production company.

5 Choose any one scene in any soap featuring a male character. Re-write the scene as if the character was a women? Would you have to change any of the character's traits?

6
DOCUMENTARY

If the term is interpreted in its broadest sense, the first films were documentaries of a sort. When the Lumière brothers gave one of the earliest demonstrations of cinema at the Grande Café, Paris on the 28th December 1895, all but one of the short films they screened were documentaries in so far as they were filmed records of actual events. In fact this kind of film became, for awhile, popular and they were known as 'actualities'. But they were not documentaries in the sense the term is generally used, as beyond showing an image of, for example, a train entering a station, a small boat being rowed out into a choppy sea, etc., they did not have anything to 'say'. Today those films do not provide us with any more knowledge about the late 19th century than surviving photographs; we have images of dress and architecture, etc., but little more. Important as they are in the development of cinema, they are nothing more than animated photographs.

Films closer to our understanding of documentaries were not long in arriving however. Before the end of the first decade of the 20th century, several of what would certainly be described now as documentaries were made in America, the UK and mainland Europe. Examples would be *A Visit to Peak Frean* (1906) and *Day in the Life of a Coal Miner* (1910). They are recognizable as documentary films both in their form and their intentions.

What does the term 'documentary' actually mean? In his book *Claiming the Real* (1995) Brian Winston usefully traces the origins of the word.

The first recorded use of the term 'documentary' is said to have been made by John Grierson in 1926 when he wrote a piece about Robert Flaherty's *Moana* for a New York Newspaper, claiming it had 'documentary value'. Grierson, himself, came to documentary film making almost by chance. At the time Grierson was in America (from 1924 to 1926) studying the formation of public opinion. Grierson was influenced by Walter Lipmann's somewhat pessimistic critique of democracy based on a perception that the ordinary voter was unable to make informed decisions because of a lack of information. He had occasion to complain to Lipmann about the difficulties he was having in researching the press. Lipmann suggested that he tried film.

Grierson does not seem to have been too concerned which of the mass media he studied, and so off he went to the West Coast where he met Chaplin, Von Sternberg and Von Stroheim. As far as Grierson was concerned, film was the answer to the problem. He saw it as being a way of speaking directly to thousands of people and a potentially very powerful instrument of education

> In English, the adjective 'documentary' was coined late, by 1802. The modern meaning of its source word 'document', is something 'written, inscribed, etc., which furnishes evidence or information' dates from only 1727. The word itself is derived from document a lesson, and enters the language with that meaning by 1450.
>
> *(Winston, p.11)*

and consequently a means of social progress. It was in the sense of revealing something about the world, that Grierson understood 'documentary value'. In the 1920s, this was not new as the Soviet Union had already discovered the power of film as an educational and propaganda tool.

Documentary form

Nichols in his book *Representing Reality* describes four basic documentary forms: expository, observational, interactive and reflexive. Nichols shows that each is dependent upon a different view of the nature of the documentary image and its relationship to reality.

The expository mode

This is the most common form of television documentary. Its most striking feature is the use of voice-over narration. The narrator may or may not be in frame, but is nevertheless, speaking directly to the audience. Other characteristics employed by this form are very familiar to anyone who has seen a conventional television documentary; indeed they are employed by television news. The expository documentary usually draws upon photographs, letters, official documents, newspapers, diaries and so on, in other words, the kind of evidence used by journalists and historians. The function of the narration is to harness this 'evidence' to the service of whatever case or argument the film is making. That is, after all, what 'expository' means – to make an exposition, 'an explanation or commentary'. The relationship between narration and the ancillary evidence is reciprocal: the narration is endorsed by the evidence, and in turn the evidence is validated by the narration. Such documentaries rarely allow the audience room to question either the apparently 'objective' evidence being offered or the legitimacy of the narration. It can only be accepted or rejected at face value and cannot be argued with or interrogated.

The Falklands War is an example of an expository documentary. It was a four part documentary series made by the BBC in 1992, ten years after the war. It sets out its agenda in the title of the opening episode: *An Unnecessary War*. Each episode commences with a title sequence. First the title, *The Falklands War* comes up over a blue map of the South Atlantic. This is followed by a brief sequence that neatly encapsulates the course of the war, from images of the initial invasion, to a British flag being raised. A sequence of images of the island ends with a series of three shots, sequenced as jump cuts, of the Falklands military cemetery. It is not that this or any other such film is not 'truthful', rather that they offer a *version* of the truth, a 'take' on it with which other journalists, historians, etc., can (and do) argue with.

The observational mode

Another widely broadcast form of documentary is the observational mode. In the mid-1990s this form of documentary became ever more popular. Observational cinema attempts to record events as they unfold with the minimum interference by the film maker. These films are seductively realistic and it is easy to understand why fiction film makers have adopted the stylistic traits of these films to make their own appear more authentic.

Direct cinema

Direct cinema was essentially a journalistic enterprise. A group of filmmakers in the 1960s, funded by *Time-Life*, made a series of frequently controversial films that would prove to be immensely influential, not only on documentary film making, but also on fiction film. The group was the Drew Associates who included Robert Drew, Richard Leacock, David and Albert Maysles and Don Pennebaker. Over time the leading protagonist of direct cinema modified the claims they made for it, but it is clear that in its earliest manifestation there was a clear aim: to capture unmediated reality, directly, through the camera lens with minimum intervention by the film maker. Direct cinema was an attempt to record '....life observed by the camera rather than, as is the case with most documentaries, life recreated for it.' (Taylor, C., 1971, p.571). The film maker Don Pennebaker is even more explicit about the camera's ability to capture reality: 'It's possible to go to a situation and simply film what you see there, what happens, what goes on...' (cited in Winston, p.149).

The first film made by the Drew Associates was *Primary* (1960) which seemed to be new because of its apparent immediacy and the access to political inner circles granted to the Drew Associates. The film follows the 1960 Wisconsin Democratic primary election battle between John Kennedy and Hubert Humphrey. The film has the appearance of objectivity. Much of it was shot in available light and with synchronised sound, including shots of Humphrey in a car. Winston shows, however, that the film is not as 'immediate' as it might seem.

The apparent newness of this, masked the fact that *Primary*, in some respects at least, was in a direct line of continuity from Grierson. Leaving aside the question of manipulation, as Winston points out, the politics of *Primary* are hidden, just as with the Grierson documentaries of the 1930s, such as *Housing Problems* and *Night Mail*, there is no social and political analysis, just a kind of description. To be fair to Grierson and the filmmakers who worked with him, even this had some value, especially with a film such as *Housing Problems*, as it revealed to many an image of poverty they did not know existed. For Grierson that would have been the point of the film.

> This is true of the film's most famous moment, the *locus classicus* of the direct cinema 'follow-the-subject shot' – a 75 second unbroken take of Kennedy pressing the flesh as he makes his way through a crowd to a stage. The camera is held high over the operator's head and an extreme wide-angle lens captures the candidate, centre screen, with people reaching to him from either side. Whistling and chatter is heard and snatches of talk: 'Ah! Ah! I can't wash my hands', and the like. Yet this, the classic demonstration of what could apparently be done with the new equipment, is not actually a synch shot. Rather, it demonstrates what Jeanne Hall has called (1991, p.30) 'a strategy of (direct cinema) self validation' involving 'the paring of asynchronous sounds and images for conventionally realistic effects'.
>
> *(Winston, p.152)*

Direct cinema in the 1960s was essentially dramatic. It sought out subjects that had an inherent quality of dramatic tension, a 'crisis structure'. *Primary*, of course, was a good example. Others included *The Chair*, which followed through the final appeal of a condemned man. This has inevitably carried over into television observational documentary, where some kind of narrative 'hook' is needed to retain an audience. In *Driving School* (BBC, 1997) one of the central characters was Maureen, who clearly did not find the business of learning to drive particularly easy. Her efforts formed a unifying element across the whole series, which featured many other learner drivers.

The interactive mode

The interactive mode of documentary is a form of observational cinema, but the emphasis is much more on the relationship between the film maker and the subject. If the relationship of direct cinema to reality is one of *observer*, with the interactive mode, it is one of *participant observer*. In its purest form, direct cinema attempts to record an event as it unfolds, without any intervention on the part of the film maker. The event has a reality separate and distinct from the film maker who is merely an objective observer. The interactive film maker (cinéma vérité) takes a different view as s/he regards the activity of film making as *changing* the reality being observed. Something is being observed, but that *something* is not what would have been had the film maker with his/her camera not been there. The filmmaker, in a very real sense, is *making* the film. Through the process of selection and decision making that s/he must go through, beginning with the choice of subject, followed by the detail of what to film, angle of vision of the camera, what is in or out of frame and so on, s/he is undertaking 'the creativity treatment of actuality'.

CASE STUDY

The Cruise

The Cruise is an interesting example of observational cinema. It is an example of 'docu-soap'. By the end of 1998 the term was widely used to describe a form of observational documentary that through its emphasis on character and narrative continuity, had some formal similarities with soap opera:

- one primary location
- a group of main characters
- continuous narrative(s)
- several plot-lines

The cruise necessarily has one primary location – the ship itself. There are, as in 'soaps', others and these are the ports visited by the cruise. There is a small group of main characters who appear in several episodes. These tend to be people employed on the ship, mainly in service roles, rather than as crew. The actual working of the ship is largely absent. The captain has a brief appearance in the first episode, but is not seen again. Other members of the crew are only occasionally glimpsed but they do not form part of the continuing narrative. This is because the series is not about the running of the ship (as a more traditional documentary might have been). It is not even really about a community, rather, it is about individuals who happen to be living and working on the ship. The focus is on their personal dramas; their aspirations and struggles and that becomes the point of identity between the audience and character. As in 'soaps', they are ordinary people made extraordinary by television. They seem comfortably familiar – they are like 'us' – yet at they same time the are transformed by the circumstance of being on the ship in the first place and being on television.

Figure 6.1 The Cruise: *'docu-soap'*   *Source:* © *BBC*

As with all docu-soaps, the characters we get to 'know' are those who have been picked out by the film makers, because they are 'telegenic'. This is an inevitable part of the process. One of the best ways of structuring such a series is do so around a few key figures. Virtually all 'docu-soaps' are worked around personalities as seen in *Driving School, Hotel, The Clampers, The Vets, Airport, Paddington Green,* etc. The frequency of some people making careers based on their appearance in a 'docu-soap' is quite high. When a new programme is transmitted, the game is to spot the new star. For example, Jane MacDonald's singing career was given a considerable boost. Several have made television appearances on chat and game shows, invited to do so for no other reason than being famous for being famous. The basis of this is the power of television to create the illusion experienced by audiences that they know the personalities that appear on their screens and in other media.

Formally, *The Cruise* is an example of the observational mode. It sets out to be a filmed account of a cruise ship and some of the people who live and work in it. However, it is a long way from the direct cinema of Leacock and Wiseman (an American documentary maker). It bears traces of the formal characteristics of all four of Bill Nichols documentary modes. In any one episode there are features that are expository, observational, interactive and, occasionally, reflexive.

Double or quits

Each episode begins by drawing attention to the 'soap' elements of *The Cruise* with a title sequence consisting of shots of the ship with superimposed ringed close-ups of the individuals featured in that particular episode. *In Double or Quits* (1998) for example, we have 'Starring Jane MacDonald' followed by Dale and Mary Nathan together and Edwin Consalves. These are the main characters in this episode. Jane MacDonald, a singer contracted as a ship's entertainer, was one of the few characters who was in the whole series. The main narrative interest built around her was, will she be a success? Dale and Mary Nathan were in several episodes: they worked in the ship's casino. Edwin Consalves was a steward. The element of a continuing narrative is made evident from the beginning. A sub-title 'the story so far' appears on the screen and a voice-over introduces the episode, saying that for passengers and crew alike 'life is unfolding like a drama...'.

One of the distinguishing features of observational documentary is the long take. There are obvious practical reasons for this. *In situ*, with only one camera, and not knowing how a situation is going to develop, there is a tendency to hold a shot for some time and this is frequently reflected in the editing. But this was not so with *The Cruise* where one of the formal novelties is the way that rapidly cut sequences are constructed. Stylistically, this is reminiscent of fiction rather than observational documentary. Such a sequence opens the *Double or Quits* episode, serving the function of introducing the main characters and establishing the 'narrative'. Jane MacDonald, Dale and Mary Nathan and Edwin Gonsalves are shown in quick succession. MacDonald is shown with Tarot cards; Dale is shown in the casino, working on a slot-machine ('I'm vandalising this machine!'); Dale and Mary are shown in their cabin, commenting on the day. Next is an exterior shot of the ship moored at the quay side. This is followed by a high, overhead shot looking directly down on a line of five musicians. Most of what follows is a fairly rapidly cut sequence moving alternately from shots of Edwin and crew members shifting luggage, to Jane MacDonald in her cabin and Dale and Mary Nathan in theirs.

Throughout, characters address the camera with accustomed informality. This can be seen to be functioning both interactively as there is a constant exchange between the film maker and his 'subjects'. But watching the film, we are aware that we are watching a reality that is not the same reality had the camera not been there. There is a moment, for example, when Jane MacDonald goes to her door and lets in a women friend. They both walk back from the cabin door and speak very casually to the camera man, McDonald's friend smiling and saying a friendly hello. The camera follows them to the right where its reflection is caught in a mirror. Here the documentary filmmaker is a kind of participant observer; his presence is acknowledged not merely in the relatively trivial sense of being seen in a mirror, but in the way he is seen to impinge upon the event, to show us a reality that includes the camera rather than pretending that it is not there. Later in the film, Jane McDonald is preparing for a performance. She has been talking to the cameraman all the time, when she has a problem pulling up the zip at the back of her dress. Suddenly, from the bottom of frame, a hand thrusts forwards and pulls up the offending zip: it is, of course, the cameraman and provides a delightful moment of reflexivity.

The reflexive mode

This is the most challenging of Nichols' four documentary modes. These are films that eschew the dominant conventions of film and television. Film makers such as Jean Luc Godard consider that *form* itself is an embodiment of certain ideological positions. Naturalism, in documentary and fiction, with its ordered and linear patterns of narrative and its coherent visual structures implies a way of looking both at the world and reality itself. The audience is encouraged to perceive the text as a *reflection* of reality rather than as a specific representation based upon certain visual and narrative codes and conventions. Reflexive films draw attention to themselves as artefacts. In so doing they attempt to make problematic the relationship between the film and the reality it seeks to examine. An example of this kind of film making is *The Thin Blue Line*.

The Thin Blue Line

On the face of it, *The Thin Blue Line*, which was made in 1988 by Errol Morris, appears to be a straight forward expository documentary employing the usual techniques, including extensive interviews and a comprehensive package of objective evidence such as newspaper cuttings, photographs, a coroner's report and much more besides. It is a documentary that appears to be testing out the claims made by two people who were allegedly involved in the murder of a police officer. One is Randall Adams, who was serving a life sentence for the killing at the time the film was made and David Harris, who was too young to be indicted with first degree murder, but was anyway in prison for a subsequent crime. It is, however, the very notion of a documentary film being able to provide unambiguous truth that Morris sets out to question. *The Thin Blue Line* is not so much an investigative film in search of the truth, as a demonstration that 'truth' is very elusive. The apparent 'objectivity' of the evidence disintegrates as the film progresses.

Figure 6.2 *Scene from* The Thin Blue Line
Source: BFI

The film opens with an unidentified man wearing a white shirt describing events that happened to him one night in 1976. It becomes apparent that this is Randall Adams who had been convicted of the murder of a police officer. The way it becomes apparent is by carefully listening to what is said and placing it within the context of what the viewer already knows about the case. It is reasonable to presume that an audience will not see the film without knowing something about it, through reviews, publicity or word-of-mouth. The whole film works in this way. Unusually for a documentary, characters are not identified and the audience has to deduce who they are from what they say. Therein lies the reason for such a strategy. The audience has to *work*: to listen and watch very carefully, taking nothing for granted.

The film is equally enigmatic visually. It is unusually stylised. Early in the film there is a sequence showing the exterior of some modern buildings. The way these buildings are framed accentuates their geometric shapes. In each shot there are intense blues and touches of red which effectively colour codes them. These shots are so stylized that they appear as abstract shapes, an impression reinforced by Philip Glass' hypnotic sound track. The buildings cease to be buildings, but become abstract images, mysterious configurations of line and colour. It could be argued, however, that it works the other way around; that it is as abstractions that these images are *first* seen and it is only through actively looking at them that they begin to take on the form of buildings. Either way, the acute level of aesthetisization in *The Thin Blue Line* is, in itself, a reflexive device. Throughout the film our attention is drawn to its status as an *aesthetic* object rather than a *real* object. This is further borne out in the 'reconstructions' shown in the film. There are eight in all, each one a reconstruction of the same incident (the killing of the police officer) yet each one is different. Not only is each version different (each one challenging the authenticity of the others) but, again, they are highly stylised, using the same reds and blues. The brooding, atmospheric lighting and oblique camera angles give each version of the reconstruction a noirish, impressionistic quality, far removed from conventional documentary images. Just as each reconstruction is different, so is each witnesses' account of events.

Adams initial description of what happened to him when he was arrested and interrogated is immediately contradicted in almost every detail by the interrogating officer. The two versions are simply juxtaposed, leaving the audience to sort it in their own minds. The entire film, and it runs for ninety minutes, is an extended series of 'talking heads' that provide us with a rich concoction of 'facts', 'evidence' and witnesses' accounts that fail to add up to a single, unified truth: and therein lies the point of the film. Morris constructs a mosaic of mutually contradicting versions of the murder, offering little in the film by way of certainty that an audience can hold onto. Even Harris' 'confession' at the end is ambiguous, although an audience will find it difficult not to conclude that he was the killer. Paradoxically, given the way the film questions the nature of evidence, *The Thin Blue Line* was instrumental in bringing about the quashing of Adams' conviction and his subsequent release in 1989.

Bill Nichols wrote of Morris and *The Thin Blue Line:*

.... by 'baring the device' and making the process by which truth is constructed more evident, by showing how multiple truths based on different assumptions and motivations contend with one another, he may be inviting us to draw our own conclusions on the basis of facts and stories that do not readily admit of unequivocal resolution into a single truth. Randall Adams may indeed be innocent, but the film invites us to experience the uncertainty that licenses divergent narratives of explanation for anyone without firsthand knowledge of the original event. Morris refrains from using the power of the photographic image to appear to certify (through "authentic" re-enactments) a degree of certainty that remains unassailable outside the cinema.

(Nichols, B., Representing Reality,
Indiana University Press, 1991 p.101)

Reflexive films like *The Thin Blue Line* challenge the dominant, positivist view of knowledge and reality. 'Facts' are understood to be free-floating, anterior entities that are objectively verifiable. Historiography teaches something different about 'facts' and that is that they are not necessarily value free or ideologically 'innocent': they are subject to interpretation. The way 'facts' are presented or 'packaged' can determine how they are interpreted and understood. In any case, 'facts' about events – and people – are forever changing. Take any historical event and our knowledge of it has constantly changed. What then, of our belief in the epistemological inviolability of documentary? How can it present *the* 'truth'?

Drama documentary

Drama documentary means 'dramatised documentary', in other words an approach to documentary film making that involves a measure of dramatisation. On the face of it, that would seem simple enough, but few television forms have provoked more controversy, usually over the issue of the mixing of fact and fiction. Yet documentary films have always employed elements of dramatic reconstruction.

Dramatised documentary is perhaps the dominant way of representing history within popular culture. It is not difficult to see why. When dealing with events where participants are no longer alive, or for whatever reason are reluctant to participate, dramatised reconstruction is a workable solution. Alternatively, one might opt for a different approach and that is to make a film which, whilst not based on actual events, is a fictional narrative representative of events, characters and conditions which actually do exist. In other words, the film is *typical* or what happens in reality. As with dramatised reconstruction, this kind of film has a long pedigree. 'Progressive realism', 'social realism', 'documentary drama' are terms variously applied to this kind of film. They are generally (but not always) fictions rooted in contemporary reality. Generally associated with television, this is another documentary based genre that started in cinema. It was fully developed by the 1940s and became an important facet of war-time British cinema. A large number of British films of the period were, for all intents and purposes, documentary dramas, with the explicit intent of representing aspects of live, social reality. Examples are *Love on the Dole* (1941) and *Millions Like Us* (1943).

With Humphrey Jennings' *I Was a Fireman* (1943) (also known as *Fires Were Started*) we have something closer to a contemporary idea of documentary drama. Although not based on a particular incident, the film sets out to portray the typical conditions and events that beset the Auxiliary Fires Service of the early 1940s. Jennings used real firemen rather than actors and managed to achieve a convincing sense of authenticity. In films of this type, the realistic quality of the image is as important as it is in more conventional documentary. The point is to create the illusion of reality. Such films declare, through various realist devices (location shooting, available light, etc.), that what is being seen is *similar* to the actual reality.

A distinction has been drawn by John Caughie between 'dramatised documentary' which are films based on actual events and 'documentary drama' which is fiction, but made with a 'documentary look.' A further documentary claim is sometimes made on behalf of documentary drama makers insofar as it refers to some aspect of social reality, usually by invoking the notion of 'typicality'. In such films, fictional characters and events are intended to be representative of such people and events that really do exist. Up to a point this distinction works. The films of Leslie Woodhead, made at Granada, such as *Why Lockerbie?* are clearly based on actual events. *Why Lockerbie?* was a serious piece of journalism, a drama documentary investigating the circumstances of the disaster.

Likewise, Peter Watkins *Culloden* (1964) is based on a rigorously researched account of the battle. On the other hand, *Cathy Come Home* (1966) was a drama based on the appalling conditions endured by the homeless in the 1960s. The characters and events were fictional but the circumstances and conditions these fictional characters were seen to endure were *typical* of what was actually happening in society at the time. Likewise, *The Spongers* (1978) and *United Kingdom* (1981) appeal to anterior reality through typicality and a style reminiscent of observational documentary. The casting and acting style of these films were also distinctive. These films were cast with largely unknowns. Ken Loach still has this approach to casting and also using actors who have regularly appeared in social realist dramas. Actors thus cast do not bring to the films any baggage of previous performances: for the audience the actor and character are as one.

CASE STUDY

There are films that challenge the distinction between drama documentary and documentary drama. Peter Watkins' film, *The War Game* (1965) is a case in point. *The War Game* is certainly fictional and is about a nuclear attack on Kent. But its research credentials are impeccable. It is based on data from nuclear tests, the attacks on Hiroshima and Nagasaki, and the massive bomber raids on Dresden and Hamburg in WW2.

In its style it is more like a documentary than a drama (in the credits Watkins refers to the film as a documentary). Throughout the film, there is voice over narration superimposed over grainy, verite type footage of seemingly actual events unfolding in front of the camera. Its degree of realism is uncompromising and, even today, some of the scene of the attack itself and the immediate aftermath can still be disturbing. The film was in fact denied a screening by the then Director General, Hugh Green.

Watkins' method, however, is to not allow the audience to become immersed in the horror. Throughout the film, distancing devices are employed to confront the audience with the issues at stake. An example is during the truly horrific fire-storm sequence. As a women slowly drops to the ground amidst a vision of hell worthy of Dante, the audience is suddenly confronted with the question of retaliation. There is a short sequence of 'vox pop' talking heads of people giving their views on whether or not it would be right to respond, and 'kill people in this way.' Similar devices are used throughout the film. All the way through the audience is forced to consider the events unfolding in a broader context. There is a cut to an expert who speaks of post-war preparations being made for World Wars 3, 4 and 5. Another shows a clergyman, introducing a moral dimension, paraphrasing 'If I hit or kill a man I am responsible; the situation does not change if people are killed in my name and on my behalf.' The film is also 'interrupted' with a great deal of statistical information, the implications of which are forcefully presented in the film.

There are relatively few major drama documentaries compared with the number of 'straight' documentaries. Two films made by Granada, *Who Bombed Birmingham?* and *An Explosion of Guilt* made a real contribution to the quashing of the convictions (after seventeen years imprisonment) of the 'Birmingham six'. What was novel about these two films, both about the same subject, was that the former was a 'straight' documentary whilst the other one was a drama documentary. The choice of form depends on a number of factors including the nature of the evidence available and the audience/market the film is aimed at. Some drama documentaries made for television, have had a cinematic quality including well known actors, lavish sets and locations and generally very high production values. These tend to be films, like *Lockerbie*, that are very expensive to make and need to recoup their costs, if not make a profit, through overseas sales.

ESSAY QUESTIONS

1 Observational documentary is more realistic and truthful than conventional expository documentary. Discuss.

2 Discussing actual examples, why would a film/programme maker make a drama documentary rather than a 'straight' documentary?

3 What stylistic elements of documentary film have been appropriated by fiction film makers and why? Give examples.

4 What has been the impact on documentary film making of direct cinema in the 1960s.

5 What differences are there in the philosophy and approach of the Drew Associates and Grierson?

SHORT ANSWER QUESTIONS

1 How many docu-soaps or other observational documentaries are there on television this week.

2 What might have made them attractive to producers and audiences?

3 Who, allegedly, coined the term 'documentary' and what did this person mean by it?

4 What are Nichols four documentary forms?

5 What is a 'docu-soup'?

FOLLOW UP WORK

1 Choose a subject and produce/script two documentary sequences: one giving it a positive representation and the other a negative representation.

2 Take a segment from any drama-documentary you have seen and, in script form, turn it into a sequence from a conventional expository documentary.

3 In what ways do documentary/drama documentary films create their realism?

4 Argue for and against the proposition that docu-soaps are not legitimate documentary films but just a prurient form of light entertainment.

5 Using examples, discuss the difference between drama documentary and documentary drama.

7
TELEVISION NEWS

Television, for many, is the primary source of news and is the most trusted. It took a relatively long time for television news to develop into a form that would be recognisable today. Even when television was reintroduced in 1946, radio was regarded as the 'natural' medium for the presentation of news. There had been no pre-war television news other than, with the agreement of Movietone and Gaumont-British Film Companies, two newsreels that were screened twice a week. Fearing competition from television, this arrangement was not reintroduced after the war. In 1946, when television was reintroduced, since they could not use cinema newsreel, the BBC started to produce their own. There was an emphasis on pictures for their own sake. The stories covered included rescues at sea, rail crashes, fires and earthquakes. There was a stress on actuality and wherever possible live sound was recorded with speech or background noises recorded on the spot. One Newsreel Manager, Harold Cox, drew a distinction between 'newsreel' and the 'news bulletin': the former placed an emphasis on pictorial values and the latter on news values.

The early days

If anything, early television news, prior to these newsreels, was no more than illustrated radio bulletins. There was nothing distinctively 'televisual' about them. They were introduced by a disembodied voice, reading over a still of the BBC icon and presenters were never used. From January 1948, these bulletins were supplemented with a newsreel. The oddity at this stage, though, was that whilst the News Division at Broadcasting House was producing the news bulletin, the newsreel was being made by the Television Film Department at Alexandra Palace. In July 1954, the News Division gained control of newsreels. This meant that for the first time BBC News was making its own visual material. The title of the evening news programme was changed to *News and Newsreel* and lasted for twenty minutes.

The first BBC Television News Editor was Tahu Hole, who was regarded as being rather cautious and as 'a man of rigid views on the sanctity of news and the importance of keeping it undefiled by such things as persons'. Definitely a man of the 'old school', Hole must have looked wistfully back at the pre-war days when announcers were never identified and wore dinner jackets. The practice of identifying news readers was introduced on radio at the start of WW2, largely as a security measure in case of invasion; presumably an early sign of the BBC being overrun by an invading force would be the strange voice reading the news. The BBC was for a long time, 'word' bound and Hole was placed firmly in that tradition. Images were not so much distrusted, as associated with the trivial. The development of news on television was also not helped by opposition from radio reporters to the introduction of television techniques. Television news would remain in the shadow of radio news until the introduction of ITN in the mid-1950s.

What news was like at this time is described by Burton Paulu.

Paulu also writes of the impersonal, sober, and quiet manner of the newsreader, a reflection, as Schlesinger, notes 'of the revived policy of anonymous news reading, which, in radio, was to last until 1963. The style was like a foreign office communiqué.....Human interest and accident stories never take precedence over or crowd out significant developments, BBC news programmes never become entertainment broadcasts; "shows" are never built around personalities...'

> In the main, programs are devoted to international and foreign events – including much news from the United States, especially if it relates to the United Kingdom; news of the British Commonwealth; home, political, and industrial events; significant developments in literature,the arts, science and other fields of learning; and the activities of the royal family (though the BBC does not report, while still in the gossip stage, such things as Edward VIII's abdication or Princess Margaret's romance with Peter Townsend).
>
> *(Paulu, B. in* Putting Reality Together, *R. Schiesinger (ed.), 1978, pp. 160–162)*

The potential television had for reporting events was, as we have already seen, strikingly realised with the coronation of Elizabeth II. This was not the first time the BBC had covered such an event. In 1936 the coronation of George VI naturally generated much interest at the time and did something to promote an upsurge in television receiver sales. It was, however, not covered on the same scale as in 1953 and television cameras were not allowed in Westminster Abbey. But the real shock to the BBC's news service came in 1955 when independent television started its own news service, ITN (Independent Television News) and what became its flagship programme until 8th March 1999, *News at Ten*.

The arrival of *News at Ten*

News at Ten began in May 1955. Its first editor was a journalist and former MP, Aidan Crawley. He had been impressed by the very different attitude towards news in the USA, with its use of personalities and often dramatic 'actuality' footage, and sought to instil some of these traits into ITN news programmes. He claimed that 'still pictures would never be shown; everything would be live'. *Year One* (Granada, p.28). Of the team he put together, many would rapidly become household names like Robin Day, Christopher Chataway and Barbara Mandell. Crawley also introduced into British Television News something of the American way of working. He was particularly influenced by the news practices and styles of ABC and CBS, which were a long way from the stiff formality of the BBC. In the BBC the announcer did nothing other than read the news. At ITN they were actively involved in its production, sometimes working as journalists (as in Robin Day's ground breaking interview of Egypt's President Nasser in 1956) but always being involved in the preparation of the bulletins. They were referred to as 'newscasters' not 'newsreaders' in order to suggest this greater involvement. ITN was also less deferential when interviewing public figures such as politicians and heads of state.

An example of ITN's new style came in 1957. After the abortive invasion

For Day, too, the interview was a triumph, proving that the ITN style would be applied even to the heads of state. When Day asked whether Nasser accepted Israel's right to exist, the president accused him of 'jumping to conclusions'. No, Day replied, 'I am asking a question'.

(Wheen, F., Television, *Century Publishing, 1985 p.72)*

of Egypt by the British and French, ITN had a world exclusive when Robin Day interviewed the Egyptian president, Gamal Abdel Nasser. Only a few months before, the British and French had suffered a humiliating withdrawal having attempted to force Nasser to lift the blockade of the Suez Canal. The interview generated wide interest, as diplomatic relations between Britain and Egypt had yet to be restored. The interview was a clear demonstration of the new, combative style.

Television news became more populist with news beginning to acquire some of the values of 'entertainment'. The newscaster's 'professional grasp of his (*sic*) material, and his lively interest in it would make the news more authoritative and entertaining.' (Robin Day, quoted by Schlesinger 1987). ITN, in fact, made much of personalities. There was the athlete, Christopher Chataway, who held the world record for the mile and Ludovic Kennedy who drew attention to himself when he married the dancer, Moira Shearer. Other 'colourful' characters included Reginald Bosanquet who wore a toupee and slurred his speech. Later, in the 1970s, when Anna Ford became engaged to another journalist, it became a front-page story. In 1976 Angela Rippon got star billing on the *Morecambe and Wise Christmas Show* and the Daily Mirror devoted most of its front page to a picture of her in a high-split evening dress, doing a dance routine.

The ITN news bulletins began to contain more 'human interest' stories. The on-the-spot interview became much used and visual material was generally more lively. The fresher approach adopted by ITN, in particular *News at Ten*, meant that the BBC also had to adapt. In the early years of ITV, the BBC was losing its audience to its competitor. Presenters on BBC news first appeared in September 1955, but it was not until 1958 that major changes were made when Stuart Hood was made Head of News. The team of presenters he brought together included Robert Dougall, Richard Baker, Kenneth Kendall and Michael Aspel. These names, like their ITN counterparts, would soon become very familiar. The era of personality led news programmes on the BBC had begun.

Aside from the result that presenters were used for the first time, ITN impacted on BBC television news in other ways, as in style. In ITN:

Newscasters....were encouraged to write informally and use colloquialisms. Their voices lacked the clerical blandness of many BBC announcers. They were permitted touches of humour and even of disrespect....Their stories were illustrated by film shot in a more realistic way with more impact and above all more sound. The impact on both the profession and the public was sensational

(Hood, s. and Tabary-Petersson, T., On Television, *Pluto Press, 1997)*

For a while, ITN led the way, but it was not long before ITN and BBC news were on a par with each other. Ever since there has been a rivalry between them, each alternately stealing a march on the other.

News values

'News' is what journalists define as news, or to put that slightly differently, news which appears on the television, radio, Internet or in newspapers. Everyday, around the world, an uncountable number of events unfold but not all is 'news'. What is it that makes one event worthy of coverage by a journalist, but not another?

News values are the criteria by which journalists decide whether or not an event is 'newsworthy'. The degree to which a story matches these criteria will determine its relative importance and its position in a bulletin's running order. There have been several attempts to describe the characteristics of a 'news story'. The most influential was that undertaken by Johan Galtung and Mari Ruge, first published in 1965. Although Galtung and Ruge's research was carried out in the press, it is also applicable to television. They concluded that there are twelve basic criteria which journalists use to assess the newsworthiness of an event. The first eight can be applied universally, that is to say they are true of any news organisation anywhere in the world. The other four are mainly relevant in the west.

1. **Frequency** – the time-span taken by an event. Murders, catastrophic accidents, earthquakes, etc., take little time and their meaning is clear. They easily fall within the production cycle of the news media, especially now there is 24 hour radio and television news.
2. **Threshold** – the size or scale of an event. A small car crash will not attract much interest but a calamitous pile-up on a major motorway will. If an event falls below a certain threshold of size, it will not be reported 'more added drama is needed to keep it going' (Hartley, 1982, p.72). After the Gulf War in 1991, the Americans imposed a 'no fly zone ' in Northern Iraq to protect Kurds and to suppress any potential threat to US forces. At first, attacks by one side on the other were regularly reported but this stopped. In 1998/9 there were almost daily attacks by the US aircraft on Iraqi anti-aircraft and radar facilities. These were largely unreported and at the time of writing remain so: it will take a 'scaling up' of incidents before they register in the news again.
3. **Unambiguity** – the clarity of an event. The simpler and narrower the range of the possible meanings of an event, the more likely it is to be reported. To some extent this depends upon the news values of a particular news organisation. Broadsheets and *Newsnight* are more likely to report complex events than tabloids
4. **Meaningfulness** – events that accord with the culture of the news gatherers are more likely to be reported. Hartley (1982) gives an example: 'Islamic, third-world and oriental events may not be seen as self-evidently meaningful to western reporters.' Culturally remote events will be reported, however, if there is a measure of national interest. In 1999 Salmon Rushdie finally had the fatwa that had been imposed on him because of his book, *Satanic Verses*, lifted. Before the Rushdie affair, few people in the UK knew what a fatwa was or anything else about Islam.
5. **Consonance** – events which match our expectations are more likely to be selected. If the media expect violence at a demonstration, that is what will be reported. For example, the 'poll tax' demonstration in London in 1990 was reported, by most of the media (including television) almost entirely in terms of the violence.

6. **Unexpectedness** – so long as an event satisfies the criterion of meaningfulness, a rare or unexpected event is likely to be reported.
7. **Continuity** – once an event is covered, it will continue to be so, even if its importance diminishes.
8. **Composition** – news reports are generally balanced. Foreign stories will run with domestic stories. If there happen to be a lot of foreign stories (American, European, etc.) then a less significant domestic story will be included for the sake of balance.
9. **Reference to elite nations** – stories about countries important to the UK such as the US, the rest of Europe, Russia, China, etc. are more likely to be reported.
10. **Reference to elite persons** – even stories that would be normally judged to be insignificant will be covered if they concern an 'elite' person. For example if a Royal Prince breaks his leg it will be a 'story': if you break yours, it probably won't.
11. **Personalisation** – events are frequently explained in terms of the actions of individuals, who are easier to identity than faceless structures or forces. The Government, for example, often becomes just Tony Blair.
12. **Negativity** – bad news is good 'news'.

Television, however, has a 13th news value, which in the last few years has also become relevant to the print press, especially tabloids:

The primacy of the visual image – a story is more likely to be covered if it is accompanied by 'strong' pictures. In some instances it will assure the running of a story even if, in itself, it is not very significant. A good example of this was when the O.J. Simpson story broke. A one time successful American football player and film star, Simpson's wife had been found murdered. On the morning of this discovery, Simpson fled his house, beginning a long car chase. This was televised from a helicopter and these pictures screened live for some considerable time. Yet nothing was actually happening, other than a car being driven down a road. The hopeful anticipation was, of course, that something dramatic *would* happen. The story was *only* the pictures which could not tell the audience anymore than what was known already which was that Simpson was on the run.

The live story – *actuality* – has become a major factor in news coverage, both in television and radio. The problem with this kind of story is the extent it marks a shift from news as *analysis* to news as mere *spectacle*. News, thereby, becomes a means not of understanding events, but instead being entertained by them.

In addition to these general values, different newspapers and other news organisations will have their own news values depending on the market in which they are operating. The news values of an early evening news programme are different to those of *News Night* or the Channel Four evening news. Even more marked are the differences between the 'popular' press, such as *The Sun* and the 'quality' press such as *The Guardian*. *The Sun* places much more emphasis on human interest stories and entertainment. *The Guardian* will have more detailed political, economic and foreign news stories.

A brief history of war reporting

War reporting in the 1980s and 1990s has put many of the issues surrounding news into sharp focus. Questions of censorship, bias and the uses of technology (or not) were all controversial during the Falklands, Gulf and Kosovo wars.

Wars, in all cultures, have always been reported. Evidence for this lies in primitive cave paintings, the tombs of Egyptian pharaohs and the chronicles of numerous campaigns fought during the eras of classical Rome and Greece. These accounts would, however, be produced to praise the exploits of leaders or for some other propaganda purpose. War reporting as we now understand it, as an activity conducted by relatively impartial professionals, is a recent phenomenon.

The Crimean War (1854–1856)

This was the last major international conflict of the 19th century involving the UK. France and the UK were lined up against Russia, ostensibly in defence of Turkey, but really for the 'usual reasons' – national self interest. In some respects it was a curious conflict. On the one hand it was the last traditional war – involving sieges, lines of infantry confronting each other and, memorably, the rush of cavalry – and on the other it foreshadowed wars to come. It was not, after all, an opposing cavalry force that decimated the Light Cavalry: it was the destructive power of artillery. High-tech warfare was on the way.

The way wars were reported also changed. For the first time a major conflict was photographed. In terms of journalism the most memorable figure was William Howard Russell, the Special Correspondent despatched to the Crimea by *The Times*. He sent back a number of shocking reports critical of the way the war was being prosecuted and the conditions endured by the troops. There was no formal censorship: before Russell there had been no need so he was able to speak directly with anyone who was prepared to talk to him. Russell can be regarded as the first modern war reporter insofar as he was not a 'mouthpiece' for either British politicians or the army and was a professional journalist trying to report what he saw. Russell was aware of the problems in covering a war in which 'your side' is a participant. Journalism is always placed in a difficult position during a war. The needs of the journalist are often opposed to the needs of the military. The journalist seeks to *reveal* and the military to *conceal,* fearing that information may be published that is of use to the enemy. For both the military and politicians alike, there is an understandable tendency to hide mistakes and highlight successes.

Where does a journalist draw the line between telling the truth and the risk of undermining the war effort? Is the 'war effort' any business of a journalist at all?

Russell, himself, clearly struggled with these issues. In November 1854 he wrote from Sebastopol:

Although it may be dangerous to communicate facts likely to be of service to the Russians, it is certainly hazardous to conceal the truth from the British people. They must know, sooner or later, that the siege has been for many days practically suspended, that

our batteries are used up and silent, and that our army are (*sic*) much exhausted by the effects of excessive labour and watching, and by the wet and storm to which they have been so incessantly exposed.

(Hudson, M. and Stainer, J., War and the Media, *Sutton Publishing 1997 p.17)*

There was no formal censorship during wartime until WW1. In both the American Civil War and the Boer War, censorship as such was not needed as commanders did the same as Wellington – keep correspondents away from the front and insist that news came only from official sources. This did not happen in the Crimea because of the special status enjoyed by *The Times*, and Russell exploited it to the full. The freedom of movement, access to senior officers and the freedom of disclosure enjoyed by Russell would not happen again until the Vietnam War, and has not reoccurred in the UK media. Official censorship would be feature of all subsequent wars involving the British.

The First World War (1914–1918)

Photography was used first in the Crimea and the American Civil War. The Boer War was the first war to be filmed, but not very extensively. It was in WW1 that cinema really came into its own with films such as *The Battle of Somme* (1916) which were very popular. But these films had little to do with journalism: they were propaganda.

Figure 7.1 *A war photo, of the Battle of the Somme, staged by real soldiers, to send home*

The *Battle of the Somme* presents the battle as a glorious victory. In fact it was, at best, a marginal success and more like a stalemate. The film makes no reference to the cost, although it could not have been long before it became known. 60 000 British troops were killed or wounded by the end of the first day of a battle that would last from 1st July 1926 to November. Newspapers did little to tell the truth about this or any other battle. As one correspondent, Philip Gibbs, put it:

We identified ourselves absolutely with the army in the field... we wiped out of our minds all thoughts of personal scoops and all temptations to write one word which would make the task of the officers and men more difficult or dangerous....There was no need of censorship of our despatches. We were our own censors.

(Hudson and Stanier, p.47)

The feelings expressed here would be familiar to almost any correspondent operating in the field. For television, radio and print journalists alike, strong attachments often develop between themselves and the military. This is not surprising as they share the same conditions and risks but when it comes to writing a report, the task is to maintain professional detachment, which is not always easy.

The Second World War (1939–1945)

WW2 was the making of the BBC as radio became the dominant news service. BBC news expanded rapidly during the six years of conflict. At the beginning there were only a handful of correspondents. By its conclusion it had grown into the worlds largest news organisation. At D-Day, for the first time, BBC radio correspondents outnumbered the press and the media campaign was planned as carefully as the military one. The BBC had full co-operation from every section of the military; they had correspondents in bombers, gliders, landing craft, anywhere, in fact where a journalist, with his new piece of technology, the 'miniature', could find a place. The miniature was a small, portable recorder (not a tape recorder, this had not yet been invented) which recorded sound directly onto a record which then had to be played in a mobile transmitter.

The handling of news was more rigorously thought out during WW2 than it had been 20 or so years earlier. The Government had set up the Ministry of Information which had the dual role of managing censorship and propaganda. Every news organisation had its MOI 'minder' who censored every report. The policy had been adopted to tell the truth whenever possible and deliberately misleading propaganda was generally avoided. But censorship was strict. One BBC radio correspondent, Frank Gillard, who went over with mostly Canadian commandos on a disastrous raid on Dieppe in 1942, which resulted in terrible casualties, was not allowed to report what he saw. He had to give an upbeat account, which only talked about the air operations, the only aspect of the mission that was more-or-less successful.

But WW2 *was* different to previous wars. It was a war of national survival and the consequences of defeat were unthinkable. It is not surprising that every possible weapon was brought to bear to win it – including the media. It is very unlikely, however, that even a war such as WW2 would be reported in the way it was in the 1940s.

> To say that we are closer to victory today is to believe, in the face of evidence, the optimists who have been wrong in the past. To suggest we are on the edge of defeat is to yield to unreasonable pessimism. To say that we are mired in stalemate seems the only realistic, yet unsatisfactory conclusion.
>
> *(From 'Who, What, When, Where: Report from Vietnam by Walter Cronkite' cited in Hallin)*

Vietnam (1964–1975)

Vietnam was the first television war. Korea was covered by television, but to a much lesser extent and in any case, television ownership did not begin its rapid expansion until after that war. The USA were involved from 1964 until 1975, when they withdrew, defeated by the North Vietnam Army (NVA) and the Viet Cong (VC) which was largely a civilian guerrilla force. Television was blamed. Partly because the war began unofficially, with only a few 'advisers' being sent in 1964 to help train the South Vietnam Army, no formal system of censorship was ever put into place. By 1966 the USA was firmly committed to fighting the war. The 'spin' it used to justify their engagement was the 'domino theory' which claimed that if non-communist, USA-supporting South Vietnam fell to the communist north it would not stop there. Next would be Cambodia, Laos and then onto other Pacific rim countries. The 'nightmare scenario' was that America would be surrounded by communist regimes. History shows that it did not work out that way.

In the early 1960s there is evidence to show that most Americans supported the war. By 1968, when the Americans suffered a number of set backs, this scenario had changed. Opposition grew through the end of the 1960s into the early 1970s. For some embittered soldiers and politicians, the rot really set in when, on 27th February 1968, the highly respected journalist and CBS 'anchor man' Walter Cronkite reported from Vietnam that the Americans were in trouble. President Johnson is said to have remarked that, 'If I have lost Cronkite, I have lost America.' By 1975 it was all over.

Television was blamed because it allegedly undermined the will of the American people to continue to prosecute the war. Television screens were filled with often disturbing footage of combat and its consequences. However, experience from WW2 and Vietnam itself suggests that if a population supports the aims of a war it will tolerate casualties. In the case of Vietnam, it is probably the case that television *confirmed* many people's view that the war had to end, rather than *created* that view.

The Falklands War (1982)

When Britain undertook to oust an Argentinean Invasion force from the Falkland Islands in May 1982, the ghost of Vietnam stalked the minds of politicians and the military alike. The military, especially the navy, were opposed to the task force carrying any journalists at all. The army were less worried, in part because of their long experience dealing with the media in Northern Ireland which was effectively a combat zone. Notwithstanding an in-built hostility by the navy towards the media, there was a problem with time – everything happened very quickly.

The Argentinean invasion happened on Friday, 2nd April 1982. After an action lasting several hours, in which a detachment of Royal Marines managed to initially resist the Argentinean force, the islands were captured. Prior to this intelligence had alerted Downing Street that the invasion was imminent and the previous Wednesday, 31st March, the Prime Minister and her advisers had been told by the First Sea Lord, Sir Henry Leach, that a task force, if required, could be ready to sail within forty eight hours. On

Saturday, 3rd April, Parliament sat (for the first time on a Saturday since the Suez crisis of 1956) and the decision was made that, should negotiations fail, the islands would be forcefully recaptured. Orders were issued for the task force to sail and make best speed for the Falkland Islands. On Sunday the first ships, with troops and Special Forces aboard, left for the South Atlantic. The remainder of the task force was despatched on the Monday.

To begin with there were to be no journalists at all. After some forceful representations by the press to Downing Street, it was decided to send six journalists, apparently all chosen at random and in some haste. The media, however, were not appeased by this concession and after further expressions of outrage, the number was increased to twenty nine. No foreign journalists were allowed.

There was little time for preparation and most of the journalists were lucky if they had more than a few hours. A correspondent from *The Sun* turned up at Portsmouth in a pair of shorts astride his motor bike: hardly adequate for the South Atlantic!

Pressure in high places and forceful arguments had resulted in the Royal Navy allowing journalists to go with the task force but even then arrangements for the media continued to be controversial. Before giving an account of these, the point needs to be made that the Falklands War was extremely unusual, and probably unique. The media were absolutely dependent upon the military – without them they could get nowhere near the scene of battle. The journalists did not only rely on the military for getting there and getting their stories back to the UK but for food, clothing and everything else. Just as the task force was put together in a hurry, so were arrangements for reporting its activities. To begin with, both military and press did not believe that there would be a war. It is said that some Fleet Street editors sent relatively inexperienced people because they believed that before the task force reached the Falklands, the problem would be resolved and it would simply turn around and come back.

At the beginning of the conflict, the Ministry of Defence Public Relations department was in some disarray. It was a mix of military officers and civilian information officers. The civilian head had left, but had not yet been replaced so his position was filled by his deputy, Ian MacDonald. It had been decided to impose very tight control over the media in their coverage of the war both in the Falklands and at home. In the Falklands, all television and radio correspondents were attached to a civilian Public Relations Officer who had the responsibility of screening everything that was written or recorded. Newspaper journalists in turn, were attached to specific units. The only way they could despatch their copy or film to their respective news rooms was via the warships equipped with satellite transmission facilities. Throughout the conflict, there were no transmissions of television pictures. This has been controversial, some claiming that it was technically impossible; others that it was a deliberate policy of covert censorship.

> To have done so (transmit television pictures) was well within the state of the art at the time, but would have necessitated the use of a satellite to do so. Bernard Ingham, the Prime Minister's press secretary at the time, recalls that there were constant requests for time to be allocated on one of the satellites in use for communication with the task force. Lady Thatcher confirmed 'that there were far too many other important things for which the satellites were needed to justify their use for mere television pictures.' Whether this was a preconceived policy decision or one arrived at in haste can only be a speculation at this distance.
>
> *(Hudson and Stanier, p.175)*

Arrangements had been made for the Navy to use a civilian marine satellite, MARSAT for transmitting copy. Sending television pictures would, it seems, have involved sending sound and picture separately. Getting copy to the ships in the first place often depended on the goodwill of Navy helicopter pilots. Print journalists, once cleared, had their stories transmitted directly to their newspaper offices. Not so television.

Radio and television transmissions were sent to the MOD for further clearance before being allowed to be broadcast by the BBC and ITN. In London, press briefings were handled by Ian MacDonald. The trickle of news was often meagre and slow, causing resentful frustration amongst news editors.

On the 4th May 1982 a Royal Navy destroyer, The *Sheffield*, was sunk by an Excocet missile. The day before a nuclear attack submarine, *HMS Conqueror* had sunk the pride of the Argentinean navy, *The General Belgrano* and the *Sheffield* had been marked out for revenge. The sinking of the General Belgrano was an example of news management that later misfired. The story re-emerged some time later, much to the embarrassment of Margaret Thatcher and her Government (see Chapter 8 for more details). Few dispute, however, that she was a legitimate target.

The paucity of news gave rise to an unforeseen problem. 'Hard' news was so scarce that the media, especially television, began to rely on speculation. Normal television schedules were severely disrupted and the priority became news and current affairs programmes. But without solid information, television resorted to bringing into the studios numerous experts, typically retired senior officers or military academics, to speculate on the progress of the war and the moves that the opposing forces might make. It occurred to the MoD that some of the speculation was a little too accurate and there was the very real possibility that, inadvertently, Argentinean intelligence might have been given a helping hand.

Where they were given a helping hand was Goose Green. This has become a test case in how *not* to use the media and an excellent example of how tensions can arise between the politicians and the military, with the media in the middle. As the end of May approached, the British advance had stalled but too much delay would have put pressure on the British Government to accept a cease-fire that was not entirely advantageous. A military success was urgently needed. An attack on an isolated hamlet called Goose Green was ordered. On the 28th May, just as the 2nd Parachute Battalion (2 Para as they are generally known), were making their final preparations for the assault, they heard on the BBC World Service that British forces were about to attack Goose Green. Doubtless, the Argentineans were listening as well. The source of this leak and the motive for it has never been explained. Alistair Milne, the then Director General of the BBC, is adamant that it was a leak from the MoD. Others go further and claim that it was a leak from Downing Street done to alert the world that aggressive action was occurring and that Britain was not willing to compromise. Perhaps the timing was wrong; it will be a long time, if ever, before we find out what really happened. As it was, after a ferocious and costly battle, the paras prevailed, to find that they had been fighting a force far larger than intelligence had indicated.

The Falklands War was, of course, a success for the British. The way the media was handled, however, gave rise to much criticism. The lessons learned, along with America's experience a year later in the invasion of

Granada (they did not allow any civilian media at all) greatly influenced the reporting of the next major conflict: Iraq.

The Gulf War (1991)

The Gulf War embodied all that had been learned from previous conflicts about managing the media in a war. It is a model of how future wars are likely to be reported. It is almost certain that it would have been applied if the Kosovo conflict had deteriorated into a full-blown ground war. The Gulf War was also the first satellite war.

During the early morning of the 2nd August 1991, invoking what Saddam Hussein claimed to be a historical claim to the territory, the Iraqi army invaded Kuwait. There was no resistance and the Emir of Kuwait escaped by helicopter to neighbouring Saudi Arabia. Almost immediately the United Nations Security Council passed Resolution 660 which condemned the invasion and demanded an immediate withdrawal. This was not forthcoming. Meanwhile, plans were made and forces mobilised. On 29th November a further Security Council Resolution was passed. Resolution 678 gave Iraq until 15th January to withdraw. This did not happen.

At 3 a.m. in Baghdad, 7 p.m. in Washington and midnight in London the largest aerial attack since the 1940s was unleashed on Iraq. At exactly the same time a well planned media campaign was launched. Both the military and media campaigns had been under preparation for months; this was not going to be another Falklands. This time the media was needed by the military and politicians. As the war progressed, clear war aims for the media took shape. One aim was to maintain public support for the war both in the USA and in Europe. Another was to assist in maintaining the cohesion of the coalition against Iraq that had formed between the west and friendly Arab states.

In order to maintain public support in the west certain features of the war had to be constantly reinforced by the media.

- **It was a just war** – Iraq had committed an act of aggression that could not go unpunished and had to be forced to withdraw from Kuwait.
- **It was a war fought to protect democratic freedom**.
- **It was a relatively bloodless war**. Military deaths, though regrettable, were acceptable if kept low. Civilian deaths were not acceptable.

Figure 7.2 *TV news crew filming in the Gulf*
Source: Associated Press

All these claims were arguable. It was not regarded by everyone as being a *just* war; although supporters of the war were in the majority (because of how it was reported?) there was widespread opposition. Some critics have argued then and since that Iraq was implicitly encouraged to attack Kuwait in order to create a scenario in which Iraq could itself be attacked. Another, more exotic view has it that the war was deliberately started by the USA's industrial-defence complex. Others have argued, less controversially, that the war aims could have been achieved by other means, such as further negotiations and the imposition of economic sanctions. Also the final point was incorrect as there were a great many civilian deaths.

So far, it might look as if the media were willing collaborators in a massive conspiracy to artificially stimulate public support for a dubious military adventure. It is never that simple and wasn't then. All of what is stated in the bullet list above about the war was, in a general sense, true. After all, Iraq did invade Kuwait; there was a sense in which freedom and democracy were being defended and, notwithstanding the substantial number of casualties, these were fewer than would have been the case if an older generation of weapons had been used. However, this is only part of the truth. It is also true that the war was fought over oil and political hegemony, about who would dominate the region. This part of the agenda remained largely unreported.

Managing the media

The Gulf war was the most extensively reported war in history. It was also the first satellite war. In order to cope with the huge number of journalists that descended upon the Gulf States, news gathering was based on a pool system. Every journalist had to be credited as an official war corespondent. Some of these were assigned to specific units, so Kate Addie (BBC) found herself with an armoured brigade; Mike Nicholson (ITN) was on a Royal Navy destroyer. All of the stories coming from these correspondents were pooled, and made available to all correspondents. Those who were not 'in the field' with combat units attended numerous press conferences arranged by the various member nations of the coalition. Some journalists, determined to get a story wherever they could find it, acted outside the pool system. The military referred to them as 'unilaterals'. They tended to be distrusted by the troops and their material was not always used by the media. But they did make some important contributions to the reporting of the war, taking some risks in the process. The Geneva Convention of 1949 makes provision for the humane treatment of captured correspondents. Correspondents have the same rights as any prisoners of war but this is 'contingent upon captured correspondents possessing authorization from the armed forces they are accompanying, attesting to their status.' (Robertson, G. and Nicol, A. *Media Law*, Penguin 1992). This is why, when operating with forces in or near the front line, official war correspondents wear a uniform.

In military operations that fall short of a formally declared war (and there has not been one of these since

---

Non-releasable information for Gulf reporters

1. **Number of troops**
2. **Number of aircraft**
3. **Number of other equipment (e.g., artillery, tanks, radar, trucks)**
4. **Names of military installations/specific geographic locations of military units**
5. **Information about future operations**
6. **Information about security operations**
7. **Photography showing the level of security installations**
8. **Photography that would reveal the name or specific location of military forces**
9. **Rules of engagement details**
10. **Information on intelligence collection**
11. **Information on 'in progress' operations**
12. **Information on special units, unique operations methodology/tactics**
13. **Information identifying postponed operations**
14. **In case of operational necessity, additional guidelines may be necessary**

(MOD)

WW2) there are few legal constraints imposed upon correspondents, other than those already in place such as the Official Secrets Act. Severe censorship can, however, be imposed by military authorities. During the Gulf War the MoD issued a list of guidelines concerning the categories of information that could not be published.

None of these are at all controversial; they are all to do with the reporting of operations. In previous wars they have been more severe and gone beyond the maintenance of operational security to include a prohibition on anything that may damage morale. But, in part, this is the difference between total war, in which national survival is at stake, and a relatively contained regional conflict about which there will be differing opinions as to its moral/political legitimacy and the manner of its prosecution. In a democracy, it could be argued that it is the moral, as well as the professional, duty of the journalist to inform people as much as possible about a war being prosecuted in their name and on their behalf. Where this fits into putting operations at risk and thereby getting people killed is an often intractable question. There are similar, very difficult arguments about what should and should not be shown either in photographs or on television. There seem to be two basic positions on this:

1. If a war is being prosecuted on behalf of a people, it is their moral responsibility to know what is actually happening in their name. This means showing, rather than concealing, the real effects of war. War is a nasty business and should always be a last resort. It is less likely to be resorted to if people know just what it means.
2. On the other hand, to show the horror will upset people, especially relatives.

This is a very difficult issue that will never be fully resolved. In any conflict there will always be a shifting line between exposure and concealment. In practice, it will probably always be the case that it will be after any war that the 'truth' seeps out.

In the Falklands the 'minders' were civilians (Public Relations Officers), but on this occasion they were military officers rather than civilians. On the whole the briefings given by these military officers were trusted except there was a feeling that, although they were not being told lies, correspondents were not being told everything. It was generally known, early on in the war, that the USA military were being very selective in their choice of the cockpit videos that were released to the media. All of them showed 'smart' weapons striking their targets with stunning accuracy. Journalists had seen, 'off the record', other cockpit videos which were not so accurate.

We have seen that one of the aims of the 'media war' in the Gulf was to represent the conflict as being relatively bloodless. The air war was represented as a precision war, as a series of 'surgical strikes' in which only military targets were 'taken out'. Saddam was the enemy, not the Iraqi people.

There was one other effect derived from the way the war was reported. There is evidence that shows that most of the population got most of the news about the war from television. This was also the most trusted news. It is probable that because of the speed with which television reports were released (events were reported within hours of them happening and sometimes live) and the sheer amount of television footage (not just cockpit videos) that the technology itself reinforced a belief in its 'truthfulness' .

Perhaps the technology reinforced the 'myth of transparency', the belief that television functions like a 'window on the world' rather than mediates and constructs the *representations* it gives us.

CASE STUDY: KOSOVO

Kosovo

The former republic of Yugoslavia consisted of a collection of culturally diverse and ancient states: Slovenia, Croatia, Bosnia-Herzegovina, Montenegro and Serbia. Historically, this has always been a volatile region. In the classical era, the Balkan peninsula was split leaving the western half influenced by Rome and the eastern half by Constantinople (later named Istanbul). Later, Serbia, Bosnia and Montenegro came under Ottoman sovereignty whilst the Venetians ruled Slovenia and most of Croatia came under the Hapsburg empire. The people of the region became a mix of Roman Catholics, Greek Orthodox Christians and Muslims.

After WW2, Tito came to power and was able to hold in check the deep religious and national tensions that had always characterised the region. Tito was able to do this partly by refusing to favour one group over another, but also through the delicate position occupied by Yugoslavia, both geographically and politically. In the days of the Cold War, Yugoslavia, being just across the Adriatic Sea from Italy, was a kind of buffer zone between east and west. This made it strategically important to the Soviet Union. Tito, however, whilst leading a communist state, was not interested in being part of the Cold War and wanted to maintain a degree of autonomy from the Soviet Union. As a measure of this, Yugoslavia's defences were arranged to resist an attack from the Soviet Union. Unhappily for the future of Yugoslavia, three things happened within a relatively short period of time. Tito died in 1980, a few years later the Soviet Bloc began to fall apart (nurturing nationalist ambitions across the region) and, at the same time, the rise to power of Slobodan Milosevic was consolidated. Milosevic was born in 1941 and rose through the ranks of the Communist Party under Tito. In 1986 he came to power as head of the League of Communists in Belgrade (later to be known as the Socialist Party of Serbia – the SPS). He was both ambitious and nationalistic. Milosevic not only wanted to control Yugoslavia with Serbia as the dominant nation, he wanted a 'Greater Serbia'. Milosevic gained control of the Belgrade media, including the most prominent newspapers, *Politika* and *Politika Ekspres*. The Politika group was the largest media organisation in Yugoslavia and included not only newspapers, but also a radio and television station. Milosevic forced out the group's Director General and Editor in Chief, replacing them with his own people. He now controlled the Serbia media. Kosovo became Milosevic's first target.

Kosovo is symbolically very important to the Serbs. It was in 1389 that the Serbs were defeated by the Ottoman Turks at the Battle of

Kosovo Polje. Defeat or not, Kosovo Polje took on immense importance as a symbol of national identity. Also within Kosovo is Pec, regarded as 'the cradle of the Serbian Orthodox Church'. Despite its symbolic value, over the years the Serbs had virtually ignored Kosovo and it became largely autonomous. By 1986 only 7% of the population was actually Serb, the majority being ethnic Albanians, many of whom, in turn, claimed the country as their own and had ambitions of Kosovo eventually being absorbed into Albania, whilst others wanted complete independence.

Through his exploitation of the media and public demonstrations, Milosevic was able to turn Kosovo into a focal point of Serb nationalism. The culmination of nationalist propaganda and intimidation culminated in the Kosovo parliament itself being ringed by Serb tanks and buzzed by MiG jets as a response to a strike by Albanian workers. The Kosovo parliament was forced to accede to a union with Serbia. Meanwhile, both Slovenia and Croatia were getting nervous about what was happening to Kosovo. Both countries held democratic elections and opted to break away from Yugoslavia. On 25th June 1991 both countries, through prior agreement, declared their independence. Early on Thursday, 27th June 1991, the Yugoslav National Army (JNA) invaded Slovenia. What followed was really a succession of separate conflicts, leaving the former Yugoslavia consisting of nothing more than Serbia and Montenegro, with two largely autonomous states Kosovo and Vojvodina which were, in any case, effectively annexed.

Within a month of attacking Slovenia, a ceasefire had been arranged and the Serbs withdrew. The Serbs then gave their support to Serb minorities in Croatia which led to a further conflict of great ferocity. By 1992, the Balkan tragedy had drawn in Bosnia. The population of Bosnia was more or less equally divided between Serbs, Croats and Muslims. In 1992 the government held a referendum on whether or not Bosnia should, like Slovenia and Croatia, declare independence. The Bosnian-Serbs, under their leader Dr. Radovan Karadzic had a separate policy. Karadzic's aim was to purge Bosnia of all non-Serbs. Before the referendum, he declared that certain parts of Bosnia should be controlled by the Serb National Council, of which he was the president. Bosnian-Serbs were instructed not to vote. Largely because of this, only 63% of the country voted and of these 99% voted in favour of independence. On the 6th April 1992 the USA and the European Community recognised Bosnia as a sovereign state. This led very quickly to open warfare between the vying groups when the Bosnian-Serbs refused to recognize the country's new status. Caught in the crossfire was UNPROFOR (The United Nations Protection Force), which included British troops, who had recently arrived to protect the inhabitants of United Nations Protection Areas in Croatia. It was about now, in 1992, that the British media began to pay closer attention to the Balkans and afforded it a much higher profile in newspapers and television bulletins. This appalling, protracted war lasted until December 1995, when a peace treaty, which had been negotiated between the warring parties at the Wright-Patterson Airforce Base in

Dayton, Ohio, was signed at the Elysee Palace, Paris. In order to maintain the precarious peace, a NATO led International Force (IFOR) of 60 000 was committed to Bosnia. IFOR began to move into Bosnia at the beginning of January 1996. By 1997 it had given way to a smaller Stabilising Force (SFOR).

Aside from the appalling death and destruction that ripped the Balkans apart during much of the 1990s, another part of the legacy was Kosovo where another crisis began to develop between the Serbs and Muslims with the Serbs trying to force out the ethnic Albanians.

On Wednesday, the 25th March 1999 at 19.00 GMT the aircraft of six nations attacked Serbia. There were eighty aircraft in the first wave, launched mainly from Aviano in Italy and carriers in the Adriatic Sea. The code name of the mission was Allied Force. Along with the military campaign went the media campaign. As in the Gulf, the war of opinion was crucial. In order to sustain and win the conflict it had, once again, to be seen as a morally just war, winnable and at minimum cost. A crucial element of the 'cost' were Serb civilians as well as the Kosovo people. However it was also clear that too many allied military casualties would not be acceptable. The US were particularly worried about this as there was a concern that there would be a public reaction against the operation if too many body bags started coming home. The military and political solution was a precision air war. Using the latest in 'smart' weapons and flying well above the range of ground missiles it was felt that so many key military and support installations could be 'taken out' that Milosevic would sue for peace within days. Critics of this strategy argued that no air campaign in history had worked in this way and it was folly to declare, at the outset, that there would be no land campaign. It was felt that with this knowledge Milosevic had only to 'sit tight', take the damage and hold out until NATO backed off.

To begin with the war did not go very well for NATO (incidentally, the first time that NATO, as an organisation, had gone to war). It even seemed to be counter-productive, apparently provoking the Serbs to escalate their campaign to drive ethnic Albanians from the country; more and more reports of atrocities began to emerge. Both sides were fully aware of the importance of the media and the propaganda war. To begin with, the Serbs ordered foreign journalists out of the country. Perhaps aware of the negative publicity this measure would provoke internationally, they drew back on this and allowed many to stay. Television pictures, however, were not allowed to be transmitted. This element of the media remained firmly in the control of the Serbs throughout the war. Except in a relatively few instances, television pictures were released exclusively by Serb Television. Western television journalists, such as John Simpson of the BBC, had to content themselves with telephoning reports from their hotel rooms, only rarely being allowed to do a television piece, presumably when it showed NATO bomb damage.

The air campaign extending into weeks without apparently damaging Milosevic was bad enough; what was much worse were the inevitable military accidents and 'collateral damage'. On the 12th April ten civilians were killed when a train was accidentally hit during a raid on a bridge. Bad as this was, NATO responded quickly and admitted responsibility, claiming it was an accident. But there was much worse to come. On Wednesday, 14th April a flight of American F-16s, operating at 15 000 feet, attacked a convoy of refugees killing seventy five. NATO public relations could not cope. Within twenty four hours there were claims and counter claims from NATO and the Serbs. That evening on the BBC 9 o'clock news it was claimed that there were JRA (Yugoslav Army) vehicles in the column that the F-16s had attacked. Another version, picked up by some of the press the following morning, was that the Serbs themselves had attacked the convoy. *The Express* was not alone in quoting a survivor shown on television news the previous evening, '''The planes were flying very low and were Serbian MiGs,' said a 23 year old man Kukes, near the border.' (*The Express*, 15th April 1999). *The Sun* carried a front page headline with yet another 'spin' on the story: 'Alive.. on day Slobba tricked Nato into bombing refugees.' (*The Sun*, 15th April 1999) The Serbs were quick to exploit the situation, bussing journalists out to the wreckage. Notwithstanding the fact that bodies had been deliberately left lying around and had probably been moved, the scenes that appeared in subsequent television news bulletins and the press were horrific. NATO had a lot of explaining to do. But nobody seemed to know what had happened: speculation was rife and it was several days before NATO cleared up the confusion and admitted that there had, after all, been an error. The delay and confusion gave the impression that NATO had something to hide. This was damaging to one of NATO's assets - they had been trusted by the press.

What had been exposed were weaknesses in the NATO media operation. This was being run from NATO in Brussels and apparently not given a very high priority by the military. The NATO spokesman was Jamie Shea. He had only a small staff without anyone of sufficient rank to demand information from the highest levels of command. After the convoy incident this changed. Both Clinton and Blair were anxious that the propaganda initiative was not to be lost to the Serbs. Blair's Press Secretary, Alistair Campbell, was despatched to Brussels to analyse the situation. He recommended that the whole media operation should be upgraded and given more resources. What came out of Campbell's review was a restructured communications operation that not only had more resources, but under Clinton's and Blair's instruction, greater access to information and the high command.

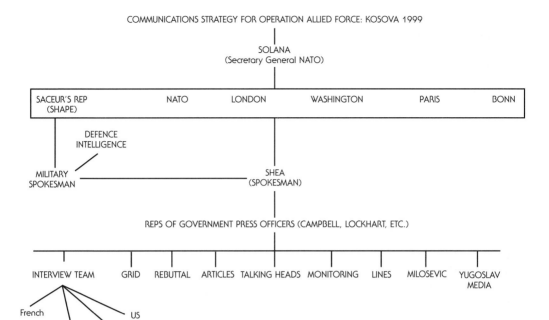

COMMUNICATIONS STRATEGY FOR OPERATION ALLIED FORCE: KOSOVA 1999

SOLANA
(Secretary General NATO)

SACEUR'S REP (SHAPE)   NATO   LONDON   WASHINGTON   PARIS   BONN

DEFENCE INTELLIGENCE

MILITARY SPOKESMAN   SHEA (SPOKESMAN)

REPS OF GOVERNMENT PRESS OFFICERS (CAMPBELL, LOCKHART, ETC.)

INTERVIEW TEAM   GRID   REBUTTAL   ARTICLES   TALKING HEADS   MONITORING   LINES   MILOSEVIC   YUGOSLAV MEDIA

French   German   UK   US

Figure 7.3 *Structure of communication for NATO*

At the top of the new structure was the Director General of NATO, Javier Solana. At the next level were the chief Press Officers from NATO, the White House, Downing Street and the German and French governments and a representative of the Supreme Allied Commander Europe (SACEUR), General Wesley Clark. The 'public face' of this structure was the next level, the spokesmen who gave the daily briefings from Brussels – Jamie Shea and a military spokesman. Then there were the representatives of the chief press officers and a whole battery of personnel organised into a variety of roles: interviewing; grid (basically planning); rebuttal (ready to deny any Serb allegations); talking heads (the monitoring of 'arm chair' ex-officers, etc, who were being interviewed by the media); monitoring (watching the international media); lines (script writing for Shea – 'sound bites', etc.); Milosevic (monitoring how Milosevic was being reported) and the monitoring of the Yugoslav media. By the time of the Chinese Embassy bombing the system was in place and working and responses to that situation were swift and focused (if not completely illuminating). What this meant in practice was that NATO spoke with one voice with everyone 'on message'. There were no contradictory accounts as with the bombing of the convoy and so this prevented a very difficult international incident from getting worse.

Perhaps even more than with the Gulf War, Kosovo changed the terms in which the West engages in international armed conflict. Traditionally, a military commander preoccupied himself with defeating the enemy. This usually meant either occupying territory or denying it to the enemy at minimum cost to himself, both in terms of personal and material. The corollary of this was maximum destruction of the enemy. This is no longer tenable. Modern communications have contributed to the military and politicians having greater accountability for their actions. By the same token, however, it also means that they have the capacity of 'constructing' their own 'reality' and 'truths' through the same media. The range of media used to prosecute a war have expanded. If Vietnam was the first television war and the Gulf the first satellite war, Kosovo was the first Internet war. Essentially, the relationship between the civil population, governments, the military and the press remains unchanged. The civil population want to know the truth via the press, politicians want to give their version of the truth and the military would rather not give away anything at all. Since the Gulf and Kosovo, the rules have changed and the media war has become almost as important as the shooting war. One question will perhaps never be resolved: how much truth of war should the media show?

ESSAY QUESTIONS

1 Note the main formal/stylistic differences between the major news programmes on any four television channels (terrestrial, cable or satellite).

2 What can be learned from their style and form about the news values that inform these news programmes.

3 To what extent is television news produced as entertainment?

4 What impact has technology had on the selection and presentation of television news?

5 Television never shows the truth about war? Discuss

FOLLOW UP WORK

1 Take any newspaper story and script/storyboard it as a television news item.

2 Analyse a television news bulletin in terms of Galtung and Ruge.

3 Should there be any limits on the freedom of the press in time of war?

4 What differences has technology made to the reporting of wars?

5 How might television journalism change in the future?

SHORT ANSWER QUESTIONS

1 When did BBC TV News and ITN start?

2 What was the first international event covered by BBC news?

3 Who was the first great war reporter. Why is he worth remembering?

4 What are regarded as the first television war and the first satellite war?

5 How many television news services are there available in the UK?

8
TELEVISION AND THE STATE: FUNDING AND CONTROL

We have seen throughout much of this book ways in which governments impinge upon the work of television owners, controllers and programme makers. There is no broadcaster in the world working completely free of some kind of state regulation. Even in a relatively free-market television provision, such as the USA, Washington, and state authorities, have bottom-line regulation, for example in the allocation of frequencies, but actually even there, it goes beyond this. British television has always been much more tightly regulated than in the USA and so it remains. British television, like all media is regulated in largely two areas:

1. ownership
2. programme content

In both areas, television is more strictly regulated than in other media such as cinema, radio, the press and book/magazine publishing.

Ownership

The ownership of television companies, in the UK (and other countries) is regulated for several reasons. One is to do with the view that ownership should not be concentrated in too few hands. As we have seen, this was one of the arguments for removing the BBC monopoly. Critics believed that the nation was being offered a limited range of social and cultural perspectives. It is clearly unhealthy for a democracy to have only a few public voices. The greater the diversity of views articulated across the airways and in the pages of newspapers and magazines, the better. Diversity is one thing but a completely unrestricted freedom of expression is another, or at least, so it can be argued. The law, as we shall see in more detail later, does impose restrictions on the freedom of expression, in order to protect freedom of expression. The problem of freedom is how far can one person's freedom be allowed to impinge upon another person's freedom? By protecting the rights of the individual to be free from intimidation, duress, slander or whatever, the freedom of others so to act has to be restricted. What applies to individuals applies to broadcasters and newspapers. Of course there is another perspective on this which does not have much to do with individual freedom, and that is the protection of the status quo. This can be inflected in different ways, from the unconscious impulses of an editor to veer one way or another in the 'spin' a story is given to the more obvious desire of a government to remain in power. 'Freedom' is a compromise, a play between constraint and liberty, to which in theory, the individual willingly accedes, but in reality is compelled, not so much by force but through the subtleties of ideology – a process of socialisation of which television forms such an important part.

This is well illustrated by the constitutional position, if I can call it that, of the BBC. It is independent of commercial pressure and government control – well, it is and it isn't.

Let's take (briefly, for now) the issue of commercial pressure. On paper, the BBC does not have to worry about where the money comes from as it comes from the licence fee and is a guaranteed source of income not at all related to audience ratings. However, none of this true. The BBC's fee has a great deal to do with audience ratings. Should its audience fall too low the licence fee (an indirect tax) would become politically untenable. The electorate would not tolerate paying for something it was not using. It follows that the BBC is very much subjected to commercial pressures.

Equally, the BBC is not free from government control. Written into the BBC's charter are quite clear limitations to its freedom. Government powers to ban programmes are written into the Licence Agreement that forms part of the BBC's Charter and the 1990 Broadcasting Act, which regulates independent television. Section 19 of the Licence Agreement enables the Home Secretary, in an emergency and if it is 'expedient so to act' to send troops to 'take possession of the BBC in the name of and on behalf of Her Majesty'. This was framed during the General Strike of 1926 and has never been used, although the Prime Minister of the day, Sir Anthony Eden, did give it serious consideration during the Suez crisis of 1956. It also provided the legal basis for the use of BBC transmitters on Ascension Island by the Government for broadcasting propaganda to Argentina during the Falklands War.

Broadcasting bans

The Government has a more dangerous power than that described in Section 19 of the Licence Agreement. Section 13(4) of the agreement gives the Home Secretary the right to ban any transmission at any time. Unlike Section 19, it does not depend upon an 'emergency' and to safeguard against political censorship, the BBC 'may' (not 'must') tell the public.

In addition Section 10 of the Broadcasting Act entitles the Home Secretary to order the ITC (Independent Television Commission) to 'refrain from broadcasting any matter or classes of matter' on commercial television. The Home Secretary cannot be challenged on this unless it can be shown that s/he has acted unreasonably or perversely.

C A S E   S T U D Y

Broadcasting bans

On 30th July 1985 the then Home Secretary, Leon Brittan, prevented the BBC from screening a programme called *Real Lives,* which included an interview with Martin McGuinness, a senior IRA officer. The programme also included an interview with Gregory Campbell, an equally 'hard-line' member of the Protestant Democratic Unionist Party. It was a typical example of British censorship. Strictly speaking, Brittan did not impose a ban; he simply 'asked' the BBC to 'reconsider' its decision to screen the film and it was subsequently banned by the BBC's own Board of Governors. In a statement made at the time he said he 'did not want to censor the corporation' (*The London Evening Standard*: July, 29, 1985). It was clear to all, however, that even though Brittan did not have to resort to his residual powers contained under Section 13(4) of the BBC's Licence Agreement, this was, for whatever the reasons, government censorship.

In 1988 the BBC and IBA were ordered not to transmit any interviews with representatives of any banned organisation, for example, the IRA and UDA or with Sinn Fein or to broadcast any statement that incited support for such groups. This prevented the re-screening by the BBC of Robert Kee's *Ireland: a television history* and Thames Television's *The Troubles* as both contained interviews with IRA veterans. In 1990 Channel Four started using actors speaking the lines of interviewees which wasn't against the ruling and this became standard practice by both the BBC and ITN until the lifting of the broadcasting ban in 1994.

The 1988 bans are the only examples of *direct* political censorship in recent times. A more subtle means of political control over the media is the Government's power to appoint key people to controlling bodies and statutory commissions set up to supervise complaints about unfair treatment. The Governor of the BBC and the Head of the Broadcasting Complaints Commission are examples of what are effectively political appointments. That is to say the people who are awarded these posts are done so as much for their political sympathies as their abilities. According to the 1990 Broadcasting Act, it is the Government that appoints both the members and the Chairman of the BCC. The BCC exists to adjudicate on any complaint made about broadcasting by any member of the public. If the BCC finds in favour of the complainant, the offending broadcaster must have published the BCC's decision.

Legislation

There exists on the statute books several acts of legislation that, whilst not having censorship as a primary function, nevertheless, are employed in that role.

The Official Secrets Act

This was very hastily drafted in 1911 in response to fears of German espionage and has remained in force ever since. Section 2 of the act had been carefully drafted some time before with the purpose of stopping leakage of official information to the press. By virtue of tortuous drafting more than 2 000 different offences were created in a few paragraphs. The 1911 Act was revised in 1989 and Section 2 has been replaced by Section 5. Broadly, this makes it a specific offence for journalists and editors to publish information they know is protected by the Act, although the prosecution must additionally prove that publication would be damaging to the security services or to the interests of the UK. This is a complex piece of legislation, not least in the necessity, at any trial, to consider the type of information disclosed and the nature of 'national interest'.

The 1989 Act came in the wake of the *General Belgrano* affair which occurred in 1982, during the Falklands War. In 1985 a senior Civil Servant at the Ministry of Defence, Clive Ponting, leaked some government documents proving that the government had lied over the circumstances surrounding the sinking of the Argentine cruiser, the *General Belgrano*, which was sunk by a British nuclear attack submarine, *HMS Conqueror*. When the ship was sunk the country was told she had been heading towards the Royal Navy and was inside the 200 mile total exclusion zone (very quickly seen not to be the case). Also the country was told that *HMS Conqueror* prosecuted her attack on sighting the *General Belgrano*. None of this proved to be true. The documents leaked proved that the *General Belgrano* was heading away from the Royal Navy towards its own base and she was attacked not on sight, but after two days of being followed by *HMS Conqueror*, under orders from Northwood (the RN Operational Head Quarters) and 'No.10'. Coincidentally, the order to attack was given within hours of a peace proposal being made in Peru. It is not yet known if there was a connection.

Ponting was duly charged with offences under Section 2 of the Official Secrets Act and brought to trial. Throughout, Ponting's defence argued that he had acted in the 'national interest': the Government had lied to the nation and Ponting had exposed the lie. The trial judge, however, during his summing-up, instructed the jury that there was *prima facie* evidence that Ponting had contravened the Official Secrets Act and further there was no distinction to be made between *national* and *government* interest – they were the same. The jury did not agree and refused to convict so Ponting was found not guilty. Under the 1989 Act, Ponting's defence is no longer possible. The defence of public or national interest has been outlawed.

DA Notices

DA Notices (formerly D Notices) are the responsibility of the Defence, Press and Broadcasting Advisory Committee. This is made up of representatives of the armed forces, senior civil servants and various press and broadcasting institutions. Its purpose is to provide 'advice and guidance to the UK media about defence and counter-terrorist information, the publication of which would be damaging to the UK's national security. The system is voluntary, it has no legal authority and the final responsibility for deciding whether or not to publish rests solely with the editor or publisher concerned' (www.btinternet.com/~d.a.notices). DA Notices currently apply to six categories of information:

1. Operations, plans and capabilities (details of present or future operations, tactics, etc.)
2. Non-nuclear weapons and operational equipment
3. Nuclear weapons and equipment
4. Ciphers and secure communications
5. Identification of specific installations
6. United Kingdom security and intelligence services

'It is also requested that where other individuals are likely targets for attacks by terrorists, care should be taken not to publish details of their home addresses without first seeking advice.' (op. cit.)

The Committee was the result of the speed with which the Official Secrets Act was passed. It was felt that its wording was too vague and therefore it was incapable of performing the functions now carried out by the Committee. It was set up in 1912, shrouded in secrecy and its existence did not become publicly known until the early 1950s. The Committee, however, has no legal force: it only 'advises'. Potentially problematic stories are regularly printed without attracting any legal proceedings. For instance, in 1980 the *New Statesman* published a series of articles by Duncan Campbell about telephone tapping despite a warning from the Committee that this contravened a DA Notice, but no prosecution followed.

The Obscene Publications Act

The definition of obscenity is contained in Section 1 of the Obscene Publications Act: 'For the purposes of this Act an article shall be deemed to be obscene if its effect ... is ... to tend to deprave and corrupt persons who are likely ... to read, see or hear the matter contained or embodied in it.'

Across all media, there have been relatively few convictions under this Act, probably because 'self censorship' ensures that things don't get that far. However, few areas of censorship and the media are so patently ideologically 'loaded'. Just *how* does one identify that which 'depraves' and 'corrupts' and what do these terms mean anyway? Does sexual explicitness in itself qualify as 'obscenity'? Once upon a time it almost certainly would have done, but seemingly not now if a case in 1991 is anything to go by, when a judge refused the police a warrant under the Act to search for 'material of a sexually explicit nature' on the grounds that such material was not necessarily obscene. This is why, for example, there was no chance of a successful OPA prosecution being brought against Madonna's book of photographs. But clearly, in practice, a line is drawn between material that is merely sexually explicit and that which is also deemed to be 'obscene' under the terms of the Act, as the police and customs officers do virtually everyday. The rights and wrongs of this represents an ongoing debate between 'libertarians' who feel that adults should be able to make up their own minds as to what they want to see and read and the 'paternalists' who feel that this isn't good enough and people should be protected from the 'harm' that such material may cause.

In the past, the most common defence of a prosecuted work (by the publishers of the work) has been that its publication was in the interests of 'science, literature or learning', a good example of such a defence (successful) was D.H. Lawrence's *Lady Chatterley's Lover* in the 1960s.

Defamation (libel law)

> 'London is the libel capital of the world. No other legal system offers such advantages to the wealthy maligned celebrity: procedures that tilt the odds in favour of the plaintiffs; a law that gives little weight to the principles of freedom of expression; and tax-free damages awarded unrestrainedly by star-struck juries who dislike newspapers.'
>
> *(Robertson and Nicol, p.38).*

Libel is the making of a false statement that is damaging to its subject's reputation. However, no legal aid has ever been available and libel cases are notoriously expensive, so only the wealthy can pursue them. If the ordinary person is libelled – tough! It has been all too easy for any litigious and powerful person to slap a writ on anything s/he doesn't like. Robert Maxwell, (the late owner of Mirror group Newspapers) was a notorious habitué of the law courts pursuing cases of libel or requesting a stay of publication on anything that he could argue was potentially libellous. He, like others, was able to do this because he could afford the legal costs. There is nothing objectionable in the principle (especially if it was available to all) that a person's reputation should be protected from a falsehood: problems arise when the procedures of libel law lead to the concealment of wrongdoing.

Blasphemy

Strictly speaking blasphemy falls within libel law. It is defined as 'outrageous comments about God, holy personages, or articles of the Anglican faith, and is constituted by vilification, ridicule or indecency'. (Robertson and Nicol). Cases of blasphemy rarely arise. In the case of film the most recent was in 1989 when a 'twenty minute video depicting the erotic visions of St Theresa of Avila' (*The Guardian*, 3rd December 1989) was refused a certificate by the British Board of Film Classification on the grounds that it was blasphemous. As in other areas of censorship, this legislation is clearly ideological, to an extent that became clear in 1989 with the case of Salmon Rushdie's *Satanic Verses*. A group of aggrieved Muslims took Rushdie to court for committing blasphemy only to discover that the law only protected Christians! The case highlighted the problem with the law. In what is now inarguably a multi-racial society, just how fair or appropriate is a piece of legislation that singles out *one* religion for special protection? It would seem clear that there are two course of reasonable action:

1. Extend its protection to all religious beliefs
2. Abolish it altogether

The second view was that expressed by the Archbishop of Canterbury in 1990 and in time the law will almost certainly be abolished. To extend it to all religions would almost certainly contravene Article 10 of the European Convention which guarantees freedom of expression. Article 9, which guarantees the freedom to manifest religious beliefs, does not protect believers from having their beliefs criticised or even ridiculed. This, itself, raises an interesting point: why should religious ideas be afforded a protection not available to other categories of ideas, such as political, philosophical, etc.?

The reason why the offence of blasphemy has remained on the statute books is probably, in part at least, due to the infrequency of cases being brought to court. Since 1922 there has only been one successful prosecution when in 1978 Mary Whitehouse brought an action against *Gay News* for publishing a poem by James Kirkup which metaphorically attributed to Christ homosexual acts. It was Kirkup's intention to celebrate the universality of Gods love to include homosexuals. Whitehouse brought a private prosecution; the jury convicted by 10 votes to 2 and the House of Lords, on appeal, confirmed the conviction by 3 to 2. It was ruled that the author's or publisher's intentions were irrelevant and that there was no need for the prosecution to prove any risk of breach of the peace.

In a report on the law of blasphemy in 1986 the Law Commission recognised three fundamental defects:

1. Its ambit is so wide it is impossible to predict in advance whether a particular publication would constitute an offence (even making 'self-censorship' problematic)
2. The sincerity of the publishers is irrelevant
3. Blasphemy protects only Anglican beliefs and the criminal law is not an appropriate vehicle for upholding sectional religious tenets

All of these legal ordinances are directly applicable to television. No case has yet been prosecuted regarding blasphemy, but it is theoretically possible. Certainly films have occasionally attracted the attention of those who have considered bringing private actions against them, for example *The Last Temptation of Christ* and *The Life of Brian*. *The Last Temptation of Christ* (1988), directed by Martin Scorsese, was based on a book of the same title by Nikos Kazantzakis. Whilst on the cross, Christ dreams of escaping his fate and becoming an ordinary person. There was uproar where the film was shown: in Paris one cinema was bombed. The book did not attract anything like the same attention as the film.

The Life of Brian (1980) was a Monty Python film that for many, was too irreligious in its treatment of the story of Christ (although there is no actual reference to him). Attempts to have the films banned were unsuccessful.

The use of the law as a means of preventing certain classes of material being broadcast in the UK has already been found to be flawed in the age of satellite. In the early 1990s a pornographic channel based in Holland for a while broadcast into the UK with impunity. The British Government eventually managed to curtail its operations by outlawing the sale of the decoder required to receive its broadcasts.

However, the point was made well enough: there are huge difficulties in legally preventing incoming satellite transmissions when they emanate from independent and sovereign powers. Clearly only international agreements can achieve this, but such agreements are going to be difficult to achieve when the nations concerned have such varying ideas about what counts as obscene. Some governments are concerned about the trans-border nature of satellite for more than ideological reasons. The Chinese, for example, have imposed a ban on the ownership of domestic satellite dishes. Satellite channels, for example Rupert Murdoch's Star, are received by the Chinese state broadcaster and relayed to homes, through cable.

The Chinese, since the BBC's vivid reporting of Tiananmen Square, are primarily concerned about news. Star had a simple solution: the BBC was removed from their schedules and they do not broadcast any news into China at all. Other countries such as Indonesia and other Asian states, are concerned about their cultures being gradually eroded by western influence via satellite. Relatively strong democracies with very rich cultural traditions, such as India, have little to fear. Their experience with cinema suggests they are able to assimilate a range of cultural influences.

CASE STUDY

The ITC

The ITC is the main regulatory body overseeing commercial television. It is not responsible for what is broadcast in terms of content, merely that broadcasts conform to criteria written into the Broadcasting Acts of 1990 and 1996. Unlike the IBA it is only a regulator. The Act also gave the ITC responsibility for cable and satellite television. The Act enjoins the ITC to:

- regulate commercial television (terrestrial, cable and satellite)
- ensure a range of services is offered
- license contractors (franchise holders) to broadcast programmes
- ensure the regulation of taste and decency
- ensure impartiality in matters of politics
- enforce rules governing the depiction of violence and sexual conduct
- ensure no political advertising
- ensure audience research is carried out
- ensure sufficient news and current affairs programming
- ensure regional programming is included
- ensure that programmes of European origin are broadcast
- ensure schools programmes are included

Regulation of programme content

The ITC does not have the power of 'pre-publication' censorship: it can only act after the event. The ITC was enjoined by the Act to establish a Code setting out minimum standards of programming:

General provisions about licensed services

-6— (1) The Commission shall do all that they can to secure that every licensed service complies with the following requirements, namely –
    (a) that nothing is included in its programmes which offends against good taste or decency or is likely to encourage or incite to crime or to lead to disorder or to be offensive to public feeling;

    (b) that any news given (in whatever form) in its programmes is presented with due accuracy and impartiality;

    (c) that due impartiality is preserved on the part of the person providing the service as respects matters of political or industrial controversy or relating to current public policy;

    (d) that due responsibility is exercised with respect to the content of any of its programmes which are religious programmes, and that in particular any such programmes do not involve –

        (i) any improper exploitation of any susceptibilities of those watching the programmes, or

       (ii) any abusive treatment of the religious views and beliefs of those belonging to a particular religion or religious denomination; and

    (e) that its programmes do not include any technical device which, by using images of very brief duration or by any other means, exploits the possibility of conveying a message to, or otherwise influencing the minds of, persons watching the programmes without their being aware, or fully aware, of what has occurred.

Anyone, should they believe that an infringement of the code has occurred, is entitled to complain to the ITC. The Act goes beyond this, however, and extends the Obscene Publications Act (1959) to cover broadcasting (radio and television). In the case of the Obscene Publications Act, 'broadcasting' is taken to mean 'publishing': 'For the purposes of this Act a person also publishes an article to the extent that any matter recorded on it is included by him in a programme included in a programme service.'

Regulations regarding 'editorialising' are much stricter with television than the press. Newspapers are free to offer an opinion on matters relating to politics, etc. but this is not the case with television. There must be 'due impartiality…on the part of the person providing the service as respects matters of political or industrial controversy or relating to current policy.' However, as the Act states, 'due impartiality does not require absolute neutrality on every issue or detachment from fundamental democratic principles.'

The ITC expects all franchise holders to respect the 9 o'clock threshold, before which programmes unsuitable for children will not be shown.

The ITC has a separate regulatory code for programmes, advertising and sponsorship.

ESSAY QUESTIONS

1 Which aspects of media law do you think are likely to be the most troublesome for journalists?

2 What sort of legal problems must programme makers be wary of?

3 What do you consider to be the role of the media in general elections?

4 What role does, or should, government have in the running of television?

5 If you could revise a piece of legislation that would affect the media, what would it be and why?

FOLLOW UP WORK

1 Through your own research, find out when and in what circumstances broadcasters and government have clashed.

2 In what ways does new technology potentially threaten the government's ability to regulate television?

3 If a television journalist receives a leaked document from a government department, what should s/he do with it? Try and find some instances where this has occurred. What are the possible consequences if it is published?

4 Choose one other country apart from the UK and the USA. What role does the government play in the running of its television service?

5 Through your own research, find examples, either in the UK or in the USA, where television has been censored.

Advances in technology have impacted on television at every level: production, distribution and reception. Since the middle of the 1980s new technology has been dominated by satellite, but as it establishes itself, new technologies are being developed and modified at an astonishing rate.

Fibre-optics

There are two kinds of cable: coaxial and fibre-optic. Coaxial cable is made from copper and the amount of information it can carry is limited. Fibre-optic cable is made from glass. The information is carried as light-impulses and its capacity is massive. Future developments in telecommunications depend on fibre-optics, because this is the only terrestrial means by which large amounts of information can be carried. The global communications systems rapidly being constructed depend on fibre-optic technology. 'Most Washington experts take the position that it makes no more sense to delay the installation of fibre-optic wire than it does to stop paving roads.' (Doyle, M., *The Future of Television*, NTC Business Books, 1992, p.161). Interactive telecommunications depend on fibre-optics.

Digital/interactive television

Public awareness of interactive television goes little further than the prospect of using the television for shopping. This, of course, is already with us as is (of 1999) interactive sport. The centre of interactive television will be ICTV (integrated computer television). ICTV will enable all communication sources, incoming and outgoing, to be controlled by a computer – the computer being the television itself. Progress in this direction is already advanced. By the early 1990s, Radius, a California based company, had devised such a system. 'The system puts all the video and TV sources, like camcorders and video cassettes, broadcast stations and cable stations, under the control of a Macintosh computer.' (Doyle). According to Nicholas Negroponte, the director of the MIT Media lab, the television set itself will become 'smart'.

On buying a new television, the new owner will feed into the television's computer a detailed profile about his/her interests, tastes, etc. Thereafter, on switching on the television a menu will appear tailored to the user's interests.

> By comparison with some of the more modern appliances in your home I bet that most of us have televisions that, on a per-cubic-foot basis, are the dumbest appliances in our homes. We really don't put very much computing in the receiver.
>
> *(Doyle, p.138)*

The television will also have stored other programmes. Films, for example. The television/computer's menu will also indicate appropriate films or even extracts:

In 1999 Sky was first to provide an interactive facility in its coverage of some football matches. This is sure to be extended to a range of games and other events. Regardless of how many cameras are covering a game, of whatever sport, the viewer will be able to decide, with the push of a button, which shot s/he wishes to see on screen: the viewer will become, in effect, the director, creating his/her own televised version.

In the early 1990s in America, the Federal Communications Commission (FCC) approved an interactive broadcast service in Virginia. A two-way television shopping service, based on a digital television signal, has been developed by TV Answer. The system employs a set-top computer for processing orders. A convergence of television and computer based technologies will almost certainly be the next major development in television.

Until the mid 1990s interactive television was thought of in terms of fibre-optic cable. Now there is an alternative and cheaper form of delivery: digital television. Each analogue television channel uses 6 megahertz of the electromagnetic spectrum. Digital television transmits audio and video in computer language which is made up of just ones and zeros. Digital technology enables the signal to be compressed so that many digital channels can take up the same spectrum space used by just one analogue channel. Whether carried by satellite, fibre-optic cable or terrestrial means, the number of television channels available could run into the hundreds.

> The first item on the menu may be today's news program, but you will not have to wait until 6 p.m., or 6.30 p.m. All you will do is push a button and your news will begin. The computer will have monitored and stored every news story, from every news program, that came into your house that day ... You will simply be presented a customised, personal news program that only contains the information you told your computer you are interested in.
>
> *(Doyle, p.160)*

> You get home at night and your television says to you: 'Nicholas, while you were away I looked at 350 hours of television this afternoon and I have this great twenty minutes which I think you'll be interested in seeing...Prime time is your time.'
>
> *(Nicholas Negroponte cited in Doyle, p.159)*

HDTV

High Density Television, of all recent technological developments in television, is the one not yet to have made much impact on domestic markets. This is largely due to cost. Notwithstanding the huge investments required to lay cable, the domestic user only has to pay a modest subscription fee; the same applies to satellite used, along with the additional cost of a set-top decoder which is about £200 at the time of writing – this is also about the cost of a digital box needed to receive digital channels. None of these systems of reception require a new television. This, however, is not the case with the HDTV, for which a new set is required. They are presently neither cheap nor small.

The story of HDTV is a salient case-study in the relationship between science, economics and politics. The Japanese came late to television. They inherited a system of 525 lines from the post-war occupation and even by the mid-1950s, relatively few house-holds possessed a receiver. This changed at the end of the decade. As in the UK, Japanese television received a substantial boost from a royal wedding, on this occasion, the wedding of the Japanese Crown Prince. Another boost to sales happened in 1964, when the Japanese hosted the Olympics in Tokyo.

Two factors now came into play that would lead to the eventual development of HDTV. Japanese engineers were dissatisfied with the system they had been left with: '... TV cannot be compared with movies or printing in terms of picture clarity, impact, or immediacy' (Brinkley, p.13). HTV, the Japanese television service, were also victims of their success. By the 1970s, domestic ownership reached saturation point and sales levelled off so revenues from receiver fees set by the Diet (the Japanese parliament) began to decline. Something was needed to regenerate turnover. HDTV would be it.

Research was carried out into screen sizes, shape and the distance at which a viewer would have to sit in order to obtain the optimum image. One realisation that emerged from this work was that the human field of vision was wider than the normal television screen. The Japanese concluded that in order to enhance the television image, the number of lines had to increase and the screen's aspect ratio had to change: the picture would have to become wider. They opted for 1125 lines with 60 fields (frames) a second and an aspect ratio of 16 × 9 – almost the same as cinema. With twice as many lines as a conventional television, each one was only half as wide so the screen would show twice as much detail. But there was one problem: an HDTV signal of these proportions would not fit into a 6 megahertz spectrum. It would need at least fifty percent more: *two* channels would have to be used. The research and development began in earnest in the 1970s and by 1981 NHK (Japan's public service channel) was ready for its first demonstration of HDTV in San Francisco.

The Japanese wanted their system of 1125 lines and 60 fields to be established as the international standard. To begin with, before they themselves became seriously involved in developing an HDTV system, the Americans did not mind and supported Japan. America did not have a major stake in television manufacturing and, in any case, if there was one international standard, it would be easier to sell their films in video tape form abroad.

The Europeans, however, especially the French, minded very much. At stake were the European electronic industries: they were developing their own HDTV system, incompatible with the Japanese system. The economics aside, France had no enthusiasm for the cultural implications of an unrestricted flow of American films and television programmes on video tape. The European Community set up their own consortium to oversee the development of their own HDTV system. The Japanese proposal for an international standard was debated at the Consultative Committee meeting in Dubovnick in May 1986, but it was rejected out of hand.

For a while the Japanese had a head start with HDTV, there being only limited interest from the USA. However, a struggle over the allocation of spectrum space led to the Americans engaging wholeheartedly in the quest for HDTV. In the early 1980s broadcast television was threatened on two fronts. First there was the expansion of cable television, which was eating away at their audiences. Second there were mobile phones. Land Mobiles were lobbying for more spectrum space. The agency responsible for the distribution of spectrum space in America is the FCC. On the face of it the FCC could see no clear argument why Land Mobiles should not have more space. Most cities only had eight to ten television stations and about fifty channels allocated to television were not being used. Not wanting to lose any of their spectrum space, television, represented by the National Association of Broadcasters (NAB) had to come up with a persuasive reason to keep what seemed to be wasted spectrum space. HDTV was it. Originally done largely as a lobbying tactic, the NAB arranged for the Japanese to give a demonstration of HDTV in Washington. Not only were broadcasters and senators astonished by the quality of HDTV, but it occurred to many that here was a commercial opportunity that could not be missed. By now America had effectively dropped out of the electronics manufacturing industry, leaving the field to the Japanese. By 1987 the Japanese were manufacturing one third of all the television sets sold in America, but, it was argued, this should not be allowed to happen to HDTV.

HDTV quickly attracted the attention of the education, military and other agencies. The television industry lobbied the FCC to set up an official enquiry into HDTV: in 1988 the Advisory Committee on Advanced Television Service (ACATS) was established. ACATS, funded at this stage by the Committee members themselves, set up a research laboratory in Alexandria, Virginia for the testing of HDTV prototypes. Testing was due to begin in the Spring of 1990. However, some twenty systems had been proposed, some analogue and some digital. This was eventually reduced to four systems. This led to an alliance of research institutions and manufacturers: Zenith, General Instrument, AT & T, the Massachusetts Institute of Technology and a consortium led by Philips Electronics, NBC and the David Sarnoff Research Centre. They collaborated to produce a system which was acceptable to all of the networks and met an FCC requirement that any HDTV system was compatible with NTSC sets.

HDTV is technically advanced in the USA, Japan and Europe (including the BBC), but it is, at the time of writing, the least certain of new technologies. There is some uncertainty as to whether there is a sufficient difference in definition between HDTV and small domestic digital televisions to justify the much greater cost.

New markets

One obvious implication of the massive expansion of the number of television channels is an increased demand for product. This was acute during the 1980s and early 1990s which saw an unprecedented demand for programmes. This demand has been heightened by the widespread deregulation of television in this country and in mainland Europe which has encouraged the expansion of the independent production. With an increase in the numbers of providers, through cable and satellite especially, there has been a fragmentation of the audience.

The greater number of channels available through cable and satellite is going to be multiplied even further through the exponential rise in digital channels. As it is, the 1980s saw an on-going fragmentation of the traditional audience. In the 1950s and 1960s, channels – and advertisers – could rely on channel loyalty. There are (probably apocryphal) tales of people watching their favourite channel's empty screen during shutdowns during broadcasting union strikes in the 1970s, rather than watching another channel. All channels are now having to make much more determined efforts to 'brand' themselves in order to attract audiences. Audience behaviour today is far more volatile. A combination of the remote control and multi-channel choice meant the end of channel loyalty some time ago.

Before the 1980s the choice in the UK was between BBC1, BBC2 and ITV. There then followed an unprecedented expansion of television services: Channels 4 and 5, cable, satellite and digital: the last three having the potential to offer literally hundreds of channels. Added to this has been a growth in both the sale and rental of pre-recorded video tapes. In programming terms this represents a growth in Europe alone of 220 000 hours in 1987 to 500 000 in 1995. The number of available channels in Europe has grown from 26 in 1980 to 90 in the mid 1990s. The impetus of this growth has been both technology and deregulation. Volume growth, however, in terms of the number of channels and programmes available, is not the same as an increase in choice: it might mean a growth in *more of the same*. Opponents of outright deregulation argue that we are actually heading to a *reduction* of choice.

SHORT ANSWER QUESTIONS

1 What is fibre-optic cable?
2 What is interactive television?
3 What is a multiplex?
4 What is the difference between an analogue and digital signal?
5 What is HDTV?

ESSAY QUESTIONS

1 What aspect of new technology do you find the *most* interesting and why?

2 Of all the projected new developments in television, which do you think is the *least* important and why?

3 'We must be very cautious about this new technology that people are getting excited about. It can only have two consequences: greater power and control in the hands of the media moguls and the dumbing down of an entire generation.' How far do you agree with this statement?

4 What will be the next major developments in television broadcast technology?

5 Are new technologies having any impact on widening choice?

FOLLOW UP WORK

1 What impact is new technology having on viewing behaviour?

2 Examine the links between the development of new television technology and ownership of the media.

3 How might the increasing availability of new television technology influence our use of leisure and social time?

4 How might new television technology change the way we watch films?

5 What do you regard as the benefits and risks of new television technology to the way we live our lives?

REFERENCES AND FURTHER READING

Valerie Adams *The Media and the Falklands Campaign* Macmillan 1986

Robert C. Allen *Channels of Discourse* Routledge 1987

Manuel Alvarado and Edward Buscombe *Hazel – the making of a TV series* BFI 1978

Manuel Alvarado and John O. Thompson *The Media Reader* BFI 1990

Daniel Arijon *Grammar of the Film Language* Silman-Jones Press 1976

BBC *Year Book 1947* BBC

William F. Baker and George Dessart *Down the Tube* BasicBooks 1998

Tino Balio *Hollywood in the Age of Television* Unwin Hyman 1990

Steven Barnett *Games and Sets: The Changing Face of Sport on Television* BFI 1990

Erik Barnouw *Tube of Plenty: The Evolution of American* TV OUP 1982

Christopher Bellamy *A Defence Correspondent's Gulf War 1990–91* Brassey 1993

Tony Bennett *et al* (eds) *Popular Television and Film* BFI 1981

Peter Black *The Mirror in the Corner* Hutchinson 1972

David Bordwell and Kristin Thomson *Film Art: An Introduction* McGraw Hill, Inc. 1995

Pierre Bourdieu *On Television and Journalism* Pluto Press 1996

Edward Branigan *Narrative Comprehension and Film* Routledge 1992

Assa Briggs *The Birth of Broadcasting, The History of Broadcasting in the United Kingdom Volume I* OUP 1961

Assa Briggs *Sound and Vision, The History of Broadcasting in the United Kingdom* Volume IV OUP 1993

Joel Brinkley *Defining Vision* Harcourt Brace & Company 1997

David Buckingham *Public Secrets: EastEnders and its Audience* BFI 1987

Tom Burns *The BBC: Public Institution and Private World* Macmillan 1977

Andrew Cassell

Seymour Chatman *Story and Discourse* Cornell University 1978

Richard Collins *Television: Policy & Culture* Unwin Hyman 1990

Jim Cook (ed.) *BFI Dossier 17: Television Sitcom* BFI 1982

John Corner *Critical Ideas in Television Studies* Clarendon Press 1999

Andrew Crissell *An Introductory History of British Broadcasting* Routledge 1997

Bruce Crowther *Hollywood Faction: Reality and Myth in the Movies* Columbus Books 1984

Bruce Cumings *War and Television* Verso 1992

Eddie Dyja *Film and Television Handbook* BFI 1999

Anthony Davis *Television: the First Forty Years* ITV 1976

Marc Doyle *The Future Of Television* NTC Business Books 1992

John Eldridge (ed) *Getting the Message* Glasgow University Media Group Routledge 1993

John Ellis *Visible Fictions* Routledge 1992

Jane Feuer, *et al* (eds) *MTM 'Quality Television'* BFI 1984

John Fiske *Television Culture* Routledge 1987

Roger Fowler *Language in the News* Routledge 1991

Bob Franklin *Newsak & News Media* Arnold 1997

Andrew Goodwin and Garry Whannel *Understanding Television* Routledge 1990

Granada *Year One* Granada 1958

Jeanne Hall Realism as a Style in Cinema Verité: a Critical Analysis of Primary (to be supplied) *Cinema Journal* Vol. 30 No. 4

Daniel C. Hallin *The Uncensored War: the Media and Vietnam* University of California Press 1989

John Hartley *Understanding News* Methuen 1982

John Hartley *Tele-ology Studies in Television* Routledge 1992

John Hawkins *New Technologies, New Policies?* BFI 1982

Stuart Hood and Thalia Tabary-Petersson *On Television* Pluto Press 1997

Miles Hudson and John Stainer *War And The Media* Sutton Publishing 1997

Albert Hunt *The Language of Television* Eyre Methuen 1981

John Izod *Reading the Screen* York Press 1989

Steven D. Katz *Film directing shot by shot* Michael Wiese Productions 1991

HR.F. Keating *Crime Writers* BBC 1978

Douglas Kellner *The Persian Gulf TV War* Westview Press 1992

Richard Kilburn and John Izod *An Introduction to Television Documentary* Manchester University Press 1997

Stephen Lambert *Channel Four: Television with a Difference* BFI 1982

James Ledbetter *Made Possible by ..... The Death of Public Broadcasting In the United States* Verso 1997

C.A. Lewis *Broadcasting from Within* George Newnes 1924

Alan Lovell and Jim Hillier *Studies in Documentary* BFI 1972

Brian MacArthur *Despatches from the Gulf* Bloomsbury 1991

Kevin Macdonald and Mark Cousins *Imagining Reality* faber and faber 1996

James McDonnell *Public Service Broadcasting* Routledge 1991

Robert McKee *Story: substance, structure, style and the principles of screenwriting* Methuen 1997

Brian McNair *News and Journalism in the UK* Routledge 1944

David McQueen *Television: a Media Student's Guide* Arnold 1998

Brian Marjoribanks, *et al. The Future of Broadcasting in Britain* Centre for Theology and Public Issues Occasional Paper No:24 May 1991

Len Masterman *Teaching the Media* Comedia 1985

David E. Morrison and Howard Tumber *Journalists at War: The Dynamics of News Reporting During the Falklands War* SAGE Publications 1988

David E. Morrison *Television And The Gulf War* John Libbey 1992

Bill Nichols *Representing Reality* Indiana University Press 1991

Michael Nicholson *A Measure of Danger: Memoirs of a British War Correspondent* HarperCollins 1991

Burton Paulu in *Putting Reality Together* R. (ed.) Schlesinger 1978

Steve Peak and Paul Fisher *The Media Guide* Fourth Estate 1999

Monroe Price *Television, the Public Sphere and National Identity* Clarendon Press 1995

John Reith *Broadcast Over Britain* Hodder & Stoughton 1924

Michael Renov (ed) *Theorizing Documentary* Routledge 1993

Geoffrey Robertson, QC, and Andrew Nicol *Media Law* Penguin 1992

Alan Rosenthal (ed) *New Challenges for Documentary* University of California Press 1988

Alan Rosenthal *Writing Docudrama: Dramatizing Reality for Film and TV* Focal Press 1995

Paddy Scannell and Cardiff *A Social History Of British Broadcasting: Volume I Serving the Nation* Blackwell 1991

Philip Schlesinger *Putting 'Reality' Together* Constable 1978

David Self *Television Drama: An Introduction*

William Shawcross *Murdoch* Pan Books 1992

Vikto Shlovskly *Theory of Prose* Dalkey Archive Press 1990

Anthony Smith *British Broadcasting* David & Charles 1974

Anthony Smith (ed) *Television: An International* History OUP 1998

Raymond Steadman *The Serials: Suspense and Drama by Installment* University of Oklahoma Press 1977

Ian Stewart and Susan L. Carruthers (ed) *War, Culture and the Media* Flick Books 1996

Wyle Sypher *The Meaning of Comedy*

Philip M. Taylor *War and the Media: Propaganda and Persuasion in the Gulf War* Manchester University Press 1992

Robert J. Thompson *Television's Second Golden Age* Syracuse University Press 1997

Alex Thomson *Smokescreen: The Media. The Censors. The Gulf* Laburnham & Spellmount Ltd 1992

John Tulloch *Television Drama: Agency, Audience and Myth* Routledge 1990

Mike Wayne *Dissident Voices: The Politics of Television and Cultural Change* Pluto Press 1998

Francis Wheen *Television* Century Publishing 1985

Granville Williams *Britain's Media: How They are Related* Campaign for Freedom in the Press and Broadcasting 1996

Raymond Williams *Television: Technology and Cultural Form* Wesleyan University Press 1974, 1992

Brian Winston *Claiming The Real* British Film Institute 1995

Admiral Sandy Woodward *One Hundred Days: the Memoirs of the Falklands Battle Group Commander* BCA 1992

Will Wright *Sixguns and Society: A Structural Study of the Western* University of California Press 1977

Peter R. Young (ed) *Defence and the Media in Time of Limited War* Frank Cass 1992

GLOSSARY

Access cablecasting access to cable television by either individuals or local groups or organisations. In America cable operators are obliged by Federal Communications Commission rules to make available space on cable for local community use.

Actuality recorded material of actual events used in radio and television news broadcasts, or other programmes based on such material.

Aerial shot an extreme high angle shot, looking directly down on the subject, taken from a plane, helicopter or elevated camera position.

Agenda setting the process of selecting and giving special emphasis to issues and events in preference to others by news, political and public relations organisations.

Anchor the link presenter in an American news programme.

Angle of view the field of vision covered by a lens. A wide angle lens has a wide angle of view, while a telephoto lens has a narrow angle of view.

Broadcasters' Audience Research Board (BARB) undertakes audience research for both ITV and the BBC.

British Broadcasting Corporation (BBC) the UK public service broadcaster. From 1922 to 1926 it was a private company regulated by the Post Office (it was called the British Broadcasting Company). In 1926 it became a public corporation.

Back lighting lighting used to illuminate an actor/action from behind in order to create a sense of depth (see also **key light** and **fill light**).

Blocking a scene the organisation of positions and movements of actors, props, etc., in a scene. This may include the camera.

Broadcasting Standards Commission (BSC) the BSC was formed on the 31 March 1997 when the Broadcasting Complaints Commission (BCC) merged with the Broadcasting Standards Council (BSC).

BskyB British Sky Broadcasting. A satellite broadcaster owned by News Corporation.

Budget the amount of money allocated to pay for the production of a media product, such as a film or television programme.

Cable cable was first used in the UK in the 1930s for relaying radio broadcasts. Cable is a means of transmitting signals through underground cables, of which there are two kinds: coaxial and fibre optic.

Cathode ray tube used in television and radar, it is a vacuum tube that, when placed in a magnetic field, emits a stream of electrons. These appear on a screen as pictures. The pictures are made up of 'lines' of electrons. The greater the number of lines, the greater the clarity of the picture. British television uses 625 lines; HDTV uses 1000 or more.

Ceefax the BBC's teletext service ('seefacts'). See also **Teletext**.

Cinema verité (cinema truth) a form of observational documentary filmmaking that, unlike direct cinema, acknowledges the presence of the filmmaker and his/her involvement in the process of filmmaking. More or less contemporaneous with American direct cinema, it was associated with the French filmmaker, Jean Rouch.

CNN Cable News Network, founded by Ted Turner in June 1988, it began as a relatively modest cable service, initially serving less than two million homes. Turner's original plan was only for a domestic service. However, his operation rapidly expanded.

Cover shot see **master shot**.

Continuity editing this is dominant form of editing whereby shots are juxtaposed into sequences, so as to construct a coherent sense of space and time. It is sometimes referred to as invisible editing.

Conglomerates usually large multinational companies, bringing together under single ownership a number of different, but usually related, commercial interests. News Corporation, for example, owns, amongst other things, a film studio (Twentieth Century Fox), satellites (BSkyB and Star) and many newspapers.

Cross-cutting the alternating of shots from two or more scenes to suggest separate actions occurring simultaneously.

Crossing the line shooting a scene from opposite sides, such that characters appear to keep reversing their position. Likewise with eyeline matches and the movement of characters, direction is seemingly reversed from one shot to another.

Cutaway a shot inserted into a sequence that interrupts the flow of action. It shows a detail or a new location relevant to the action.

Dead donkey usually an inconsequential, 'soft' story that concludes a television news bulletin. Generally the first to go if other stories 'break', hence the title of the nineties situation comedy, *Drop the Dead Donkey*.

Denotation in semiotics this is the first order of meaning of any sign. It is the surface meaning, the 'thing in itself'.

Depth of field the distance between the furthest and nearest points in an image that are in focus.

Deregulation the removal or weakening of rules that place limitations on the ownership of the media. It also refers to the weakening of regulations that protect the public services, including broadcasting, usually by introducing an element of privatisation, that is, the selling off of services to private, commercial interests.

Diegesis that which belongs to the world of the film or TV programme. Diegetic sound will be 'motivated' and seen to come from a recognisable source, such as a radio. Non-diegetic sound would include underscoring ('background' music).

Direct Broadcasting satellite (DBS) geostationary satellites that broadcast directly to earth without having to be relayed through ground stations.

Direct cinema observational documentary associated with Robert Drew and his associates in the 1960s. Its aim was to minimise the intervention of the film-maker and to capture realty directly.

Discourse:

1. the minimum unit of speech that can be subjected to analysis, i.e. anything larger than a sentence or a single utterance. Discourse analysis is the study of everyday language.

2. a specialised form of language that draws upon its own rules and conventions of use. This would include professional modes of language, such as business, law, medicine, etc., as in 'the discourse of medicine' or 'medical discourse'. It can also refer to the language of particular social groupings or interests such as 'feminist discourse'. Discourse analysis is not only concerned with the rules and content of language use, but also with the way in which language operates symbolically in, for example, the expression of power relations between individuals and social groups.

DA Notice formally D Notice, these are issued by the Defence, Press and Broadcasting Advisory Committee as advice to editors on matters that ought not to be published in the interests of national security. A DA Notice is a request and not a legally binding instruction.

Documentary a film, television or radio programme.

Documentary drama a television drama presented in the style of observational documentary. Real locations tend to be used with either little known actors (or even non-professionals), or those associated with realist drama, such as Ricky Tomlinson.

Drama documentary literally 'dramatised documentary' - a film or television drama based on an actual event.

Electronic News Gathering (ENG) television news gathering that relies on lightweight video or digital camcorders instead of separate film cameras and sound recorders. In the days of film, it could take several hours before images could be broadcast as, for one thing, film had to be processed first. With ENG, in conjunction with small satellite dishes, images can be transmitted immediately and fed into a news bulletin while it is on air.

Establishing shot a long shot that establishes location, general mood and relative placement of subjects in a scene.

European Broadcasting Union an association of, mostly, Western European broadcasters.

Fairness Doctrine an obligation imposed by the Federal Communications Commission on American broadcasters to present differing views on controversial issues. With the deregulation of American television in the 1980s, the FCC dropped this requirement.

Federal Communications Commission (FCC) the regulator of American broadcasting. The British equivalent is the ITC.

Fibre-optics an integral part of digital communications, fibre-optic cable is made up of strands of glass fibre, each capable of carrying a huge amount of information in the form of impulses of light. Conventional cable, coaxial, is made from copper wire which carries a tiny fraction of the amount of information born by a fibre-optic cable.

Fill light secondary lighting that literally fills in unwanted shadows. However, in certain circumstance it can become the primary lighting, such as when a dark, high contrast image is required, as in some thrillers.

Focus pull/follow focus the refocusing of the lens during the course of a shot to keep a moving subject within the depth of field.

Format:

1. refers to the way a programme is organised i.e. an episode might be part of a serial or a series.

2. the concept or idea behind a programme.

Genre a way of categorisation texts according to recurring stylistic, formal and thematic elements.

High Definition Television (HDTV) digital television systems based on 1000 lines or more, thus producing greatly enhanced (high definition) images.

Ideology the ideas, values and beliefs that sustain relations of power within a society.

Infotainment the mixing of information and entertainment.

Insert/insert shot generally a close-up showing an important detail of a scene.

Internet the 'Net' began as a US military project in the late 'sixties (the ARPA Net) which sought to create a communications system able to survive the highly destructive electro-magnetic impulses generated by nuclear explosions.

Intertextuality the reference within a text to another text, in order to create meaning.

Independent Television Commission (ITC) the ITC is the regulator of British commercial television. The ITC superseded its predecessor, the Independent Broadcasting Authority, on 1 January, 1992. The ITC was one of the changes to British broadcasting brought about by the Broadcasting Act of 1990. The ITC is responsible for licensing all independent television operators, including cable and satellite.

Jump cut a cut that disrupts continuity by making an abrupt leap in either space or time, showing people or objects in new positions or locations.

Key light this is the primary lighting on a set, providing overall illumination.

Loose refers to the composition of a shot. It generally means there is a lot of space around a subject.

Master/master shot the viewpoint of a scene in which both the dramatic action and the relationships between subjects are clear within a single shot.

Match cut two shots of the same action joined in such a way that visual continuity is preserved.

Media Imperialism usually refers to the Western media and its influence on other cultures, in particular those of developing countries.

Mise-en-scéne in French it was originally a theatrical term meaning 'putting in the scene'. In film/TV it refers to the manipulation of space within the frame and includes the use of light, colour, spatial relationships between characters, objects, etc.

Montage from the French 'to assemble'. A montage sequence is usually a rapidly cut sequence of shots. In 1920s Soviet cinema it was regarded as the essence of cinema. Eisenstein base his theory of montage on conflict. The clash of two or more different shots would produce a new meaning that was not part of either of the individual shots.

Narrowcasting broadcasting targeted at specific-interest, niche audiences.

Network a number of television and/or radio stations affiliated to, or owned by, a major broadcaster on either a regional or national basis, from whom these stations receive a substantial proportion of their programming. The four major networks in the USA are: ABC, CBS, NBC and Fox Television.

Network Centre a federation of the independent television broadcasters that commissions and schedules networked programming. It was created in 1993 in order to fulfil a requirement imposed on independent television by the Broadcasting Act 1990 for it to 'commission and schedule programmes through an independent body separate from the ITV companies.' (ITV Network Annual Report 1998)

News management (see also **spin doctor**) is a means whereby organisations or individuals are shown positively through the manipulation of news, through press conferences, the staging of events (photo calls, etc.) and carefully timing the release of stories.

News values the criteria by which the news worthiness of an event is judged.

Oligarchy the domination of a market by a small number of firms.

Pilot a single episode designed to test audience reactions to a proposed new series.

Point of view shot a shot that shows the point of view of a character. This will often be shown as an over the shoulder shot; a subjective point of view is where the camera functions as the eyes of the character.

Pay TV usually associated with either cable or satellite services, where audiences pay to watch individual programmes.

Polysemy the potential of a sign to generate many meanings. Roland Barthes coined the term anchorage to describe the way in which the meaning of a sign can either be fixed or restricted, through its juxtaposition with another sign, such as in the use of captions or sounds. In this sense, editing is a form of anchorage, whereby the meaning of images is determined, in part at least, by their relationship to each other.

Production values refers to the overall quality of a production in both a technical and a cultural sense. Crudely, it alludes to the amount of money spent on the screen in terms of the quality of sets, costumes, props, cast and detail in general.

Property that upon which the film/TV programme is based, such as a book, original script, treatment or even notes for an idea.

Public Service Broadcasting (PSB) non-commercial broadcasting whose primary concern is the public rather any commercial or political interest.

Referent if, in semiotics, the signifier refers only to a concept, the referent is the thing itself. 'Dog' refers to the concept of dog. If, however, a real dog is being alluded to, it is the referent of the sign 'dog'.

Schedule the schedule is the timetable of a production. In television this is usually the responsibility of the production manager. The order of recording is determined by such things as the locations being used, the availability of actors and transport costs. For example, all scenes that occur in the same location or on the same set, irrespective of where they occur in the plot, are recorded together.

Screen time the time taken to run the film or television programme.

Semiology/semiotics the study of sign systems and their function in society.

Social realism a long standing tradition in British film and television drama that affected a documentary realism in its depictions of largely working class life. The 1960s is often cited as an important period of such filmmaking, but it can be found much earlier in British cinema of the 1940s.

Soundbite many people who in the course of their work deal with the media (such as politicians, military officers, public figures, etc.) are often trained in the art of the radio/television interview. One way to make sure that something of what you say is actually broadcast in the way you want it said, is to encapsulate it in pithy 30 second statements that can be easily quoted: that is a soundbite.

Spin doctor usually a senior press officer. The term was coined in the USA in the 1980s. He or she has the task of promoting a positive image of the person or organisation for whom he or she is working (see also **news management**).

Stereotype an image that incorporates, in a simplistic way, the supposed attributes of a group. Stereotypes are generally thought of as being negative, but this is not necessarily always the case.

Storyboard the pictorial representation of a film, video or television programme done in such a way that each image represents a shot. In large scale productions these are often realised in some detail with a good deal of artistry; however, simple sketches can function well enough.

Story time the time that unfolds in the world of the narrative (diegetic time). The screen time for an episode of a television drama might be fifty five minutes. Story time, however, could be anything: five minutes, five hours, five years or five centuries. 'Real time' is where, as in *The Royle Family* for example, screen time is the same as story time. The term is equally applicable to documentary film.

Synergy a business concept, whereby related activities are brought together within the same organisation. An example is News Corp: they own Twentieth Century Fox film studios and BskyB. Another example is Viacom, which owns several television cable channels and Paramount film studios. Early in 2000 Warner Brothers merged with the Internet company AOL and EMI, anticipating an expansion in the transmission of media products on the Internet.

Teletext television data service provided by both the BBC and ITV (see also **Ceefax**).

Textual analysis the process of identifying and explaining the internal operations of a text so as to assign it a meaning(s) and make an evaluation. Increasingly, this has come to be understood as something other than an end in itself, but part of a process of understanding ways in which readers/audiences relate to a text.

Three point lighting the basic arrangement of lights in a studio: key, fill and back lighting.

Treatment an outline of a film or television drama. It is something more than a plot synopsis, usually including ideas about characters, locations, etc.

Two shot a shot framing two people.

Voice over (VO) the voice of an unseen narrator.

Vox pop from the Latin, *vox populi* meaning, 'voice of the people', usually presented in films or TV programmes as a sequence of 'talking heads' of members of the public responding to a question or giving an opinion.

Wrap:

1. the conclusion of filming/recording either on location or in a studio.

2. an item in a news programme that starts with the news reader, cuts to the location reporter and/or an actuality sequence and then goes back to the new reader.

Zoom lens a variable focal length lens. By manipulating the lens, objects/characters are seen to either recede into the distance or come nearer. A shot with a zoom lens is not to be confused with a dolly or tracking shot, where the camera is physically moved either on wheels (dolly) or along a track.

INDEX

Headings in italics refer to TV programmes unless otherwise stated. Page numbers in italics indicate illustrations or diagrams.